THE ORIGINS OF
THE LABOUR PARTY
1880–1900

THE ORIGINS OF
THE LABOUR PARTY
1880 – 1900

BY

HENRY PELLING

FELLOW AND TUTOR OF
THE QUEEN'S COLLEGE, OXFORD

CLARENDON PRESS · OXFORD

1965

Oxford University Press, Amen House, London E.C. 4

GLASGOW NEW YORK TORONTO MELBOURNE WELLINGTON
BOMBAY CALCUTTA MADRAS KARACHI LAHORE DACCA
CAPE TOWN SALISBURY NAIROBI IBADAN ACCRA
KUALA LUMPUR HONG KONG

First edition   1954
published by Macmillan and Co.
Second edition   1965

PRINTED IN GREAT BRITAIN AT
THE UNIVERSITY PRESS
ABERDEEN

PREFACE

This book is an attempt to describe how the Labour Party came into existence. It is primarily a study in the development of new political structure. Although it has a good deal to say about the social, religious and economic environment of Socialist and working-class politics, it does not pretend to provide a complete picture of the growth of the labour movement as a whole in the later nineteenth century.

Even within its limits, however, the task has presented considerable difficulties. The unpublished source material is very scattered, and, unless great efforts are made to look after it properly, much of it may in the future become even more scattered and in many cases may be lost. At the same time, there remain several important private collections of documents which are not yet available for research. In kindred fields of study, much remains to be done. Trade union histories are rarely adequate, and numerous problems in the economic and social history of the period remain unsolved.

I believe, however, that the main lines of the story can now be established. While interpretations are bound to differ, and details may be altered by the additional material that may appear in the future, I am confident that little would be gained by postponing publication in the expectation that fresh evidence would radically alter the account contained in the following pages.

It is impossible for me to enumerate all those who have assisted me in the course of my work. My sense of obligation is none the less real. Acknowledgement is made in Appendix C (List of Unpublished Sources) to those who have facilitated my task by allowing me to see, and in most cases to quote from, the documents in their possession. I am especially grateful to Mr. Francis Johnson, for many years Secretary of the I.L.P., for his great generosity, over a period of five years, in lending me books and documents from his remarkable library. Mr. Johnson, whose knowledge of this period of labour history must be unique, has also helped me in the choice of illustrations. Mr.

The Origins of the Labour Party, 1880–1900

Laurence Thompson has unstintingly shared with me his knowledge of the personalities and documentation of the *Clarion* movement. I have also been fortunate in being able to draw upon the memories of some of those who took leading parts in the events that I have recorded: the late Mrs. Bruce Glasier, Mr. Edward Pease, Mr. Fred Henderson and Mr. J. S. Middleton have all given me the benefit of their personal reminiscences.

My thanks are also due to Mr. R. V. Clements, who spared the time from his own researches to undertake work on my behalf in the Henry Demarest Lloyd papers at Madison, Wisconsin, U.S.A.

As an 'advanced student' of Cambridge University in 1947–50, I had the good fortune to be supervised by Professor D. W. Brogan, and could draw upon his wide range of historical knowledge. Mr. Asa Briggs very kindly read my manuscript before it went to press and made a number of most useful suggestions.

I am happy to acknowledge the cordial co-operation of the secretaries and headquarters staff of the I.L.P., the Fabian Society and the Labour Party; and I must not close without recording the patience of the library staffs whom I have most frequently troubled, especially those of the British Museum, the British Library of Political and Economic Science, the Cambridge University Library, the Bodleian and Nuffield College Libraries, Oxford, and the International Institute of Social History, Amsterdam.

May 1953   H. M. P.

PREFACE TO NEW EDITION

In this edition, which has been entirely reset, I have taken the opportunity to make a number of alterations to the text and footnotes, and also to Appendices A and C. The only considerable addition, however, is in the form of a bibliographical essay, which tries to take account of all relevant published work in the field, including that which has appeared since the first edition of this book.

September, 1964   H. M. P.

vi

CONTENTS

LIST OF ILLUSTRATIONS

CHAPTER I

Introduction

(1)

ALTHOUGH the period between the Reform Acts of 1867 and 1884 is within the lifetime of many living persons, the present-day observer cannot but be struck by the enormous changes in the political scene which have taken place since those days. In the first place, it was not then possible to speak of Britain as a democratic country, although it was on the way to becoming one. The democratic experience of the United States and the Australian colonies, and the ancient example of Greece, were anxiously being analysed by British political leaders who were pondering the advisability of a further advance towards full universal suffrage. As late as 1880 Queen Victoria was setting her face against the full implications of the trend of political change: she declared with emphasis that she '. . . *cannot* and will not be the Queen of a *democratic monarchy*'.[1]

The political parties, too, bore little resemblance to those of today. Extra-parliamentary organization was only just beginning to develop on the national scale. Previously, government had been effected by bargaining between Parliamentary groups, and there had been little semblance of party discipline as we know it today. It was only in the 1860's that what was to become the Liberal Party began to crystallize as an alliance of Whigs, Radicals and Nonconformists; and Gladstone's role in politics can be better appreciated if he is regarded as the leader of a 'connexion' of the old eighteenth-century type rather than as the manipulator of a modern political machine.[2]

The working class in this twilight period of democratic development still had no direct part in the government of the country.

---

[1] *Letters of Queen Victoria*, 2nd ser., iii (1928), p. 166.
[2] For a brief statement of this view see A. F. Thompson, 'Gladstone', in P. Quennell (ed.), *British Prime Ministers* (1953).

The substantial extensions to the franchise in 1867 were expected to lead to great changes at Westminster, for in many borough constituencies working men in possession of the household suffrage now formed a majority of the electorate. But, as after the reform of 1832, a mere extension of the electorate did not necessarily remove the existing political groups from the seat of power. In spite of the efforts of the London Working Men's Association, which urged the direct representation of labour in Parliament, the few working men who stood in the 1868 election were heavily defeated at the polls. In 1869 a more extensive organization, the Labour Representation League, was set up with the object, among other things, of promoting the registration of the working-class vote 'without reference to opinion or party bias'.[1] But the League's task was a difficult one, for it had not the finance to make its candidatures a success. In those days the candidate had to find, not only his election expenses, but also the returning officer's fees and, if elected, his own maintenance as Member of Parliament. Further, if he was to win a real grip on the constituency, substantial contributions to local charities and social bodies were a necessity. Nor was this all: until 1883 the laws of bribery and corruption were dangerously ineffective, and considerable loopholes in the law still remained, to be taken advantage of by many of the candidates.

In these circumstances, the cause of labour representation was seriously handicapped, and the Labour Representation League faced an awkward dilemma. To be effective it must have strong financial backing: but this could not be obtained from inside the working class, not even from the trade unions, which were not yet well enough off to risk any of their resources on purely political objects. The contributions of the ordinary members of the League were not ample enough to go very far, and if there were any persons of wealth who promised their support, it was normally on condition that the League should abandon its attempt at political independence. The League had therefore the alternative of dependence on an existing political

---

[1] 'Prospectus of the Labour Representation League', reprinted in A. W. Humphrey *History of Labour Representation* (1912), p. 189.

Introduction

party, or immediate collapse owing to poverty. In either case it
was doomed to failure in its original object—the organization
of the labour vote as a separate Parliamentary force.

In view of the difficulties, it is not surprising that in the
1870's there were few labour leaders who regarded the establishment of an entirely independent workers' party as a practical
possibility. Most of them accepted the leadership of Gladstone,
for it was he who had championed the cause of working-class
suffrage in the previous decade, and on many issues of policy
the leaders of the artisans found themselves in alliance with the
Liberals. The Liberal Party was not a monolithic structure:
and the acceptance of the leadership of Gladstone on general
questions did not necessarily mean that the labour interest need
forego its special organization. In the circumstances of the time,
there was no reason why the Labour Representation League
should not continue to exist among, and indeed to struggle
against, the other elements of the Liberal Party. This struggle
could and did continue at the constituency level.

The failure of the Labour Representation League to maintain itself even on these terms indicates the unwillingness of the
Whigs and middle-class Liberals to see working men elected as
their representatives. John Bright himself accused the League
of 'disorganising the party, unless what are called working-
class representatives could be returned'[1]; and Henry Broadhurst, the Secretary of the League, in his rejoinder, admitted
the failure of its policy:

> Up to the present, the number of seats contested by labour
> candidates have been very few, and in some of these cases the
> seats sought to be won were those held by the Conservatives,
> and in many of those instances we singularly enough found
> large numbers of the middle class electors preferred voting
> for the Tories rather than support a working-class candidate.
> Surely, then, we are the aggrieved party. . . .[2]

It was indeed true that the policy of finding Liberal seats for
labour candidates had few successes and many failures. At the

[1] *The Times*, 29 Jan. 1875.
[2] Letter to John Bright, 2 Feb. 1875: copy in L.R.L. Minute Book, Brit. Lib.
Pol. Sci.

1874 election two miners were elected, Thomas Burt for Morpeth and Alexander McDonald for Stafford; but this was a miserable showing for an electorate, the majority of which now consisted of members of the working class.

(2)

To a large extent this lack of political militancy was a reflection of the prosperity of the country under *laissez-faire* conditions. The industrial advances of the middle-Victorian era eliminated the immediate risk of serious social discontent among the workers, and especially among their potential leaders, the skilled artisans and the factory employees. Yet in a country like Britain, with a long-established aristocracy and a traditional class system, no very high degree of social fluidity could be attained even in the heyday of early industrial capitalism. On the contrary, large-scale industry developed a class solidarity among the workers which in the end facilitated effective political action in the interest of labour as a whole. The events of the late 1860's and early 1870's clearly indicated the path of future development. By 1871 the Trades Union Congress had been established and accepted as the central parliament of labour, meeting annually, and its Parliamentary Committee was the recognized agent for applying political pressure on behalf of the trade unions at the centre of government. By the Acts of 1871 the trade unions secured a legal status; in the same year the engineers of north-east England revived the Nine Hours movement and won a strike for this object. The boundaries of trade unionism widened: the Amalgamated Society of Railway Servants was founded in December 1871, and a few months later Joseph Arch began to organize the agricultural labourers. A Gas Stokers Union was formed in London, but it was broken up by prosecutions for breach of contract, which led in turn to an agitation for a further amendment of the law in favour of the unions. In 1875 a Conservative government, showing itself as sensitive as the Liberals to the pressure of the unions in industrial matters, passed two Acts which satisfied the unions in respect of breach of contract and picketing.

Introduction

Then, so far as class-conscious politics are concerned, a closer inspection of the evidence shows that remnants of Chartism survived long after the debacle of 1848, and that there were always some advocates of an independent labour party—for instance, George Potter, the editor of the vigorous labour paper the *Beehive*, and the members of the short-lived Land and Labour League, founded in 1869 by the British members of the First International. There were also a few local labour associations active in securing representation for working men on local authorities, and sometimes, as at Birmingham in the 1870's, they carried on their work without any understanding with an existing party.[1] There were even signs of the development of sympathy for Socialism at the time of the Paris Commune. This was largely to be found in a wing of the Republican movement which sprang up in these years and which resulted in the establishment of a large number of Republican clubs throughout the country.[2] Eventually the disagreement of the Republican leaders on the issue of whether or not they wanted a social revolution was such that it led to a division in their ranks, and by the mid-seventies the movement, for this and other reasons, was in decline. For the most part its Socialist doctrine was limited to a vague Owenism, for although Marx was living in London his works were little known in England. Still, it was not entirely uninfluential: it is in this period that we find many of the trade unions taking up schemes for co-operative production, and buying collieries and engineering works in order to try out their ideas.

In the later seventies, the activities of the labour movement were curtailed by the severe trade depression. In the years 1874 to 1880, while the Liberals were out of power, it was in any case difficult to assert the special character of labour opposition as distinct from that of other Liberals. The Labour Representation League lingered on, but in an ever-weakening state: by 1878 it had entirely ceased to attract public notice, while the agitation of the Eastern Question had rallied the working-class

[1] W. A. Dalley, *Life Story of W. J. Davis* (1914), pp. 47 ff.
[2] Mr. E. G. Collieu kindly informs me that he has traced 84 Republican Clubs founded in Britain in the period 1871–4.

leadership into full support of Gladstone. The more politically aggressive trade unions—usually those which were most vulnerable to adverse trade conditions—were killed off by the bad times: the remainder, husbanding their resources for industrial needs, were even more unwilling than before to embrace any political designs. There was a heavy reduction in the membership represented at the Trades Union Congress. Arch's Agricultural Labourers Union was especially hard hit by the depression and its membership quickly declined. Extreme radical politics were also on the wane: as we have seen, the Republican movement was disintegrating. It is clear that the immediate onset of what economic historians now call the 'Great Depression', so far from encouraging Socialism and the break-up of the Liberal Party, actually discouraged working-class militancy and destroyed the 'advanced' elements then in existence.

A consequence of this state of affairs was that the acceptance of Liberal political guidance by the labour leadership was never more complete than in 1880. It is true that this was never more than a limited acceptance: the Chartist tradition of independent labour politics was not entirely extinct, nor was the entire working class Liberal in sentiment. It must be remembered that in some areas Tory Radicalism had a real significance for working people who recollected the agitation of such leaders as Richard Oastler. This sympathy for Toryism was reinforced not only by the social policy of Disraeli but also by the conflict of interest between the indigenous population and Irish immigrants, especially in industrial Lancashire. The association of Nonconformity and the Temperance movement with the Liberal Party gave its opponents the support of the inn and the parish church, both of them important factors in the social life of all classes. Still, when it came to a choice between the existing parties, most of the better-off industrial workers and artisans, who alone were organized in trade unions and who therefore provided the articulate leadership of the working class, felt themselves to be more closely akin to the Liberal middle class, whose sober habits and dissenting religion they commonly shared. There was, in any case, no distinctive labour political creed, for the Owenite Socialism of the time, identified as it was with Utopian experiments and lacking any systematic economic theory, could hardly form the basis for a practical political programme. Writing in 1881, Engels, who was normally an optimist about the growth of Socialism, felt bound to admit that the working class of this country had become the 'tail of the great Liberal Party'.[1]

It is this check to labour's political progress in the later 1870's which has led some observers to assume a full generation of quiescence since the days of the Chartists, and to find in the early 1880's a great turning-point of working-class behaviour. In reality, throughout the last half of the century the effective political strength of labour was almost constantly increasing: the growth of industry, the improvement of real wages and conditions, and the extension of educational facilities all combined to maintain this long-term trend. There were, it is true, periods of apparent set-back such as the later 1870's; but to make up for them there were other periods of increased tempo of advance, such as 1865–73. It was to be expected that these periods of accelerated progress would be repeated whenever better times returned. The early 1880's obtain an accidental significance in working-class history by contrast with the previous few years, and because there now appeared the beginnings of organized Socialist politics—an important development for the future of working-class politics, but in itself, as we shall see, largely a middle-class phenomenon. On the whole, the workers did not suffer as a result of the so-called Great Depression which, except in the later 1870's, was a period of continued advance in real wages. This twenty-year period, extending into the middle 1890's, was called a depression because there was a notable decline in the return on industrial investments, which hit the middle class. So far as the workers were concerned, the cyclical slumps of the late seventies, middle eighties and early nineties caused a temporary high level of unemployment, especially in heavy industry, and agriculture was permanently depressed owing to the competition of foreign wheat. But neither the general average of unemployment nor the cyclical 'peaks' appear to have been much, if any, higher than in the

[1] *Labour Standard*, 23 July 1881.

middle-Victorian era of expansion[1]; and while in general money wages stood still, real wages increased with the fall in prices, and the workers were substantially better off as a class in the nineties than they were in the seventies.[2] The period of their greatest political and industrial advance (1888 to 1891) was a period of comparative prosperity.

(3)

An examination of the general social thought of the period, that is to say, the opinions current among the more educated elements of society, reveals a considerable change in the course of the eighties. This was principally due to the concern that was felt in industrial and commercial circles which had been adversely affected by the impact of the depression. It had been difficult to criticize the principles of *laissez-faire* capitalism while it was bringing a steady increase of wealth to the country, and such criticisms as were made, for instance those of John Stuart Mill, were easily ignored. But when the intervention of foreign competition began to put a term to this type of uncontrolled expansion, and to cause a reduction of industrial profits, *laissez-faire* at once became less popular. It was not accidental that the development of the Fair Trade campaign took place at the same time as the formation of the first Socialist groups, both of them appearing in response to the awkward problems suggested by the trade depression. Indeed, one of the most striking intellectual developments of the period was the abandonment of classical conceptions by the younger economists, and their attempt, following the lead of Cliffe Leslie, to base economic analysis upon the examination of historical processes rather than upon *a priori* theory. Toynbee, Cunningham, and Ashley were at one in the view that the old 'hair-splitting analysis of abstract doctrine' was out of date[3]: and, whatever,

---

[1] J. H. Clapman, *Economic History of Modern Britain*, ii (1932), p. 455.
[2] A. L. Bowley, *Wages and Income in the United Kingdom since 1860* (1937), p. 94, gives the following index figures for real wages: 1880, 70; 1881–5, 77; 1886–90, 89; 1891–5, 98; 1896–1900, 104.
[3] The phrase is from an interesting discussion of Socialism in a letter of W. J. Ashley to his future wife, quoted in A. Ashley, *William James Ashley* (1932), p. 35.

their differences of political outlook, it was from them that the early Fabians borrowed many of their ideas.

The new orientation of economic thought was influenced not only by the impact of the depression but also by the fact that long-term changes in the structure of industry were taking place which earlier economists had not bargained for. The family firm was being replaced by the impersonal limited company, in which ownership was divorced from managerial skill and from direct contact with labour. As a result, the opportunities of social advancement were curtailed and the workers' class solidarity was increased. This did not happen uniformly in all industries, and by the mid-eighties it was common only in iron, shipbuilding and heavy engineering. But the tendency was the same everywhere, and it seemed very possible that it might lead to the substitution of monopoly for competition in the end, as Marx had forecast.

Another important factor was the development of State intervention in the economic sphere for various *ad hoc* purposes connected with the welfare of the community. The work of the Benthamites in the middle of the century laid the basis of the local government system. The growth of the professions, an increasing proportion of whose members were in public employment, encouraged the discussion of standards of human welfare and the creation of a sensitive social conscience. The age of social surveys and public statistics was at hand. The existence of bad living and working conditions could no longer be ignored, even if things were not so bad as in earlier times. The slum-dweller and the sweated worker were still frequently to be met with, and they became more obvious as it became a duty to investigate 'Darkest England'. In this sense there is much truth in Toynbee's remark that in economics 'it was the labour question . . . that revived the method of observation. Political economy was transformed by the working classes.'[1]

The work of the economist was of limited political significance, however, until it was popularized; and at the beginning of the 1880's the most effective popular critic of classical economics

[1] A. Toynbee, *Industrial Revolution in England* (1884), p. 10.

was the American, Henry George, whose principal work, *Progress and Poverty* (1879), advocated a tax on land as the cure for all economic ills, arguing that the origin of land values was primarily to be found in the growth of society as a whole and not in the virtue of the individual landowner. George's writings, appearing in Britain during the most acute phase of the agricultural depression, and further advertised by his own vigorous and effective campaigning tours in the areas of special distress, Scotland and Ireland, were remarkably influential in setting people thinking about political economy on lines that often led them much farther than George himself would have wished. Although he was not a Socialist, he was responsible for the early political education of many of the subsequent leaders of the Socialist movement in this country.

Finally, in this brief outline, a word must be said about the more purely literary influences at the popular level. There were always those who maintained that the existing industrial system was unjust or ugly or both. The most notable of the writers who took this view were Carlyle and Ruskin, and both of them were very popular in the later nineteenth century. Carlyle denounced the state of affairs whereby the only contact of master and servant was that afforded by the 'cash nexus': he regretted the passing of the old paternal relationships of pre-capitalist society. Although he was struggling against the current of contemporary change, he expressed a point of view with which many could sympathize, and his criticisms of industrialism were real and forceful. Ruskin, writing for the most part rather later than Carlyle, showed more recognition of the need to build a new order of civilization, even if it be on an old pattern. As befitted a Professor of Fine Art, his criticism focused on the ugliness of existing society, and he envisaged an industrial system based on his conception of the medieval guilds, in which, he believed, the dignity of craftsmanship received due recognition. He founded a Utopian experiment, St. George's Guild, and bought a farm where a little group of Sheffield Socialists attempted without success to set up a self-sufficient community. His essays on political economy, *Unto this Last* (1860), and his letters to working men, known as *Fors Clavigera* (1871–84), did

much to encourage the growing sentiment in favour of collectivism. They revived, in simple and impressive language, many
of the criticisms of classical economics which had first been
voiced by Thompson, Hodgskin and the other 'Ricardian
Socialists' of the 1820's. Not that Ruskin had read the works of
these writers, who were completely forgotten in this period except
for an occasional footnote in Marx. Ruskin, indeed, was the
great amateur of political economy, but none the less influential for that. It was not without reason that Keir Hardie
and many other labour leaders regarded Carlyle and Ruskin as
more important in shaping their political views than any
writers more fully versed in the abstractions of economic theory.

Still, in assessing the importance of all these influences on
the development of the political labour movement, we must distinguish between the foundation of permanent Socialist organization on the one hand, with all that that implied for the
future of the Labour Party, and on the other hand the 'socialistic' and humanitarian sentiment which was common in political circles and which accounted for the spasmodic and hap-
hazard action of the legislature in extending the sphere of State
activity. It was in the latter sense that Sir William Harcourt
could say in 1889 that 'we are all Socialists now'. This tenta-
tively collectivist outlook was so widespread and so vague that
it cannot be said to have had any special significance in the
development of the Labour Party. It is interesting to observe
that the political theory of T. H. Green, who modified the
doctrine of Liberalism as if to fit in with the contemporary
change of attitude to the function of the State, had an influence
upon the intellectuals of the older political parties, such as
Balfour and Haldane, but his work was not read either by the
members of the working class, who could not have understood
it, or by the active middle-class Socialists, who rarely proceeded
further into philosophical speculation than was required to
appreciate the ethics of Comte or Spencer. The influence of
Idealism did not help to found the Labour Party, though it may
have helped to split the Liberals twenty years later. It would,
indeed, be difficult to maintain that any of the British labour
leaders at the end of the nineteenth century, except for a very

few Marxists, were able to build their political views upon a reasoned philosophical basis. Their motivation is to be discovered rather in the failure of existing political bodies to recognize, as the Socialists were prepared to do, the continually increasing importance of the 'labour interest' in a country which, with a maturing capitalist economy and a well-established class system, was now verging on political democracy.

We can suitably proceed, therefore, to an examination of the beginnings of Socialist organization at the opening of our period.

CHAPTER II

The Socialist Revival

(1)

ONLY the closest inspection of the British political scene affords any indication of Socialist activity in 1880. What interest there was in Socialism sprang very largely from the success of the German Social Democratic Party, which in 1877 had polled nearly half a million votes, and had won thirteen seats in the Reichstag. In 1879 an old Chartist, John Sketchley of Birmingham, published a pamphlet entitled *The Principles of Social Democracy*, which seeks to show, from the example of the German party, what the programme of a similar party in Britain would be. The pamphlet gives a London address of 'The Social Democratic Party', but the address is that of the little club in Rose Street, Soho, where a group of German exiles gathered to keep their Socialist ideals alive in the frigid political climate of England.

The British Socialists at this time were indeed a small and scattered minority. The London Commonwealth Club, which John Hales represented at the Ghent Socialist Congress of 1877, seems to have died out before the end of the decade.[1] A few old Chartists still met in London under the leadership of the two brothers Charles and J. F. Murray, in a small group called the Manhood Suffrage League, apparently a successor to the National Reform League: their discussions had a distinctly Socialist flavour.[2] At Birmingham, Sketchley was trying to

[1] G. M. Stekloff, *History of the First International* (1928), p. 340. Hales, who led the opposition to Marx in the British section of the International, tried to revive it by founding an International Labour Union in 1877–8, but this was a very short-lived affair, although it secured the support of advanced Radicals like Bradlaugh, Mrs. Besant, and Stewart Headlam. See M. Nettlau, 'Ein verschollener Nachklang der Internationale', *Archiv für die Geschichte des Sozialismus* (Leipzig, 1921), p. 134.
[2] Meetings of the League were reported in the *Labour Standard* of 1881. W. K. Lamb, 'British Labour and Parliament, 1865 to 1893' (1933, unpublished, Brit. Lib. Pol. Sci.) quotes a reference in *Industrial Review*, 24 Mar. 1877. The League was still in existence in Aug. 1885, when it met to hear Charles Murray read and comment on an 1850 address by Richard Oastler (*Democrat*, 5 Sept. 1885).

organize a Midland Social Democratic Association.[1] Other Socialist propagandists of the time were Henry Travis, a doctor, who published occasional pamphlets on Owenism[2]; and a young journalist, Ernest Belfort Bax, who knew Germany well, had read Marx's *Capital* in German, and had written articles on Marxism in the monthly magazine *Modern Thought*.[3] There was hardly any other evidence of interest in Socialism, unless we count the inchoate economic discontent of the Commons Protection League, and the supporters of the Tichborne claimant.[4] It is true that a body called the Hebrew Socialist Union existed among Jewish immigrants in Whitechapel for a few months in 1876[5]; and also that in the course of 1880 the Rose Street club of German exiles developed an English section, and also expanded considerably owing to the influx of exiles from the repressive legislation in Germany and Austria. Indeed, from 1879 until 1882 the club had a weekly journal of its own, *Freiheit*, which was edited by the German Socialist, Johann Most.[6] But when in 1881 Kropotkin visited England and lectured on Socialism, he found himself addressing 'ridiculously small audiences'[7]; and Marx's death in London two years later would have passed unnoticed by *The Times* had not the Paris correspondent sent a paragraph on his European reputation.

Clearly, in 1880, Socialism in Britain was as yet a movement without indigenous strength. Ruskin's letter to the trade

[1] Its manifesto and programme are discussed in the *Republican* of Jan. 1879. A link with Birmingham politics of a previous generation is indicated by its adoption of a proposal for a paper currency.

[2] H. Travis, *The Co-operative System of Society* (1871); *English Socialism*, a collection of tracts (1880).

[3] *Modern Thought*, Aug. and Oct. 1879.

[4] For a more detailed catalogue of British Socialists or sympathisers at this time see M. Nettlau, *Anarchisten und Sozial-Revolutionaire* (Berlin, 1931), p. 340. *De Morgan's Monthly* (1876–7) airs the views of a socialistic economic rebel. Support for the claimant to the Tichborne baronetcy and estate was strong enough to secure the return of a 'Tichbornite' at a by-election in 1875. See *Annual Register*, 1871–5.

[5] P. Elman, 'Beginnings of the Jewish Trade Union Movement in England', *Transactions of the Jewish Historical Society of England*, xvii (1951–2), 57.

[6] Most was imprisoned in 1881 for incitement to murder because he acclaimed the assassination of Alexander II of Russia. In 1882 he was expelled from Britain, and emigrated to the United States, taking *Freiheit* with him. See *Dictionary of American Biography* for a summary of his career. While he was in prison an English edition of *Freiheit* was produced for some weeks by F. Kitz, the founder of the English section of the Social Democratic Club (F. Kitz, 'Recollections and Reflections', *Freedom*, Jan.–July 1912).

[7] P. Kropotkin, *Memoirs of a Revolutionist* (1899), ii. 252 f.

14

unions[1] may have occasioned a slight stir among the organized workers, and may have reminded the older of them, if they read it, of their forgotten ideals: but the climate of politics seemed still unpropitious for any labour attempt to take up the general social question. In 1880 there was a General Election, and the hold of the Liberal Party over the working-class vote was shown to be stronger than ever. Only three working men were returned, all of them as Liberals: Henry Broadhurst, by this time Secretary of the T.U.C., joined Thomas Burt and Alexander McDonald at Westminster, but as McDonald died in 1881, and was not succeeded by a labour man, the labour M.P.s again numbered only two. The elections showed the strength of Chamberlain's new Radical pressure group, the National Liberal Federation, which dominated the constituencies in the middle-class interest, to the alarm of Whigs and labour leaders alike. So far as the issues of the election were concerned, however, Gladstone's personality and the trade depression dominated the voting: the Liberals had a clear majority of seventy-two seats in the new House.

In late 1880 a new weekly paper, the *Radical*, was established in London. The paper was run by a working man, F. W. Soutter, who says in his memoirs that it was founded to support the Anti-Coercion Association, which united the 'advanced' Radicals with the Irish in opposition to the new Liberal government's policy of applying coercion in Ireland.[2] The leading article of the first issue deplored the small number of labour representatives in Parliament.[3] We can see, from a meeting of the Anti-Coercion Association in February 1881, who were the protagonists of this alliance of Radicals and Irish: Miss Helen Taylor, John Stuart Mill's stepdaughter, took the chair, and T. P. O'Connor, F. W. Soutter, and the old Chartist Charles Murray were among those who spoke.[4]

Just at this time the suggestion arose that a more permanent organization of 'advanced' Radicalism should be formed. The idea seems to have originated with H. M. Hyndman, a Tory

[1] *Fors Clavigera*, Letter 89, Aug. 1880.
[2] F. W. Soutter, *Recollections of a Labour Pioneer* (1923), p. 99.
[3] *Radical*, 4 Dec. 1880.   [4] *Radical*, 12 Feb. 1881.

Radical who was defeated at Marylebone at the 1880 election, and his friend H. A. M. Butler-Johnstone, for many years M.P. for Canterbury. The views of these two men on the Eastern Question provided a link with Karl Marx, whose advice they anxiously sought.[1] On 2 March, in response to their invitation, delegates from various London clubs and associations met at the headquarters of the Social Democrats in Rose Street in an attempt to 'unite, if possible, all societies willing to adopt a Radical programme with a powerful Democratic party'.[2] The outcome of the meeting was that a committee was appointed to see Joseph Cowen, Radical M.P. for Newcastle, who was said to be willing to assist. A few days later another meeting was held, this time with Cowen in the chair. It was explained that the earlier meeting had 'urged the necessity of the formation of a New Party, the grand object of which should be the direct representation of labour. In addition to Parliamentary reform, the new party would, of course, have to deal with the question of improvement in the social condition of the people.' More specific grievances were now stressed by a member of the Lambeth Democratic Association, who observed that:

> the people of London were compelled to change their residences more frequently than the inhabitants of the manufacturing districts, and thereby frequently became disenfranchised; also, under the caucus system it was impossible for a labour candidate to run for a seat with any degree of success.[3]

The upshot was that a resolution was passed without opposition in favour of an attempt to establish 'a labour party', and a committee of nine was appointed to draft a programme. The

[1] Butler-Johnstone to Marx, 7 and 15 Mar. 1881; Hyndman to Marx, 28 Feb. and 6 Mar. 1881 (Marx Correspondence, Int. Inst. Soc. Hist.). Butler-Johnstone became Conservative M.P. for Canterbury, formerly his father's seat, in 1862, and held it until 1878, when he resigned owing to differences with his party. In 1880 he stood as an independent but was defeated. See Report of Commission on Corrupt Practices, Canterbury (*Parliamentary Papers*, 1881, xxxix. 172 ff.). Butler-Johnstone's own reputation did not emerge entirely unscathed from this enquiry which he was responsible for initiating.
[2] *Radical*, 5 Mar. 1881.
[3] Ibid. 12 Mar. 1881; Engels to Bernstein, 12 Mar. 1881 (E. Bernstein (ed.), *Die Briefe von Friedrich Engels an Eduard Bernstein* (Berlin, 1925), p. 21).

committee was to include Cowen; Professor E. S. Beesly, the
Positivist, who had befriended the trade unions in the 1860's,
but who was no Socialist; J. Lord, the President of the English
section of the Rose Street club, and a few other working-class
Radicals; and Hyndman and Butler-Johnstone.

The foundation conference duly took place on 8 June 1881,
and a long advertisement in the *Radical* beforehand invited delegates from 'advanced political organizations, trade societies,
and clubs' throughout the country. The statement opened by
saying:

> At the last General Election, held during a period of great
> public excitement, a vast number of members were returned
> to the House of Commons who represent any interest in the
> country but that of the working class.

It advocated a 'social and political programme which shall
unite the great body of the people, quite irrespective of party':
this programme was to include attention to labour interests,
economy, constitutional reform, the end of coercion in Ireland,
and full publicity for the discussion of imperial and foreign
affairs.[1] The hand of H. M. Hyndman can be detected in the
phraseology of the statement, and it is evident that he was
taking an active part in the shaping of the new party.

When the conference took place, it was decided that the new
body should be called the Democratic Federation. It is not unreasonable to find, in this name, a deliberate attempt to copy
and rival Chamberlain's National Liberal Federation, which
had proved all too successful in establishing the hold of the
middle classes on the constituencies. In the N.L.F. there was
plenty of local autonomy for the constituent associations or
'caucuses', which, while often containing a number of working
men, were normally dominated by their wealthier members.
The Democratic Federation imitated the machinery of the
N.L.F. but proposed to make its appeal primarily to the working
class. Cowen himself, an independent Radical who had numbered many Chartists among his friends, was already facing the
great struggle with the Newcastle caucus that was to lead to his

[1] *Radical*, 28 May 1881.

retirement from Parliament in 1886.[1] The Democratic Federation may therefore be regarded as the product of a reaction against the Chamberlain caucuses—a reaction occasioned by the Liberal government's policy of coercion in Ireland, with which Chamberlain, as a member of the Cabinet, was necessarily associated.

(2)

In its first year of life the Democratic Federation devoted much of its time to the two problems of coercion in Ireland and agricultural distress. A deputation was sent to Ireland to investigate conditions there, and protest meetings were held, not only in London, but also in the larger provincial cities, where attempts were made to establish branches or affiliated societies.[2] So far as agricultural distress was concerned, the remedy advocated was land nationalization, which had been proposed by Professor A. R. Wallace as the solution to the Irish land problem.[3] As often happened in nineteenth-century politics, proposals to solve the difficulties of Ireland were the thin end of the wedge for new principles in British government. About this time, too, the gospel of Henry George began to be heard from America: as already mentioned, *Progress and Poverty* found an eager audience at a time when political attention was focused on agrarian disorders in Ireland, crofter distress in the Scottish Highlands, and a severe agricultural depression everywhere. George's remedy, the Single Tax, was not so drastic as land nationalization: but his propaganda attracted attention to the subject, and his arguments could be applied, as has already been suggested, to a more thoroughgoing programme.

At the same time, principally under Hyndman's lead, a new Socialist group was beginning to develop. Hyndman, a graduate of Trinity College, Cambridge, came of a family of Ulster

---

[1] M. Ostrogorski, *Democracy and the Organisation of Political Parties* (1902), i. 231 ff.
[2] E.g. Herbert Burrows lectured at Liverpool: *Radical*, 24 Dec. 1881. Engels had now decided that the Federation was 'quite without significance' because it could only arouse interest on the Irish question (Engels to Bernstein, 3 May 1881: Bernstein, op. cit. p. 70).
[3] *Contemporary Review*, Nov. 1880; A. R. Wallace, *My Life* (1908), pp. 320 ff.

origin, enriched by a fortune made by his grandfather in the West Indies.[1] His father left a considerable sum to endow churches of the Establishment in the poorer parts of London. Hyndman himself, now almost forty, had knocked about the world as a company promoter or as a journalist—he had visited Italy during the *Risorgimento* and had also spent some time in Australasia and in the United States. He had become a Radical, but he had no sympathy for Gladstone, and he first took up public speaking to denounce the Russians and to support the foreign policy of Disraeli. On a trip to America in 1880 he read Marx's *Capital* in the French edition, a copy of which had been given him by Butler-Johnstone. His conversion to Marxian Socialism followed, and in January 1881 he published an article in the influential monthly, the *Nineteenth Century*, which he entitled, 'The Dawn of a Revolutionary Epoch'. In June of that year, at the inaugural conference of the Democratic Federation, he distributed to all the delegates a little book he had written called *England for All*, in which he expounded the views of Marx without mentioning his name. This annoyed Marx, whom he had already met, and their relations became strained. Marx wrote to his friend Sorge in some irritation:

> In the beginning of June there was published by a certain Hyndman (who had earlier intruded himself into my house) a little book: *England for All*. It pretends to be written as an exposition of the programme of the 'Democratic Federation' —a recently formed association of different English and Scottish radical societies, half bourgeois, half proletarian. The chapters on Labour and Capital are simply literal extracts from, or circumlocutions of, *Das Kapital*, but the fellow mentions neither the book nor its author, but to shield himself from exposure remarks at the end of his preface: 'For the ideas and much of the matter contained in Chapters II and III, I am indebted to the work of a great thinker and original writer', etc., etc. As to myself, the fellow wrote stupid letters of excuse, for instance, that 'the English don't like to be taught by foreigners', that 'my name was so much detested', etc. For all that, his little book, so far as it pilfers *Das Kapital* makes good propaganda, although the man is a weak vessel,

[1] See his autobiography, *The Record of an Adventurous Life* (1911).

and very far from having even the patience—the first condition of learning anything—to study a matter thoroughly.[1]

In this way Hyndman lost the friendship of Marx, and as a
result that of Engels as well. Marx died in 1883, but Engels was
to live on in London until 1895, aspiring to direct the Socialist
and labour movements from behind the scenes; and his hostility
to Hyndman was to have important consequences. Marx and
Engels were not easy people to get on with, and they were sometimes very poor judges of character. Hyndman nicknamed
Engels the 'Grand Lama of the Regents Park Road' because of
his seclusion in his house there,[2] and Engels spoke of Hyndman
as 'an arch-Conservative and an extremely chauvinistic but not
stupid careerist, who behaved pretty shabbily to Marx, and for
that reason was dropped by us personally'.[3] Hyndman was by no
means a careerist, as his subsequent unrewarding toil in the
Socialist movement was to show: Marx was perhaps nearer the
truth when he described him as 'self-satisfied and garrulous'.[4]
He was, as we would say, a man with a bee in his bonnet, ex-
cessively talkative, quite insensible to the feelings of his audience
—in his later agitation he would quote Virgil at the street-
corner to the working men of London—but, for all that, quite
unselfishly devoted to his cause. Bernard Shaw classified him:

> . . . with the free-thinking English gentlemen-republicans of
> the last half of the nineteenth century: with Dilke, Burton,
> Auberon Herbert, Wilfred Scawen Blunt, Laurence Oliphant:
> great globe-trotters, writers, *frondeurs*, brilliant and accom-
> plished cosmopolitans so far as their various abilities per-
> mitted, all more interested in the world than in themselves,
> and in themselves than in official decorations; consequently
> unpurchasable, their price being too high for any modern
> commercial Government to pay.[5]

Hyndman's Conservative leanings made him suspect to many
of the Radicals, who mostly preferred the Liberals if they had

[1] To Sorge, 13 Dec. 1881 : *Selected Correspondence of Marx and Engels* (1936), p. 397.
In some cases of quotation from this volume the translation has been modified.
[2] Hyndman, op. cit. p. 252; *Justice*, 1 Apr. 1893.
[3] To Bebel, 30 Aug. 1883 (*Selected Correspondence*, p. 389).
[4] To his daughter Jenny, 11 Apr. 1881 (*Selected Correspondence*, p. 389).
[5] Book review in *The Nation* (1911), reprinted in Bernard Shaw, *Pen Portraits
and Reviews* (1932), p. 129.

to choose between the parties. His Marylebone election address of 1880, which declared opposition to disestablishment and to Irish Home Rule, was a source of later suspicion and was not forgotten by some of his contemporaries.[1] It is true that under the influence of Marxism he soon gave up these points of his programme. In the course of that year, however, he was still sufficiently Conservative in his leanings to arrange a meeting with Disraeli, now the Earl of Beaconsfield, and to pour forth his views to him in the hope that the Conservative Party might take them up. The ex-Premier listened to him with patience, but told him that there was little hope, warning him of the 'phalanx of the great families', and of the fact that 'private property which you hope to communize, and vested interests which you openly threaten, have a great many to speak up for them still'.[2] So Hyndman turned his back on the Conservative Party, but he always disliked them less than he disliked the Liberals, a feature which was to distinguish his politics from those of many of the other British Socialists.

(3)

Hyndman, as President, was directly in control of the organization of the Democratic Federation, and paid the rent of its office and the salary of its secretary[3]: but until 1883 it was not committed to Socialist principles, for its other sponsors were not prepared for that. Hyndman himself devoted much attention to the land question, and republished Spence's lecture on the common ownership of land (1775) under the new title of *Land Nationalisation*. Henry George, who was visiting Britain to further his own campaign, interviewed Hyndman about the objects of the Democratic Federation, and Hyndman stated that 'at present the principal cause of its existence [is] the action of the Government in relation to Ireland'.[4] The arrest of Parnell and

---

[1] See e.g. A. G. Barker's leaflet, *The Father and Founder of the Modern English Socialist Movement* (1912). The Marylebone election address is reprinted in H. W. Lee and E. Archbold, *Social Democracy in Britain* (1935), p. 275. It is very similar to Butler-Johnstone's address at Canterbury, for which see *Kentish Chronicle*, 20 Mar. 1880: both of them, for instance, speak of the colonies as 'the special heritage of the working classes'.　　[2] Hyndman, op. cit. p. 244.
[3] Ibid. p. 253.　　[4] *Radical*, 1 Apr. 1882.

other Irish leaders in late 1881, and the suppression of the Land League, caused the Federation to redouble its protests against coercion. In June 1882 a large demonstration under Cowen's chairmanship was held in Hyde Park to protest against the new coercion measures which followed the Phoenix Park murders. Other meetings were held to consider questions of constitutional reform, which bulked large in the Federation's programme.[1]

Still, the number of Socialists was slowly on the increase. The German colony of exiles in London contained some energetic propagandists, and there was a small fringe of native working-men Radicals who fell under their influence. Among them were Joseph Lane and Ambrose Barker of the Marylebone Democratic Association, which had helped to convene the foundation conference of the Democratic Federation. They distrusted Hyndman and founded their own organization, first the Homerton Socialist Club and then the ambitiously-named Labour Emancipation League, which cheerfully sought to enrol the working class by propaganda on Mile End waste.[2] This tiny body can claim the title of being the first indigenous Socialist organization in the revival of the 1880's, for along with the Chartist programme of constitutional reform which it shared with the Democratic Federation, it demanded, for the sake of the 'Emancipation of Labour', a collectivization of the 'Instruments of Production and the Means of Employment'. Its connexion with the Democratic Federation only developed when many of the other Radicals had withdrawn.

For the fact was that the Democratic Federation's intransigent opposition to the Liberal Party became unpalatable to many of its promoters and early members. Its vigorous support for a Land League candidate against the Liberal nominee at a by-election in Tyrone, and its denunciation of 'capitalist radicalism' in a special manifesto on this occasion (autumn 1881), led to the defection of all the Radical clubs except that of

[1] Report of D. F. Executive, *Justice*, 9 Aug. 1884.
[2] Lee and Archbold, op. cit. p. 50; Lane's reminiscences in letters to A. G. Barker, 22 Mar. and 12 Apr. 1912 (Nettlau Collection, Int. Inst. Soc. Hist.). Lane, a member of the Manhood Suffrage League since 1871, had helped in the printing of the *Radical*; with Kitz he formed a Workmen's Propagandist Committee, which had a small printing press and produced leaflets.

Stratford.[1] Cowen and Butler-Johnstone had dropped out of the
Federation, and gradually, as its original membership con-
tracted and as Socialism began to spread, it became possible for
Hyndman to convert it into an openly Socialist body, which he
did at the annual conference in 1883. Already, earlier in that
year, it had begun to concentrate on topics such as Housing and
the Eight Hours Working Day, which showed that the emphasis
was no longer on purely political Radicalism. The Federation
now accepted Hyndman's declaration of principles, *Socialism
Made Plain*, but it did not change its name until the following
year, when it became the Social Democratic Federation.

The new recruits to Socialism who joined Hyndman in running the Federation included a number of young public school
men, such as J. L. Joynes, who had been a master at Eton, and
R. P. B. Frost and H. H. Champion, who had been contemporaries at Marlborough. A more notable convert, more of
Hyndman's age, was William Morris, already a writer and
artist with a distinguished reputation and an honorary fellowship at Exeter College, Oxford. Thus as the working-class
Radicals left the Federation, the middle-class Socialists came in.[2]
It was notable that many of the latter found their way to
Socialism by way of the land reform movement: this was true
of Joynes, who had accompanied Henry George on his tour of
Ireland in 1882, and also of Frost and Champion, who held
office in the newly founded Land Reform Union, which publicized George's views in England.[3] Morris had been active in
the Eastern Question Association, which had brought him
into contact with Liberal labour leaders a few years before,
but he had not taken any part in the land agitation: Ruskin,

[1] *Justice*, 9 Aug. 1884. Hyndman wrote to Helen Taylor that 'the Liberal wire
pullers, specially paid for that purpose, are at work taking the clubs from us'. He
regarded 'Charles Murray and the '48 men' as the most reliable in spite of their
'queer ideas on the currency' (2 Oct. 1881, Mill-Taylor Correspondence, Brit. Lib.
Pol. Sci.).
[2] Hyndman wrote to Henry George on 14 Mar. 1883: 'The common English
workmen are more or less embittered against the Irish and at times I feel despon-
dent. But Socialist ideas are growing rapidly among the educated class. . . .' (Henry
George Correspondence).
[3] The Land Reform Union, founded in Apr. 1883, later became the English
Land Restoration League. In its early days Frost was its secretary, Champion its
treasurer (*Christian Socialist*, July 1883).

rather than George, seems to have been his introduction to Socialism.[1]

Champion became the secretary of the Democratic Federation, and was at this time regarded as Hyndman's *fidus Achates*.[2] In some ways their political attitudes were closely similar: Champion, the son of a major-general, was a Tory Socialist, even more than Hyndman. He had been commissioned in the Royal Artillery, but he had retired to become a politician, and his father now set him up as a publisher in London. The Federation needed publicity, and at the end of 1883 Champion arranged to take over publication of a monthly magazine, *To-day*. Shortly afterwards at the beginning of 1884, he started publishing *Justice*, a weekly newspaper and organ of the Federation, which was launched with a contribution of £300 from Edward Carpenter, a talented rebel against Victorian society who greeted the Socialist cause with enthusiasm.[3]

In 1883 the Federation continued propaganda in the provinces: it was reported to have branches in Newcastle and Liverpool and to be active in Birmingham, Bristol, Edinburgh and Nottingham. It employed the veteran John Sketchley to act as propagandist in South Staffordshire during a strike of ironworkers. It issued protests against 'wars of aggrandizement' by Britain in Egypt and by France in Tunis; it attacked with special virulence the advocates of State-aided emigration, and demanded instead an Eight Hours law and home colonies as the solution to unemployment.[4]

Yet in spite of this activity the Federation failed to win any widespread popular support. There were, by the beginning of 1884, a few working-class members of great energy and loyalty. Some of them, like J. E. Williams, had been members of the old

[1] Morris gives accounts of his political development in H. M. Hyndman *et al.*, *How I became a Socialist* (n.d.); and in a letter to Scheu, 5 Sept. 1883, quoted P. Henderson, *Letters of William Morris* (1950), pp. 183 ff. His attitude to the Eastern Question was Gladstonian, the opposite to that of Marx and Hyndman.

[2] An account of Champion's life in Britain, based on his own memoirs in the Melbourne *Trident* of 1908, is given in H. M. Pelling, 'H. H. Champion', *Cambridge Journal*, vol. vi (1953). See also, more briefly, *Dictionary of Australian Biography*.

[3] Lee and Archbold, op. cit. p. 86. For Edward Carpenter, see below, p. 142; and also his autobiography, *My Days and Dreams* (1916).

[4] *Christian Socialist*, Sept. and Oct. 1883. The Federation claimed that its 'organised opposition to State-Aided Emigration had almost prevented the holding of any more public meetings on the question' (*Justice*, 9 Aug. 1884).

Picture Post Library

Friedrich Engels

H. M. Hyndman

Picture Post Library

Picture Post Library

H. H. Champion

William Morris

Leaders of the Socialist Revival

Rose Street club[1]; others, like James Macdonald of the Marylebone Democratic Association, came over later, attracted by the
new propaganda.[2] But the Federation's first Socialist executive,
elected in 1883, was dominated by the bourgeois element, the
bulk of the working-men Radicals having disaffiliated. James
Macdonald's Marylebone club was an exception in transforming
itself into a branch of the Federation[3]; and the Labour Emancipation League was still very unwilling to co-operate.

Hyndman was aware of the Federation's weakness in this
respect, and did his best to arouse the workers to its support. A
feature was made of canvassing the delegates to the annual
T.U.C.: for instance, in 1883, when the Congress met at
Nottingham, J. E. Williams, a working-class member of the
Federation, was in the town preaching Socialism, and Hyndman
addressed a meeting on Land Nationalization. The Federation
also decided to take advantage of industrial strikes for the sake
of Socialist agitation: thus the cotton strike in the Blackburn
area early in 1884 led to a campaign there by Joynes, Williams,
Macdonald, Morris and Hyndman, and a branch of the Federation was founded in Blackburn. A similar 'mission' was made
about the same time to the miners striking in the neighbourhood of West Bromwich, and Burrows, Sketchley and Helen
Taylor took part, as well as Hyndman and Morris. Farther
afield, too, the Federation, secured support: the Austrian
Socialist Scheu, who had now moved to Edinburgh, helped to
form the Scottish Land and Labour League, which affiliated
itself to the Democratic Federation in August 1884.[4]

The Federation had also taken the final steps to make itself a
fully Socialist organization. Hyndman had persuaded the
Labour Emancipation League to send several representatives
to the fourth annual conference, which saw not only the adoption of the title of 'Social Democratic Federation', but also substantial alterations in the programme. The proposals for nationalization were no longer limited to the railways, the banks and
the land, but were extended to include all the 'means of

[1] Lee and Archbold, op. cit. p. 86.
[2] Hyndman *et al.*, *How I became a Socialist* (2nd edn., n.d.), pp. 60 ff.
[3] Lee and Archbold, op. cit. p. 85. [4] *Justice*, 9 and 23 Aug. 1884.

production, distribution and exchange'. Radical constitutional proposals remained prominent—after all, the 1884 Franchise Act was not yet in operation—and were made even more 'democratic' by the adoption of several points of the L.E.L. list, including the following:

> Legislation by the People, in such wise that no project of Law shall become legally binding till accepted by the majority of the People.
> The Abolition of a Standing Army, and the Establishment of a National Citizen Force; the People to decide on Peace and War.

These clauses, and indeed the bulk of the programme of the L.E.L., were drawn from the programme of the German Social Democratic Party as adopted at Gotha in 1875. But the Gotha programme, and that of the L.E.L., went so far as to demand '*direct* legislation' by the people, that is to say, the Initiative as well as the Referendum; this seems to have been too much for Hyndman and the Federation, who rejected it. But Hyndman could not prevent Lane, with the help of Morris, Scheu and others dethroning him from the office of permanent President and putting the Executive Council in control of the organization.[1]

As it turned out, one of the most successful methods of propaganda for the S.D.F. (as we may now call the Federation) was the public debating which Hyndman undertook with prominent Radical leaders. His first debate with Bradlaugh in 1884 gave the Socialists a good deal of publicity in the National Secular Society,[2] and the Secularists may well have been already favourably disposed to the Socialists owing to their support of Bradlaugh in the Affirmation Case. Bradlaugh himself was a vigorous opponent of Socialism, and it was largely his hostility to the socialistic tendencies of some members of the Republican

---

[1] *Objects and Programme of the Labour Emancipation League* (n.d.). Lane, in a letter to Barker published in the leaflet, *The Father and Founder of the Modern English Socialist Movement*, says of the D.F.: 'Hyndman was the permanent President until 1884 when, at his request, I went as delegate to their conference, put an end to permanent President, got it called Social Democratic Federation, and forced them to adopt our Labour Emancipation League programme, instead of their merely political one.' The new S.D.F. programme was in fact drawn up by a committee of four —Champion, Lane, Bax and Morris. See Morris to Scheu, 13 Aug. 1884, quoted P. Henderson, op. cit. p. 211.
[2] *Will Socialism Benefit the English People?* Verbatim report of a debate between H. M. Hyndman and C. Bradlaugh (1884).

movement which had caused it to split in 1873.[1] But some of his principal lieutenants in the National Secular Society, notably Annie Besant and Edward Aveling, accepted the new doctrine, and for some time the Society was itself a debating ground in which the cases for and against Socialism were argued with equal freedom. As the Society had branches throughout the country, with especial strength in all industrial areas, this was an excellent field for Socialist propaganda, which in Hyndman's cases was always hostile to religion.

Thus in 1884 the S.D.F. seemed to have every hope of rapid progress. It had secured the services of a number of able men, many of them both well-off and generous. The best-known of these was William Morris, who was appropriately elected treasurer, in which capacity he made himself responsible for making good the loss on *Justice*.[2] The Federation was not strong in numbers, but it had important footholds in the Land Reform Union and the National Secular Society, and it had both weekly and monthly journals on its side. It also had two affiliated bodies, the Scottish Land and Labour League and the (East London) Labour Emancipation League. When in March 1884 the Federation organized a procession to the grave of Marx in Highgate cemetery on the first anniversary of his death those who took part amounted, according to Morris, to over a thousand, with another two or three thousand onlookers. This was, at least, a beginning.[3]

(4)

It would have been surprising if the Socialists of the early 1880's had been able to keep together within one organization. Neither the character of the S.D.F.'s membership nor the arrangements for its control encouraged this. According to Hubert Bland:

> The Executive Committee of the Federation used to meet in a little basement room in a block of buildings in Westminster, nearly opposite the Eastern end of the Houses of Parliament. To carry out the democratic idea of its basis any

---

[1] For this controversy see *International Herald*, Jan. 1873.
[2] Report of D. F. Executive, *Justice*, 9 Aug. 1884.
[3] Morris to his wife, 18 Mar. 1884, quoted P. Henderson, op. cit. p. 195.

member of the Federation was allowed to attend their meetings, but only members of the committee might speak or vote. It was a stuffy, ill-furnished little room, illuminated only by the flickering flames of a couple of candles, stuck in common tin candlesticks. . . . There was always a good deal more friction than fraternity at Palace Chambers. . . . The type of man who has the intellectual and moral courage to join a new and unpopular movement has also fully developed the faults of his qualities—obstinacy, vanity, a sort of prickly originality, and a quick impatience of contradiction.[1]

It was, above all, the disagreement about the means of attaining Socialism that brought the clashes of personality into prominence. Hyndman had captured the Democratic Federation for Socialism, and he expected to go on dominating it and leading it along the line of policy which he favoured. He was a lot older than many of its most active members, and he expected them to respect his age and experience. But he did not find favour in all quarters: Marx and Engels, as we have seen, had never regarded him as a genuine Socialist by their standards, and although Marx's daughter, Eleanor, was a member of the S.D.F., both she and Edward Aveling, who became her partner in a 'free' marriage, regarded Hyndman with a suspicion that in Aveling's case was reciprocated, and with reason.[2] More important than this, as it turned out, was the fact that Morris himself, like Hyndman a forceful personality and actually eight years older, resented Hyndman's domineering ways and eventually decided that he could not put up with him. Finally, there was the lurking suspicion of the leaders of the L.E.L., who opposed not only Hyndman's 'views of political adventure', that is to say, his willingness to promote candidatures for Parliament and local bodies, but also his 'tendency towards National assertion'. Both these were points on which Morris was in agreement with them.[3]

[1] *Sunday Chronicle*, 26 May 1895.
[2] Some account of Aveling's character is given in E. Bernstein, *My Years of Exile* (1921), pp. 160 ff. See below, p. 159. Bradlaugh had accused Aveling of peculation from the funds of the National Secular Society, and Hyndman sought to raise this charge on the S.D.F. Council, thereby increasing the tension at its meetings (Morris to Scheu, 28 Sept. 1884; Shaw to Scheu, 26 Oct. 1884. Scheu Correspondence, Int. Inst. Soc. Hist.).
[3] The quotations are from the manifesto of the Socialist League, which is reprinted in T. Mann, *Memoirs* (1923), p. 46.

At this time the Executive Council of the S.D.F. was an unwieldy body of nineteen members—far too many for the business they had to deal with. It owed its size, no doubt, to an attempt to secure democratic control, but the attempt, which began in mutual suspicion, ended in schism. On 27 December 1884 the split took place: ten of the members of the Council resigned, denouncing what in a signed statement they called the 'attempt to substitute arbitrary rule therein for fraternal co-operation'. The signatories included Morris himself; Aveling and Eleanor Marx, and Belfort Bax, the journalist and philosopher, who was a confidant of Engels; Lane and Mainwaring, of the L.E.L., and J. L. Mahon of the Scottish Land and Labour League. A counter-statement was then made by the nine members who, led by Hyndman, took the opposite view, and remained in control of the remnants of the S.D.F.[1]

The actual points at issue between the two parties were comparatively unimportant.[2] At a meeting of the Council on 16 December Hyndman had wanted to expel W. J. Clarke, a member of that body, on the ground of being an Anarchist: but he was outvoted by 9 votes to 7. This had shown the division of the forces, and the clash was renewed a week later, when Hyndman's opponents moved a vote of confidence in Scheu, who was also suspect to Hyndman on account of Anarchist tendencies. The anti-Hyndman group also wanted to remove the control of *Justice* from Hyndman's hands. But these details were simply the excuse for the crisis which had been boiling up for months: in August, for instance, Morris was complaining about the failure to publish a verbatim report of the annual conference, while Hyndman was apparently already anxious to set aside its decisions.[3]

---

[1] The statement of the seceders appears in P. Henderson, op. cit. p. 226.

[2] See Morris's letters to Scheu and others in Dec. 1884 and early Jan. 1885 (P. Henderson, op. cit. pp. 218 ff.). Engels thoroughly enjoyed the whole business: 'On Saturday, the S.D.F. fortunately came to the split. . . . I have the satisfaction of having seen through the whole swindle from the start' (to Bernstein, 29 Dec. 1884: Bernstein, *Briefe von Engels*, p. 161).

[3] Morris to Scheu, 13 Aug. 1884, P. Henderson, op. cit. p. 211. Shaw, in the letter to Scheu mentioned above, p. 28, said that, 'But for Frost and Champion, who, though nominally, Hyndmanites, practically boss the Federation between them by sticking together and working (they have kicked up a flourishing agitation in the East End) the whole body would have gone to pieces long ago'.

Morris received an *ex cathedra* summons to visit Engels on the day of the split just before the critical Council meeting took place, and Engels gave him his advice on the way to organize a new party. Next day Morris was acquiring headquarters for it: not surprisingly, as it had the support of the two leagues of East London and Scotland, it was called the Socialist League. It at once began to publish a new journal, *Commonweal*, which was started with £300 from Morris, and thereafter required constant subsidies. The main difference between *Commonweal* and *Justice*, which the S.D.F. still managed to continue, was that *Commonweal* was, in Morris's hands, a paper of real literary merit: they were alike in that both lost money heavily. The Socialist League secured the adhesion, not only of the two leagues, but also of several former S.D.F. branches: those at Hammersmith and Merton Abbey which were under Morris's patronage, and also the branch at Leeds. Charles Faulkner, Morris's friend, who was a mathematics tutor at University College, Oxford, provided the League with a branch at Oxford by winning over a Radical association; and other branches were founded elsewhere.[1] But in spite of Morris's great activity as a lecturer up and down the country, the League did not displace the S.D.F., and after six months it had, apart from the two affiliated bodies, only eight branches with 230 members.[2] Morris was depressed about this, as he wrote to Mrs. Burne-Jones:

I am in low spirits about the prospects of our 'party', if I can dignify a little knot of men by such a word. . . . You see we are such a few, and hard as we work we don't seem to pick up people to take over our places when we demit. All this you understand is only said about the petty skirmish of outposts, the fight of a corporal's guard, in which I am immediately concerned: I have [no] more faith than a grain of mustard seed in the future history of 'civilization', which I *know* now is doomed to destruction, and probably before long: what a joy it is to think of! and how often it consoles me to think of barbarism once more flooding the world, and real feelings

[1] Morris to May Morris, 20 Feb. 1885, P. Henderson, op. cit. p. 231.
[2] Conference Report in *Commonweal*, Aug. 1885.

and passions, however rudimentary, taking the place of our wretched hypocrisies. . . .[1]

This letter explains very clearly the nature of Morris's views on the character of the future Socialist revolution. Like Hyndman, he believed in catastrophe and looked forward to it with millenniary enthusiasm, though he did not, like Hyndman, regard himself as marked out for revolutionary leadership. Rather, he believed that the immediate role of the Socialist was to educate people for the great inevitable change which would bring back the simpler, sounder society of medieval times, when craftsmen took pride in their work and when there was no capitalist exploitation or industrial ugliness. In this there is clear evidence of Ruskin's influence, shaping a criticism of contemporary society that was to form the basis of Syndicalism and Guild Socialism in the twentieth century. Morris disagreed with those who favoured Parliamentary action, that is to say, efforts to put Socialists on public bodies, because he thought that this would encourage the self-seeker and threaten the purity of the Socialist ideal with the corruption and compromise inevitably involved in politics. To his distress he found even his own Socialist League divided on this issue—a division that was to hasten its collapse at the end of the decade.

In the meantime, the activities of the League centred upon himself, controlling the purse strings as he did, and they reflected his personality in its strength and weakness. Morris was a fully convinced Socialist, and though he did not know much about Marxian economics he was quite prepared to take them on trust. His attitude is well illustrated by his answer to a Hyndmanite questioner who asked, 'Does Comrade Morris accept Marx's Theory of Value?' His reply, as reported by Glasier, was:

To speak frankly, I do not know what Marx's Theory of Value is, and I'm damned if I want to know. Truth to say, my friends, I have tried to understand Marx's theory, but political economy is not in my line, and much of it appears to me to be dreary rubbish. But I am, I hope, a Socialist none the less. It is enough political economy for me to know that

[1] Morris to Mrs. Burne-Jones, 13 May 1885 (P. Henderson, op. cit. p. 236).

31

the idle rich class is rich and the working class is poor, and that the rich are rich because they rob the poor. . . .[1]

In retrospect, Morris, with his fine literary gifts and artistic skill, seems much the most attractive personality among these early Socialists. His picturesque nautical appearance, his spontaneous generosity, his very human explosions of wrath all contributed to make him a popular propagandist and to earn him great loyalty and devotion from many of his supporters. It may seem surprising, therefore, that the Socialist League had so little success even in comparison with the S.D.F. The explanation lies principally in the fact that public opinion did not favour Morris's opposition to Parliamentary action. The S.D.F., for all its peculiarities, seemed more practical than Morris's group, many of whom were out-and-out Anarchists. Moreover, much of the League's organization was inefficient. All its literature was handsomely produced, and even its circulars to Council members were printed: but its officers were often unreliable in the performance of their duties. The *Commonweal* accounts were very badly kept and the branch membership fees were most irregularly paid.[2] Hubert Bland relates:

> The League's headquarters were in a large, barn-like loft in Farringdon St. When we called there we generally found it occupied by a touzle-haired young man in shirt-sleeves and slippers smoking a pipe over the fire. The very look of the place gave an impression of feebleness and want of method. Nobody seemed to have anything to do there. . . .[3]

(5)

There were, however, other groups of Socialists growing up without affiliation to either the Federation or the League. One of these was Stewart Headlam's Guild of St. Matthew, which

---

[1] J. B. Glasier, *William Morris and the Early Days of the Socialist Movement* (1921), p. 32.

[2] See Socialist League papers, Nettlau Collection, Int. Inst. Soc. Hist. Thus on 23 Feb. 1886 the Bradford branch secretary wrote: 'I cannot understand your bookkeeping at all. We have not had an account rendered for months. You surely do not expect us to remit for *Commonweals* etc. until after you send us an invoice!' On 31 Jan. 1887 the Leicester branch secretary complained: 'Why is it that when we send an order for literature we cannot get a reply under a month?'

[3] *Sunday Chronicle*, 26 May 1895.

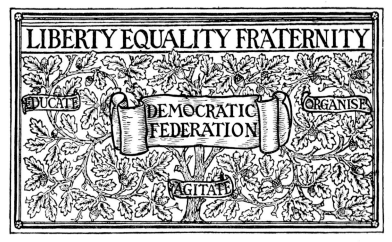

William Morris's design for the membership card of the
Democratic Federation

Walter Crane's design for the heading of *Commonweal*

Art in the Service of Socialism : *1*

needs little attention at this stage because it was primarily a religious and not a political body.[1] There were also one or two groups of independent Socialists in the provinces, such as the Sheffield Socialists, formed by Edward Carpenter in 1886, and by him carefully kept outside the controversies between the rival London organizations.[2] But there was one group, the Fabian Society, founded in London in 1884, which deserves more than passing mention. Its early history has been recounted with great clarity and in considerable detail by Edward Pease, who was for many years its secretary.[3] It sprang from a slightly older society called the Fellowship of the New Life, a vaguely Ruskinian, vaguely Owenite ethical society originally founded by Thomas Davidson, 'the wandering scholar', a Scotsman who spent much of his lifetime in America and who was responsible for the formation of several societies of this sort both there and in Britain. The first meeting of the Fellowship was held in 1883, and the group considered the idea of forming, perhaps in South America, a little Utopian community, possibly on the lines of Owen's New Harmony. A committee was appointed to make proposals, and its report was drawn up by H. H. Champion, who had lately become the secretary of the Democratic Federation. He not unnaturally directed attention to more practical issues. His proposals included the following resolution, which pointed the way towards political action and away from Utopianism:

> The members of the Society assert that the competitive system assures the happiness and comfort of the few at the expense of the suffering of the many and that Society must be reconstituted in such a manner as to secure the general welfare and happiness.[4]

After this, there was a division of opinion between those who were for placing economic problems in the first place, and those who were for subordinating them to the ethical. The latter retained control of the Fellowship of the New Life, but the

---

[1] See below, pp. 126f.
[2] Carpenter, *My Days and Dreams*, p. 125.
[3] E. R. Pease, *History of the Fabian Society* (1916).
[4] Pease, op. cit. p. 32.

former founded early in 1884 a separate society which they called the Fabian Society. The dominant personality in the Fabian group at this time appears to have been Frank Podmore, who was a student of psychical research and later a biographer of Robert Owen.[1]

The Fellowship of the New Life continued to exist in a small way until 1898, though it founded no Utopias. Its membership fluctuated round the hundred mark, and it published a quarterly called *Seedtime*, which contained articles on ethical Socialism, the Simple Life, and various humanitarian subjects. But in importance it was quite overshadowed by the Fabians.

Apart from the fact that they were Socialists, it is difficult to determine what the views of the original Fabians were. Pease maintains that right from the start the Society opposed the revolutionary views of the S.D.F.[2]; while Bernard Shaw, who attended for the first time in May 1884 and was elected to membership in September, later declared that 'the constitutionalism which now distinguishes us was as unheard of at the Fabian meetings in 1884 and 1885 as at the demonstrations of the S.D.F. or the Socialist League'.[3] It seems to be the case that although some of the members were always constitutionalists—it is difficult to imagine Pease himself being otherwise—the Society had not officially declared itself on the question, and its membership soon contained persons with revolutionary views, including some Anarchists. Podmore was responsible for suggesting the name 'Fabian'; and he explained the early tactics of the society in the following words:

> For the right moment you must wait, as Fabius did most patiently when warring against Hannibal, though many censured his delays: but when the time comes you must strike hard, as Fabius did, or your waiting will be in vain and fruitless.[4]

It is noteworthy that this declaration of Podmore did not commit the Fabian Society to constitutionalism, but only to caution.

[1] See his letter to Davidson, Thomas Davidson Correspondence, Yale University Library.
[2] Pease, op. cit. pp. 61 f., and note by Shaw.
[3] G. B. Shaw, *The Fabian Society: Its Early History* (Fabian Tract 41, 1892), p. 4.
[4] Pease, op. cit. p. 39.

There was an implied criticism of the tactics of the S.D.F.: and the principal characteristic of Podmore and his friends seemed to be that they were men and women who wanted to escape occasionally from the street-corner atmosphere of the Federation in order to think out their politics in quieter surroundings. But the society at once began to recruit a body of young, high-spirited men and women who seemed, as one member complained, 'to regard the discussions as a species of admirable drawing-room diversions. Indeed in several quarters socialism (of as extreme a type as you will) is becoming a fashion, a new sensation. Ladies are joining us in goodly numbers. . . .'[1] It is clear that the Fabian drawing-room environment, while it effectively kept out nearly all the proletarians, also attracted a very miscellaneous audience, not all of it very intellectually minded. 'It was a silly business', says Shaw:

> They had one elderly retired workman. They had two psychical researchers, Edward Pease and Frank Podmore, for whom I slept in a haunted house in Clapham. There were Anarchists, led by Mrs. Wilson, who would not hear of anything Parliamentary. There were young ladies on the lookout for husbands, who left when they succeeded. There was Bland's very attractive wife Edith Nesbit, who wrote verses in the *Weekly Dispatch* for half a guinea a week, and upset all the meetings by making scenes and pretending to faint. She became famous as a writer of fairy tales. . . .[2]

Under these circumstances it took a little time for the Society to find a steady political course. One of its earliest decisions seems to have been a resolution moved by Bland on 29 February 1884:

> That whilst not entirely agreeing with the statements and phrases used in the pamphlets of the Democratic Federation, and in the speeches of Mr. Hyndman, this Society considers that the Democratic Federation is doing good and useful work and is worthy of sympathy and support.[3]

There remains, however, no indication of what the Fabians criticized in particular in the behaviour of the Federation. The

---

[1] P. Chubb to Davidson, 4 Feb. 1884, Thomas Davidson Correspondence.
[2] M. Cole (ed.), *The Webbs and Their Work* (1949), p. 7.
[3] Pease, op. cit. p. 38.

first Fabian Tract, issued in April and entitled *Why are the Many Poor?*, simply stated the extent of wealth and poverty but offered no remedy. The second tract, issued in September, was drawn up by Shaw in his most scintillating style: it advocated Land Nationalization, State competition in industry, abolition of sex inequalities and of all types of privilege. It concluded, however, with the observation (to which Pease objected), 'That we had rather face a Civil War than another century of suffering as the present one has been'. Nor was there any indication of Fabian policy in the speeches of Shaw at the Industrial Remuneration Conference in January 1885, which he attended as a delegate of the Society.[1] At the end of 1884 the Society elected its executive committee of five members: two of them were clearly not constitutionalists—Mrs. Wilson, the Anarchist, and Frederick Keddell, the Society's first secretary and later the treasurer of the S.D.F.; the other three were Pease, Bland and Shaw himself, whose mind was probably not made up on the question.[2] Podmore had now retired, explaining in a letter to Thomas Davidson that 'the Fabian has by no means kept true to its name'.[3]

At this time Shaw was an aspiring novelist, so far unknown and unsuccessful. His political interests had first been aroused by Henry George, whom he heard speak in London in 1884:

He struck me dumb and shunted me from barren agnostic controversy to economics. I read his *Progress and Poverty*, and went to a meeting of Hyndman's Marxist Democratic Federation, where I rose and protested against its drawing a red herring across the trail blazed by George. I was contemptuously dismissed as a novice who had not read the great first volume of Marx's *Capital*.

I promptly read it, and returned to announce my complete conversion to it. Immediately contempt changed to awe, for Hyndman's disciples had not read the book themselves, it being then accessible only in Deville's French version in the British Museum reading room, my daily resort.[4]

[1] *Report of the Industrial Remuneration Conference* (1885). The Conference was sponsored by a Mr. Miller of Edinburgh, to discuss the problem of maldistribution of wealth. Mr. Miller also gave £100 to the Edinburgh S.D.F. to provide it with a clubroom (Glasier, op. cit. p. 21).
[2] Pease, op. cit. p. 48.
[3] Podmore to Davidson, 16 Dec. 1884, Thomas Davidson Correspondence.
[4] G. B. Shaw, *Sixteen Self Sketches* (1949), p. 58.

Shaw was prepared, in his enthusiasm for Marx, to defend him against all comers: and when Philip Wicksteed, the mathematical economist who was also a Unitarian minister, uttered some Jevonian criticisms of Marx in the Socialist monthly *To-day*—criticisms that were not immediately answered by other Marxists—Shaw entered the fray with a reply to Wicksteed. A further response from Wicksteed convinced Shaw that he was in the wrong, and from then onwards he accepted the Jevonian theory of Marginal Utility, instead of Marx's Labour theory of Value.[1] That was in the course of 1884–5. Already, so far as revolution by violence was concerned, Shaw was beginning to have doubts[2]: and by February 1885 he was urging the middle classes to join the Socialist movement in order to counteract the influence of ' a mob of desperate sufferers abandoned to the leadership of exasperated sentimentalists and fanatical theorists'.[3] In accordance with this precept, he brought into the Fabian Society his friend Sidney Webb, a First Division clerk in the Colonial Office, whom he had met six years before at a debating society.[4] Webb was a disciple of John Stuart Mill: he had read Marx at Shaw's suggestion but had not been converted to Marx's form of Socialism.[5] Sydney Olivier, a colleague of Webb in the Colonial Office, joined the society with him.[6] Shortly afterwards, Mrs. Besant, Bradlaugh's collaborator in the causes of Secularism and Neo-Malthusianism, also joined. All of these new and able recruits were constitutionalists: one of them, Mrs. Besant, had a long record of Radical agitation. Under their influence the Fabian Society was soon to develop a distinctive political tactic of its own.

[1] *To-Day*, Oct. 1884 and Jan. and Apr. 1885; Shaw's Appendix 1 to Pease, op. cit.
[2] Shaw regarded himself as 'at heart an Anarchist. . . . Of course I know that Collectivism and Anarchism come to the same thing practically when worked out; but I object to any name which might afford a pretext, at some intermediate phase of the Revolution, for a Committee of Public Safety composed of the Executive Council of the D.F.' (to Scheu 26 Oct. 1884: Scheu Correspondence).
[3] *Christian Socialist*, Apr. 1885.
[4] Shaw in M. Cole, op. cit. p. 7.
[5] Ibid. p. 6.
[6] Pease, op. cit. p. 46; M. Olivier, *Sydney Olivier* (1948), p. 76.

CHAPTER III

The Socialist Debate on Strategy

(1)

In 1885 occurred the first elections under the new Reform Act, which extended the electorate by about two-thirds, bringing the total number of voters up to over four millions. By this measure Gladstone enfranchised many of the agricultural labourers, and his Radical supporters set about finding a programme likely to win their approval. Jesse Collings's 'Three Acres and a Cow' was quite a successful slogan, implying a degree of landownership for all. 'Next time', said Labouchere, 'we must have an urban cow',[1] for the Liberal Party was losing its grip on the towns, and an increasing proportion of its strength lay in the 'Celtic fringe' or in the agricultural areas of England. But an 'urban cow' was just what the Liberal Party could not offer, for to provide a social programme for the industrial workers would have been to threaten the interests of the most important supporters of the party—the great industrial capitalists. The best that the Liberal Party could do, as Chamberlain realized at this time and as Lloyd George was later to perceive, was to attack the landlords and the brewers, so as to rally on their side the agricultural labourers, the miners and the Nonconformists, without alienating the industrialists. Chamberlain's 'Unauthorised Programme' of 1885 accordingly advocated social and agrarian reform along these lines, but had little to say about the grievances of industrial workers.

Some of the members of the Conservative Party were not slow to realize that there was an opportunity for them to win the urban vote, and that their own political future depended upon their doing so. This, it would appear, was the principal motive of Lord Randolph Churchill's 'Tory Democracy', which sought to win working-class support for a vague programme of social and industrial reform. This competition for the new

[1] J. L. Garvin, *Life of Joseph Chamberlain* (1932–3), ii. 124.

democratic vote was deplored by the official leaders of both parties. Gladstone regretted the 'leaning of both parties to Socialism, which I radically disapprove'[1]; while Northcote and Salisbury, the Conservative leaders, gave no countenance to Churchill's ideas. Yet the attitude of Chamberlain and Churchill was a clear indication of the great fact that now dominated the political scene—the fact that the 1884 extensions of the electorate meant the end of the already moribund principle of government non-intervention in the economic sphere. As soon as the control of elections passed out of the hands of those who paid income-tax, *laissez-faire* was dead.

It was a much larger step, of course, to Socialism in the stricter sense—either that of the Marxists, or that of the Fabians, who were more eclectic in their reading of political economy. In 1885 the Socialists were not an electoral force at all. It was ridiculous to expect a body like the S.D.F. with less than a thousand members to be able to fight a Parliamentary election, unless the members were all concentrated in one constituency. Still, the S.D.F., never having fought an election, was determined to try its luck. First of all, in October it put up four candidates for the London district school boards. All were unsuccessful, but the system of cumulative voting to some extent concealed the severity of their defeat.[2] Then its leaders began to plan the Parliamentary campaign.

The difficulty was finance, for the Federation had been in very low water since the schism, and had even had to arrange for the printing of *Justice* by the voluntary work of compositors who were members. The way these voluntary workers kept *Justice* going was a remarkable story of loyalty to their cause. While the compositors worked on the printing of the paper, the unskilled, including Hyndman himself, would be preparing the contents bills on a press given by Miss Helen Taylor, and then

---

[1] J. Morley, *Life of William Ewart Gladstone* (1908), ii. 346.
[2] The candidates, their districts, and their votes were as follows: Mrs. Hicks, Marylebone, 1,820; H. Quelch, Lambeth, 1,608; H. H. Champion, Clerkenwell, 873; H. Burrows, Tower Hamlets, 4,232. Burrows was also supported by the Tower Hamlets Radical Club; and he was the only Socialist candidate to get more than half the votes necessary for election. The programme of the Socialists included the proposal of one free meal a day for the school-child. See S.D.F. Executive Report, *Justice*, 7 Aug. 1886; *The Times*, 4 Nov. 1885.

taking part in street parades to sell the completed editions.[1] So
they could just make ends meet: but they were still short of
money for elections. There were only eighteen branches of the
party listed at the time of the annual conference in August—ten
of them in the London area; and as fast as new ones were formed,
old ones dissolved.[2] Hyndman and Champion were desperate
to find some financial resource for the Federation: they were
anxious not to let the General Election go by without some
effort. They approached Joseph Chamberlain, in the hope that
if they promised him their support he would give them a seat to
contest in the Birmingham area: but Chamberlain was too
shrewd a politician not to realize their weakness, and though he
met the Socialist leaders he rejected their proposals.[3]

Then Champion received an offer of funds through Maltman
Barry, a former Marxist and member of the First International
who was now working as a Conservative agent. The money was
offered for two Socialist candidatures in London, which the
contributors no doubt thought would split the Liberal vote.
For this object, £340 was transferred to the Federation. Accordingly, two working-men members were put up, J. E. Williams
for Hampstead and John Fielding for Kennington. Neither was a
working-class constituency; Williams, at least, conducted no
campaign[4]; and the mismanagement of the affair was apparent
when the two candidates got only 59 votes between them. Another S.D.F. candidate, John Burns, an unemployed journey-
man engineer, stood at Nottingham, and he did much better,
polling 598 votes. Part of his funds were found by Champion's
friend the soap manufacturer, R. W. Hudson, who may have
been attracted by Socialist ideas at this time, but was later to be
an active Liberal Unionist.[5]

The reaction to the fiasco of the London candidatures was

[1] *Justice*, 23 May 1885. Miss Taylor had apparently lost interest in the Federation even before the split: see Hyndman's letter to her of 25 Aug. 1884, and her
reply complaining of the *Justice* policy of 'anonymous insult and irresponsible
assertion' (Mill-Taylor Correspondence.)
[2] Executive Report, *Justice*, 7 Aug. 1886—referring to the beginning of the
twelve-month period.
[3] *Echo*, 4 Dec. 1885; Champion in *Aberdeen Standard*, 19 Oct. 1893.
[4] See his letter to *Pall Mall Gazette*, 7 Dec. 1885.
[5] Some account of this is given in J. Burgess, *John Burns* (Glasgow, 1911), chaps.
iii and iv.

immediate. Hyndman and Champion had acted without con-
sulting all their colleagues, and even the treasurer of the S.D.F.,
J. Hunter Watts, had been left in the dark. Watts publicized
the whole affair in an angry letter to the *Pall Mall Gazette*, and
it was also ventilated in the Liberal-Radical paper the *Democrat*,
where C. L. Fitzgerald, a journalist who was a member of the
S.D.F. Executive Council, denounced Hyndman and Champion for 'irresponsibility' and for 'trying to run the Federation
in military style'.[1]

The result of this so-called 'Tory Gold' scandal was that there
was almost universal execration of the S.D.F., and even the
Fabian Society passed a resolution of strong disapproval. Another secession took place from the ranks of the Federation,
this time led by Fitzgerald. A new body called the Socialist
Union was set up: one of its keenest workers was a young Scotsman lately arrived in London, James Ramsay Macdonald, who
had come across Socialist ideas a year or two before during a
stay in Bristol. Fitzgerald went lecturing in the provinces and
sought to establish branches of the Socialist Union with a purely
constitutional political method in view.[2] Socialism, he said, no
more meant 'daggers and dynamite' than did Home Rule for
Ireland.[3] The Bristol and Nottingham S.D.F. branches came
over; a new branch was formed at Carlisle; a body in Manchester called the Labour Union affiliated; and there may have
been other constituents. But there was little demand for fresh
organization, and the Socialist Union had no wealthy backers:
so it did not last long. The S.D.F. continued a precarious existence, and *Justice* was still published regularly once a week,
though its format was now smaller than ever. All in all, it did
not look as if 1886 would be a good year for the Socialists.

(2)

In spite of the divisions among the Socialists, and the especial
weakness of the S.D.F. after two schisms, Socialism was more

---

[1] *Pall Mall Gazette*, 4 Dec. 1885; *Democrat*, 12 Dec. 1885. Shaw gives an account
of the episode in a letter to Scheu of 17 Dec. 1885, and concludes: 'All England is
satisfied we are a paltry handful of blackguards' (Scheu Correspondence). See also
Engels to Bernstein, 7 Dec. 1885 (Bernstein, *Briefe von Engels*, pp. 177 f.).
[2] *Democrat*, 29 May 1886.　　　　　[3] *Socialist*, July 1886.

prominently in the public eye in 1886 than it had ever been before. The reason was that a severe cyclical depression reached its worst point in this year, and there was considerable un-employment. Throughout the country public order was threatened by desperate men who had lost their jobs and had no dole to fall back on. In London, the Federation seized the opportunity to take the lead of the agitation of the unemployed. On 8 February 1886 it held a meeting in Trafalgar Square to demand public works to absorb the workless. When the Socialists started their meeting there was already a crowd at-tending a near-by demonstration of the Fair Trade League, which urged industrial protection as the cure for economic dis-tress. John Burns and Champion made speeches on behalf of the S.D.F., and Champion, never a tactful man, gave incite-ment to violence by saying that:

> When Lords and Commons were in danger of being blown up by dynamite they passed a Bill through both Houses in twenty-four hours. What has been done once can be done again.[1]

The crowd grew rapidly, and a real danger to the peace began to develop. Burns and Champion were soon growing alarmed by the effect of their bold words, and Burns readily accepted a suggestion from the police that he should lead the mob to Hyde Park, where there would be a better chance of their dispersing peacefully. On the way through Pall Mall, however, trouble began: stones were thrown at the windows of the clubs, and later shops in Mayfair were looted. When the main body reached Hyde Park, Burns and Champion tried to pacify their following, who wanted action. Burns concluded by saying:

> We are not strong enough at the present moment to cope with armed force, but when we give you the signal will you rise? (Loud cries of 'Yes'.) Then go home quietly, and the signal will be given if the government does not act. (Cheers.)[2]

This demonstration had several immediate results. Respect-able people woke up to the existence of revolutionary Socialism in their midst, and believed that it could control great masses of potential rioters. They reacted to the crisis in various ways.

---

[1] *Democrat*, 13 Feb. 1886.   [2] Ibid.

The Socialist Debate on Strategy

The subscriptions to the Mansion House Fund for the Unemployed, which had been languishing, suddenly shot up. The Queen wrote to Mr. Gladstone, her Prime Minister, deploring what she described as a '*momentary* triumph of Socialism and disgrace to the capital'.[1] The press meanwhile demanded the trial of the Socialist leaders. After the lapse of several days charges of seditious conspiracy were prepared against Hyndman, Burns, Champion and J. E. Williams, but in the nature of things they could not be proved, for the incidents had taken place without any deliberation. The prisoners made a vigorous defence of themselves, Burns making a speech for Socialism from the dock, and in the end they were acquitted. The whole affair had given the Federation a degree of publicity which they had never previously enjoyed.[2]

In the following two years the Federation continued to take the lead in organizing demonstrations of the unemployed. There were political meetings; there were processions to the workhouse to demand relief; there were church parades of the workless, culminating in a great demonstration at St. Paul's Cathedral in February 1887.[3] The Socialists were reported to be learning to drill with broomsticks: they were practising marching for their parades. Another crisis came on 13 November 1887, when an advertised meeting in Trafalgar Square was prohibited in advance by the police. Processions organized by the S.D.F., the Socialist League, and Radical bodies interested in the fight for free speech set out from various points in North London, converging on Trafalgar Square, but they were broken up by soldiers and mounted police. John Burns and Cunninghame Graham, a Scottish Radical M.P. who had been converted to Socialism a few months before,[4] were arrested on this occasion, convicted and sent to prison. Just one week later, after a meeting in Hyde Park, a young workman, Alfred Linnell, was killed by

---

[1] *Letters of Queen Victoria*, 3rd ser., i (1930), 52.
[2] Lengthy extracts from the speeches at the trial are given in Burgess, op. cit. pp. 57 ff. A good account of the riots is to be found in G. Elton, *England Arise!* (1931), chap. vi. Socialism at once became a good theme for a popular novel, as is shown by the hasty preparation and success of George Gissing's *Demos* (1886): see Morley Roberts's introduction to the 1928 edition.
[3] Lee and Archbold, *Social-Democracy*, p. 119.
[4] For the career of Cunninghame Graham, later a successful author of travel stories, see A. S. Tschiffely, *Don Roberto* (1927).

43

being run down by the police, and he was given a public funeral for which William Morris composed a Death Song:

> Not one, not one, nor thousands must they slay,
> But one and all if they would dusk the day.

After 1887, however, the danger of violence was reduced as the immediate depression wore off and the numbers of the unemployed decreased. The Socialist bodies began to find that they had achieved remarkably little for all the energy they had expended. On the one hand, respectable people were afraid to join their organization; on the other hand, the unemployed were too poor to subscribe. The Socialists had got a great deal of publicity but very few new members. Moreover, the success of the demonstrations in intimidating the government and the upper classes was very limited: if there was a lesson to be drawn from the events of 1886 and 1887, it was that unarmed workers could not stand up to soldiers and police. In these circumstances the more far-sighted Socialists were compelled to reconsider the whole question of the tactics of revolution and the future of their movement.

The first factor that they had to take into account was the very limited size of their own organizations. It is unlikely that the S.D.F. ever numbered more than 1,000 members in the course of the decade, at any rate if we count only those who regularly paid their penny a week.[1] The Socialist League could not muster half this number[2]; the Fabian Society at its strongest

---

[1] According to Engels, Morris estimated the S.D.F. membership at the end of 1884 at 400 in London, 100 in the provinces (Engels to Bernstein, 29 Dec. 1884: Bernstein, op. cit. p. 161). In 1887 financial dues were enough to cover 689 members (Champian in *Common Sense*, 15 Sept. 1887). Twelve months later Burns noted that the annual report was 'discouraging. £98 less income, £5 only more in dues, and a weakness numerically in the branches that was depressing to hear' (Diary, 6 Aug. 1888, B.M. Add. MSS. 45335). In 1889, for the credentials to the Paris Congress, the S.D.F. claimed 1926 members, but Burns said it was 'really less than half of this' (*Labour Elector*, 3 Aug. 1889).

[2] E. P. Thompson in his *William Morris, Romantic to Revolutionary* (1955), p. 546, suggests a figure of about 700 for 1887. This compares with the Secretary's estimate of an aggregate membership in Jan. 1886 of 550. But these figures are considerably in excess of real financial membership. Inefficiency of organization, the povery of many of the members, and in some cases anarchist principle all militated against the regular collection of fees. In the second three months of 1886 the Treasurer's report shows that the total of fees that he received only covered a membership of 280. The Secretary's report, 25 Jan. 1886, and the Treasurer's report, June 1886, are both in the Nettlau Collection.

Williams, Hyndman, Champion and Burns (*seen together on the left*) appear at Bow Street after the rioting of 8th February 1886

An episode of 13th November 1887: the Clerkenwell Green contingent broken up by police in St. Martin's Lane on their way to Trafalgar Square

The Unemployed Riots

in the eighties had a membership of about 150.[1] Even if we add
in the 200 or so members of the Guild of St. Matthew,[2] and
allow for a certain number, such as Edward Carpenter's
Sheffield Socialists, who did not belong to any of the national
societies, the total does not amount to more than 2,000. Moreover, this total includes duplicated memberships, for many of
the Socialists belonged to more than one organization.

In short, the Socialists were a sort of 'stage army' in the
1880's. There were plenty of leaders, anxious to play eloquent
and dramatic parts; but the supporting cast, being very limited,
had to make up for their lack of numbers by frequent changes
of role. Certainly they were successful in creating a much greater
impression than one would expect from so small a body of
opinion. The fact was that, although it was to the interest of the
working class that the Socialists appealed, there was a very
high proportion of middle-class people among the converts of this
period, and what the societies lacked in numbers they made up
in the comparative energy, ability and financial generosity of
their members. This alone can account for the flood of Socialist
periodicals and pamphlets which already poured from the
presses. There were first of all the weekly papers of the S.D.F.
and the Socialist League, *Justice* and *Commonweal* respectively,
both heavily subsidized by the sacrifices of the faithful, but the
latter at least enjoying a circulation considerably larger than
the immediate membership.[3] Then there were various maga-
zines run by individual Socialists, such as Annie Besant's *Our
Corner*. Belfort Bax and Joynes were joint editors of *To-day*,
which was for some time published by Champion; and Thomas
Bolas, a research chemist, produced a little sheet called the
Practical Socialist and later the *Socialist*. Further, the *Christian
Socialist*, nominally an organ of the land reformers, was edited
by Champion and other Socialists for some time, and they gave
the Socialist cause a good deal of publicity. Similarly, the *Link*

[1] Pease, in his *History of the Fabian Society*, p. 60, mentions a figure of about 90 for
1886; and the Society reported a membership of 130 at the Paris Congress of 1889—
see *Report of the International Workmen's Conference* (1889), p. 1.
[2] F. G. Bettany, *Stewart Headlam* (1926), p. 81.
[3] In 1887 *Commonweal* issued 52 numbers and sold 152,186 copies. The loss on
this was £271 (*Conference Report*, 1888, p. 10).

was strictly the official journal of the Law and Liberty League, but Mrs. Besant as its editor made sure that Fabian meetings were well reported in its pages. Meanwhile, the Federation was publishing its own pamphlets and reports of debates, many of them through the convenient agency of the Freethought Publishing Company; the Socialist League also published pamphlets, and the Fabians issued tracts. One must also take into account the innumerable effusions of Socialist authors and journalists such as Carpenter, Shaw, and Hubert and Edith Bland.

In this intellectual activity lies the key to the importance of Socialism in the 1880's. It was most notable among the Fabians, but the other societies also had a high proportion of middle-class members anxious to express themselves on paper. We have, therefore, plenty of evidence from which to gauge the character of the discussions that went on. The main problem for the moment was, how could the Socialist revolution be accomplished? Could it be achieved, as Hyndman expected, by taking advantage of a collapse of the old society, rather on the pattern of the French Revolution? Hyndman saw himself as the Chairman of the Committee of Public Safety, installed in office by an untutored but enthusiastic mob aroused to violence by the bitterness of capitalistic crisis. It was an entertaining if somewhat unreal expectation that he, the City man, complete with the frock-coat and top-hat which were his customary dress, should be borne to power as the workers' choice in order to inaugurate the dictatorship of the proletariat. History has seen many ironies, but this was one that it was not to tolerate. As time went on, Hyndman's vision of the future was shared by fewer and fewer of those whose ability made them the intellectual leaders of the new movement.

(3)

The most important factor making for a reconsideration of the idea of violent revolution was, of course, the failure of the unemployed agitation of 1886–7. But underlying this there were other factors of more permanent influence, and most of them were associated with the development of political democracy in this decade. The Municipal Corporations Act of 1882 had removed the property qualifications for borough councillors. The Corrupt Practices Act of 1883 had really put a stop to most of the methods of bribery of voters, and had enormously improved the conduct of elections. The franchise legislation of 1884 had very greatly increased the strength of the working class at the polls—so much so, in fact, that if the size of the electorate is taken as the criterion no one except an advocate of women's suffrage could now deny to Britain the title of political democracy. True, the number of labour members in the House of Commons of 1885 was not large—there were eleven working-men M.P.s, all of them accepting the Liberal whip—but at least it was a considerable increase on the last Parliament which for most of its duration had only two. If eleven labour M.P.s could be elected without any separate labour representation body (for the Labour Representation League had been dead for years), how many could be elected if such a body existed and extended its operations all over the country?

Moreover, the new House of 1885 contained in the Irish Nationalist Party an example which neither Socialists nor labour leaders could miss. The Irish franchise had previously been narrower than the English: but the 1884 Acts widened it to the new general standard. There would have been a strong case for reducing the total number of Irish M.P.s, for the Irish population had decreased while that of England had rapidly increased, so that Ireland was numerically over-weighted in the Commons. This was not done, no doubt because both major parties were courting Irish support at the time. The result was that the new electorate gave Parnell, now at the height of his powers and influence, the remarkable total of eighty-six Nationalist M.P.s, all of them responsive to the model discipline of his party organization. As it happened, the Liberal Party had exactly eighty-six more members in the new House than the Conservatives: so that the Parnellites could make or mar a ministry. This brought the issue of Irish Home Rule into the foreground of the Parliamentary scene. In every way the Irish party served as a pattern for those who wanted to establish a labour party. It was remarkable for its rigid independence from

47

the Conservatives and Liberals; for its internal discipline—the pledges that were required of its members and the control exercised over them by the treasurer of the party, who paid their salaries; above all, for its success in forcing Parliament to face the issues in which it was interested.[1] It was not surprising that, from this time until the Parnell divorce case, if anyone wanted to justify the idea of founding an independent labour party, he spoke of the Irish Nationalists as a model.[2]

Another factor that must not be forgotten was the growth of a working-class public interested in political propaganda. It was not only that the workers had the vote: universal primary education was making more and more of them responsive to tracts, pamphlets and journalists. It was becoming increasingly practicable to establish newspapers as commercial ventures with the object of catering specifically for the working-class reader. An example of this was the *Cotton Factory Times*, founded by John Andrew of Ashton-under-Lyne. It was a trade unionists' paper, and the editor relied on the local union secretaries for local news and for sales publicity. But its proprietor simple regarded it as a commercial enterprise.[3] This was a significant development, for newspapers are always a sensitive index of changes in social attitude.

Finally, this working-class public, potentially capable of determining the composition of Parliament, was still deeply divided on the traditional lines of British politics: but it was never so evenly divided as after the Home Rule issue had split the Liberal Party. Although most of the Liberal Unionists had been classified as belonging to the Whig element in the Liberal Party, they were led by the man who had inspired the new Radicalism of the Unauthorized Programme, Joseph Chamberlain;

[1] For a brief account of the party organization, see C. C. O'Brien, 'The Machinery of the Irish Parliamentary Party, 1880–5' (*Irish Historical Studies*, 1946).

[2] It should not be supposed, however, that the leaders of the Irish Nationalist Party were ordinarily favourable to the formation of a new party in Britain, except when they were estranged from both Liberals and Conservatives as during the coercion crises of Gladstone's 1880 government. This is true even of the Irish labour leader Michael Davitt, although he did see the case for an independent labour party much more clearly than Parnell, and went so far as to advocate it in his *Leaves from a Prison Diary* (1885), ii. 160 f.

[3] See his speech at the dinner inaugurating a later venture, *Yorkshire Factory Times*, 5 July 1889.

and although Chamberlain had lost control of the National Liberal Federation, he carried with him the urban vote of Birmingham. Yet the Liberal-Labour M.P.s, to a man, remained on the Gladstonian side. The working class was so equally divided over Home Rule that its political influence seemed to cancel out on both sides, while the Irish issue postponed into the indefinite future the prospect of legislation for social reform. Paradoxically, this strengthened the position of those who favoured an independent party to represent labour. For the Liberals could no longer expect it to be taken for granted that they were the party of the 'labour interest'; and the case for a fresh start to find representation for labour on independent lines was accordingly improved.

The Socialists were naturally interested in this issue, for it was directly relevant to the debate on political methods in which they were engaged. It has already been mentioned that the Fabian Society, after initial doubts, began as early as 1885 to develop in the direction of the acceptance of constitutionalism, through the adhesion of new members who disliked the insurrectionary attitude of the S.D.F. Mrs. Besant, the most experienced politician among them, was forthright in her denunciation of the would-be revolutionaries. In December of that year she attacked John Burns on this subject at a Fabian meeting, and concluded:

> You who strive to keep the poor miserable, and you who drive them into revolution—you who look with satisfaction on the misery of a strike-conflict, in the hope that it may culminate in bloodshed: what shall I call you? Something far worse than foolish. Society is to be reformed by a slow process of evolution, not by revolution and bloodshed. It is you revolutionists who stem and block the evolutionary process.[1]

The suggestion that is sometimes made that Mrs. Besant was purely an agitator not interested in guiding policy appears to be unjust. She deliberately publicized the constitutional Socialists in her monthly journal *Our Corner*, and made her own position

[1] *Practical Socialist*, Jan. 1886. The Fabians encouraged non-members who were Socialists to attend their meetings, and even distributed tickets to them through the other Socialist organizations. See e.g. S. Webb to Morris, 13 Sept. 1886 (Nettlau Collection).

clear on this question at a time when Shaw for one seemed to be still doubtful. She was, however, liable to be overtaken by strong emotional excitement on occasions, and this is what must have happened early in 1887, when she was among the most vigorous advocates of carrying on the fight for free speech in Trafalgar Square at all costs. For Shaw, on the other hand, the Trafalgar Square fiasco of November 1887 was the final proof of the folly of challenging the police power.

But there were other Socialists who were on the side of constitutionalism at an early stage. January 1886 saw the first issue of Thomas Bolas's little paper, which bore the significant title of *Practical Socialist*. Bolas belonged to both the Fabian Society and the Socialist League, but he made his position clear by sub-titling his paper as 'A Monthly Review of Evolutionary and Non-Revolutionary Socialism'. It was in these pages that Hubert Bland in October advocated the formation of 'a Socialist party on political lines with a definite policy, aims and proposals. . . . Only by such a party can the real work of organization be done.'

As we have seen, the first group definitely to adopt a constitutionalist attitude was the short-lived Socialist Union, which was formed as a result of the 'Tory Gold' scandal. Its manifesto, issued early in 1886, stressed the importance of the 'intelligent and early exercise of political power'.[1] The Manchester Labour Union, its affiliate, appears to have been a derivative of the Manchester Socialist Union which Morris had lectured to in 1885 but found inclined to disagree with him about the value of Parliamentary politics.[2] The change of name from 'Socialist' to 'Labour' foreshadowed tactical developments of later years: but neither this body nor Fitzgerald's group survived for more than a few months.

Meanwhile in the course of 1886 the Fabians had reached a decision on the question of revolutionary method. In June the issue had been debated in the course of a three-day conference

[1] *Socialist*, July 1886.
[2] Morris to Scheu, 16 July 1885, P. Henderson, *Letters of Morris*, p. 237. Morris's visit resulted in the formation of a branch of the Socialist League in Aug. 1885, but less than a year later the branch was breaking up owing to its members' interest in electioneering (Branch Secretary reports, Nettlau Collection).

The Socialist Debate on Strategy

which the Fabians organized in order to bring Socialists and Radicals together. Mrs. Besant had expressed her point of view with customary force, and Dr. Pankhurst, then a Radical, had pointed to the Parliamentary success of the Irish Nationalists. But Morris, for the Socialist League, had replied that:

> The allusion to the Irish does not bear much upon the question for we all know that they have succeeded in Parliamentary agitation but we must remember that their Parliamentary representation is for a Parliamentary end. When they had a Parliament in Dublin they would be brought face to face with the whole series of economical questions which we are thinking of now.

Nor had Shaw developed into a complete constitutionalist yet, for he argued that:

> It would be most dangerous to have any sort of dependence on the present Parliament. The best thing to do instead of doing that would be to run a separate Parliament. . . .[1]

However, in September 1886, prompted by Mrs. Besant and Hubert Bland, the Fabian Society declared itself unequivocally in favour of Parliamentary action as the method of reform. The thoroughgoing opponents of this declaration inside the Society were for the most part Anarchists, but their protests were louder than their numerical strength justified, and when a Fabian Parliamentary League was formed inside the Society as a way of implementing the decision without expelling the dissentients, it soon became identified with almost the whole body of the members and so disappeared as a separate entity.[2]

This does not mean that the Fabians were necessarily in favour of trying to form a new political party. Actually, they were divided on this question. Most of them, led by Webb, held that it was their task to influence the existing parties, which were in their view too strongly entrenched to be replaced by a new Socialist or labour party. Both the Liberals and the Conservatives had already adopted various *ad hoc* measures of

---

[1] Report of the Proceedings of the Three-Day Conference, June 1886 (unpublished, Brit. Lib. Pol. Sci.).

[2] Shaw, *The Fabian Society*, pp. 12 ff. Mrs. Wilson, with Kropotkin, now formed the Freedom Group of Anarchist-Communists, and founded the monthly paper *Freedom*.

socialistic legislation: the judicious influence of the Socialists, exercised from points of vantage inside the London Liberal-Radical caucuses, could effectively encourage this tendency. The development of the system of democratic government, which culminated in the creation of the County Councils in 1889, might well make available fresh fields for the application of this policy of 'permeation': but Webb did not suppose that the Liberals and Conservatives could be elbowed aside by a new party, unless the trade unions were prepared as a body to employ their financial resources in running a political party, and there seemed little immediate likelihood of this.

But this policy did not satisfy all Webb's colleagues. Hubert Bland, unlike Webb and Shaw, a Tory by origin, saw that the tactics of 'permeation' meant, in effect, working with the Liberal Party, with which he had no sympathy. This was because many of the Fabians had close contacts with the Liberal Party, for Liberal-Radicalism was a much stronger force in the metropolis than it was elsewhere. Bland's view was that a new Socialist party was both necessary and practically possible. He had been expressing his criticism of the existing Socialist groups in a serial story that he contributed to the *Weekly Dispatch*: he regarded the S.D.F. as discrediting Socialism 'because of this silly bull-at-a-gate business of a few men'[1]; and he had nothing better to say of Morris and his followers, who had gone off 'with two sticks of brimstone and a box of matches to make a little hell of their own'.[2] His more constructive views emerged in an article which he wrote early in 1887 for *To-day*, of which he was now the editor:

> A popular organization must be created for the express purpose of working existing political machinery. Leaving to others the development of socialistic theory, it must be from the beginning free from any but immediately practicable proposals, and quite absolved from the insane delusion that changes come about in England in any other way than by the ballot box. It should abstain from denunciation of society at large, and devote its critical faculties to an argumentative exposition of political fallacies. . . .[3]

[1] *Weekly Dispatch*, 16 May 1886.
[2] Ibid. 2 May 1886.   [3] *To-day*, June 1887.

The Socialist Debate on Strategy

In other words, while not following the limited Fabian line of
'permeation', it was to be entirely different in tactics from the
S.D.F. or the Socialist League, and so required a fresh start
with new organization.

(4)

It was significant that this point of view was shared by some
members of each of the Socialist groups. The Socialist League,
as we have seen, consisted not only of Anarchists, but also of the
Marx-Engels clique, who were, of course, not hostile to Parliamentary methods, although they did not rule out the possibility
of violent revolution. Engels, a shrewd political strategist, had
already put on record for British readers his view of how the
Socialists could win power in this country. In his articles in
Shipton's *Labour Standard* of 1881 he had advised them to build
up a labour party which, provided that from the first it was
independent of the parties of the ruling class, he believed would
gradually become more and more Socialist as time went on.[1]
He now drew fresh inspiration from the example of the American United Labour Parties, and in 1887 was encouraging
Eleanor Marx and Edward Aveling in their agitation in East
London, considering that it was 'an immediate question of
forming an English Labour Party with an independent class
programme'.[2] This policy had begun to attract other members
of the League: among these, whom Engels calls 'our people',
occur the names of J. L. Mahon and Thomas Binning, trade
unionists, and A. K. Donald, all of them young men active in
the running of the Socialist League.[3] They had been largely
responsible for the formation of a 'Strike Committee' of the

[1] *Labour Standard*, 7 May to 6 Aug. 1881, reprinted as F. Engels, *The British
Labour Movement* (1936).
[2] Engels to Sorge, 23 Apr. and 4 May 1887 (*Labour Monthly*, 1934, pp. 122 f.).
Writing to Bernstein on 5 May, Engels said that the Radical clubs were 'aroused
by the American example and consequently were now seriously thinking of creating
an independent labour party' (Bernstein, *Briefe von Engels*, p. 192).
[3] Engels to Sorge, 4 June 1887 (*Labour Monthly*, 1934, p. 124). Mahon was a very
recent convert to Parliamentary action, but all the more enthusiastic. He was in
touch with Edward Pease, the Fabian, who was temporarily living at Newcastle,
and on 14 June he wrote to Engels advocating an amalgamation of 'the various
little organisations in one broad definite political platform' (Engels Correspondence, Int. Inst. Soc. Hist.).

53

League in 1886, and for the establishment early in 1887 of a North of England Socialist Federation among the Northumberland miners—another indication of a real attempt to bring Socialism to the working class, although it was put to them, unfortunately, as an alternative to trade unionism. This Northern Federation, built up jointly by S.D.F. and League agitators in the course of the great miners' strike of 1887, was the nearest approach yet made to a mass Socialist movement of the working class: but it was a transient success, for with the settlement of the strike its branches, which numbered twenty-four at the peak, rapidly faded away.

The published objects of the North of England Federation are worth noticing, as an indication of the way these young Socialists were thinking. They were four in number:

1. Forming and helping other Socialist bodies to form a National and International Socialist Labour Party.
2. Striving to conquer political power by promoting the election of Socialists to Parliament, local governments, school boards, and other administrative bodies.
3. Helping trades unionism, co-operation, and every genuine movement for the good of the workers.
4. Promoting a scheme for the national and international federation of labour.[1]

Morris was sceptical of the practicability of the first two items and expressed the hope 'that our friends will see the futility of sending (or trying to send) Socialists or anyone else to Parliament before they have learned it by long and bitter experience'.[2]

But Morris could not escape the implications of this clash of opinion inside the League: as early as March 1887 he noted in his diary, after a reference to the question, 'Whatever happens, I fear that as an organization we shall come to nothing, though personal feeling may hold us together'.[3] The issue was raised at

---

[1] *Our Corner*, July 1887.
[2] *Commonweal*, 25 June 1887.
[3] Morris's Socialist Diary, 30 Mar. 1887 (B.M. Add. MSS. 45335). The anti-parliamentarians, including Morris and Lane, controlled the Ways and Means Committee of the League; but on the Policy Statement Committee set up at the end of 1886, Lane was in a minority of one to three after Mahon's defection to the other side. Lane issued his 'Minority Report', as he called it, as a pamphlet, *The Anti-Statist Communist Manifesto* (1887). See proof copy of the Manifesto, explaining this, in Nettlau Collection.

the annual conference that year, and, on being defeated, most of the supporters of Parliamentary action retired from active participation in the running of the League. After the annual conference of the following year, 1888, when they were again defeated, their point of view was explicitly repudiated in a statement by the Council of the League, and they took no further part in its work. The Bloomsbury branch, which included the Avelings and several German Marxists, was expelled, and it transformed itself into the independent Bloomsbury Socialist Society; while Mahon and his friends, acting ambitiously on their own, seceded with what was left of the Labour Emancipation League,[1] and then formed a 'Labour Union' which aimed at national standing but which only succeeded in dragging out a few years' miserable existence as a working-class group in Hoxton.[2] Meanwhile, the withdrawal of the 'Parliamentary' element caused the Socialist League to fall more and more into the control of the Anarchists. Soon Morris himself was discomfited by their activities and their attempts to win complete control of the League. The increasing weakness of the League forced him at the same time to increase his subsidies, which by the spring of 1889 had reached a rate of £500 a year.[3] In November 1890 he decided that he could continue no longer: he withdrew from the League, taking with him the Hammersmith branch, which remained loyal to his personality. He retired into the comparative peace of the Hammersmith Socialist Society, as the branch was called on reorganization, and left the League to disintegrate owing to its lack of funds and the wild behaviour of its Anarchist members, who seemed to delight in getting themselves arrested and sent to prison.[4]

[1] The L.E.L. printed the reasons for its disaffiliation in a paper dated 23 June 1888 (copy in Nettlau Collection). Since 1885, when the Mile End branch of the Socialist League was formed, it had only one group of its own, that at Hoxton, and Lane lost control of this when he ceased to live in the area. See Lane to Secretary, Socialist League, 14 May 1885 (Nettlau Collection).
[2] See *Platform of the Labour Union* (1888). This document, which was signed by Keir Hardie and others as well as by the original promoters, said: 'The Labour Union points to what the Irish Party have achieved by a similar course of action.'
[3] Morris to Glasier, 19 Mar. 1889. (E. P. Thompson, *William Morris*, pp. 610 ff.)
[4] W. C. Hart, *Confessions of an Anarchist* (1906), p. 90. For a convenient summary of the early history of Anarchism in this country, see M. Nattlau, 'Freedom's Fortieth Birthday', *Freedom*, Oct. 1926. The remnants of the Socialst League did not unite with Kropotkin's Freedom Group until 1895.

So far, it would seem that the demand for a new, practical, political party had not got very far. The Fabians were going in for 'Parliamentary' politics, but for most of them a new party seemed impossible. The Socialist Union was dead; and the Socialist League had defeated its 'Parliamentary' minority. But in 1887 a new initiative came, this time from the ranks of the S.D.F., and from none other than H. H. Champion, previously Hyndman's most loyal associate. Champion had given up the post of secretary of the S.D.F. in 1885 at the time of the 'Tory Gold' scandal, but he was still one of its most prominent members. He had taken a leading part in the unemployed agitation, but he was soon disappointed with its failure and took the view that it was necessary either to increase the pressure on the government, by camping out with the unemployed in Trafalgar Square until something was done for them—a procedure that might well have caused serious disturbances—or to abandon that type of agitation altogether and to concentrate on winning Parliamentary seats in a completely constitutional fashion. Hyndman's refusal to accept either of these alternatives led to a break between the two men. Hyndman was prepared to talk violence, but he recoiled from action when the best opportunity occurred. Such an attitude, in Champion's view, made the worst of both worlds. In 1887 Champion began to publish a little monthly paper of his own, called *Common Sense*, and in the September issue he wrote an article advocating a policy along Bland's lines, and strongly criticizing the management of *Justice*. He pointed out that under the existing methods of propaganda the S.D.F. was making no progress, and he worked out from the total of affiliation fees for 1886–7 that the membership of the body was less than 700.

Champion's desertion was a serious thing for Hyndman. Up till recently Champion had been as bold in his utterances as anyone else, and Hyndman always retained an admiration for his ability and courage. He had inherited something of the political eccentricity of his Jacobite ancestors, the Urquharts: his distant cousin, David Urquhart, a Tory-Radical M.P., had been one of the most curious political personalities of the previous generation. Fluent and caustic both on the platform and with the pen, Champion was cool and resourceful in those crises of physical danger which his rasher utterances provoked. A Tory at heart and a Socialist by conviction, he was at the same time an ambitious politician. Being a more flexible tactician than Hyndman, he kept in touch with the Fabians, whose Society, as we have seen, he had helped to found, but he was temperamentally too sanguine to join them as a member.

But Champion went farther than Bland in wanting to set up his independent party of labour by means of association with the existing organizations of the working class.[1] This was something that the leaders of the S.D.F. and the Socialist League regarded as out of the question, for they classed the trade unions as hopelessly old-fashioned institutions with which they themselves were in competition. The S.D.F. manifesto to the trade unions, issued in September 1884, had quoted Professor Beesly on the limits to their effective value, and had declared that in the victorious outcome of the class struggle, 'trade unions as they now are cannot hope to participate'.[2] Morris's view was similar, and the early Socialists did a lot to alienate the organized workers by propaganda to the same effect. Champion's aim was to reverse this policy, and to substitute friendly co-operation for the hostility that had begun to develop.

Looking at the whole political scene from a wider strategic view-point than that of any of the other indigenous Socialists, Champion determined to make use of the Labour Electoral Committee, which had been founded in 1886 by the Trades Union Congress in the enthusiasm for increased labour representation that followed the Reform Act. Hopes had been raised that this committee might become the nucleus of an independent labour party: declarations of policy along these lines had been made by some of its sponsors. On the other hand, T. R. Threlfall, President of the 1885 T.U.C., who had taken the initiative in forming the committee, urged the Congress of the following year to remember that 'they could not contest any seat without declaring their adherence to one or the other of the great

[1] According to Burgess, *John Burns*, p. 94, it was Maltman Barry who persuaded Champion of the wisdom of this course.   [2] *Justice*, 6 Sept. 1884.

political parties',[1] and the indications were that the committee, like the Labour Representation League of the early seventies, would drift into dependence on the Liberal Party. Champion determined to rescue it from this fate, and to make it into the independent party of the working class that he now regarded as the 'next step' towards Socialism.

In 1887 the Committee developed into more permanent form as the Labour Electoral Association, and described itself as 'the Centre of the National Labour Party'. It issued a manifesto which declared:

> Recent events have shown what a united and active party can do in the House of Commons. It has practically succeeded in emancipating a people. If the British toilers wish to improve their position, they must adopt similar means. . . . Working men must form themselves into Labour Electoral Associations, as centres to organize the people. . . .[2]

This reference to the independence of the Irish Nationalists looked distinctly hopeful, and so Champion offered his assistance to the Committee of the Association and was charged with running its Metropolitan Section. Though he had spent much of the money his father had given him in setting up his London publishing business and in helping the S.D.F., he was not without further resources and he had wealthy friends. He was therefore capable of financing his own policy, and he gathered together a number of the abler young working men of the Federation and the League—among them Tom Mann and John Burns, both engineers, George Bateman, a compositor, and the members of the Socialist League minority who had formed the Labour Union at Hoxton. The policy worked out in this way: whenever a Parliamentary by-election occurred, the candidates were questioned on their attitude to labour problems, and if the replies of one of them were satisfactory he was given the support of the local adherents, if any, of the 'National Labour Party'; if neither of the candidates of the established parties proved satisfactory under the inquisition, and if circumstances were favourable, a labour candidate would be run.

[1] *T.U.C. Report*, 1886, p. 33.
[2] *Manifesto of the National Labour Electoral Association* (1887).

Champion inaugurated this policy at the Dulwich by-election in December 1887, and at Deptford in January 1888 he announced his own candidature. This aroused some general interest in the political world, and a letter from Champion giving the reasons for his stand was published in *The Times*:

> I seek to aid the working classes in forcing labour questions on the law-makers and in conquering the fortress of political power. . . . I find that Home Rule is 'practical politics' because the Irish vote counts, and that the Labour problem is not 'practical politics' because the Labour vote is not effectively organized.[1]

Finally, however, he withdrew in favour of the Liberals after they had made some concessions to the labour point of view. The concessions did not amount to very much, but they were a beginning. Arnold Morley, the Chief Liberal Whip, in a confidential letter gave Champion a promise of his sympathy:

> I am strongly impressed with the advantage of not only retaining but of increasing the numerical representation of labour in the House of Commons and although I am bound to recognize that the question of selection of candidates is mainly if not entirely a matter for the local association without interference from headquarters, I shall not fail where the circumstances warrant it, to use my influence in the direction I have indicated.[2]

In the course of the following year (1888) Champion and his agents intervened at a number of by-elections, playing a game of bluff and counter-bluff with the party organizations, and seeking to develop local opinion as well as to browbeat the candidates into support of labour demands.

At the same time Champion was devising a practical programme with a direct appeal to the working class. He was secretary of the Shop Hours Regulation Committee, which was a body interested in preventing breaches of the recent Act on the subject. He began to publish a new paper with a wider appeal, the *Labour Elector*, and in its pages he took up the demand for the reduction of working hours to eight. As early as

---

[1] *The Times*, 23 Jan. 1888.
[2] Arnold Morley to Champion, 8 Feb. 1888; copy enclosed in letter of Champion to Hardie, 16 Mar. 1888 (Mid-Lanark Correspondence).

1886 he had published a pamphlet on this subject by Tom Mann, a young engineering tradesman who belonged to the Battersea S.D.F.[1] Later, he sent Mann to obtain employment in Brunner's chemical factory at Northwich, where he suspected bad labour conditions, and he published Mann's reports in the *Labour Elector*.[2] He also encouraged Mrs. Besant to look into the grievances of the match girls employed by Bryant & May in London, and thus precipitated a strike which, as we shall see, provided the first victory of the New Unionism.

This policy of taking up industrial questions found quite a lot of support among the Socialists: but it was only Champion who had the finance to put it into effect on the national scale. Hyndman, it is true, remained strangely conservative in his revolutionary fanaticism, and would have nothing to do with Champion's new ideas. But the ablest of the S.D.F. members had learnt the lesson of its failure, though they could not win control of its policy in the face of Hyndman's opposition.

Socialists though they were, they now saw that the dogma of a new political economy, even in its modified Fabian form, should not be imposed upon all potential adherents of an independent labour policy. They realized that the workers ought first to recognize their solidarity as a class, their common interest in economic reform, and the need to remove their existing social inferiority. Hence the word 'Labour' rather than 'Socialist' should be the keynote of the agitation. Accordingly, John Burns banded together his supporters in Battersea as a Labour League; the Socialist League 'Parliamentary' minority constituted themselves a Labour Union; and Champion himself was ostensibly running a section of the Labour Electoral Association. The heterogeneity of Socialist organization in 1888 remained as pronounced as ever, but many of its leaders were beginning to develop a more practical outlook. They perceived that it was now possible for the working class, equipped with the vote and primary education, to control the political future of the community. The first stages of the Socialist revival were over: the agitation of Trafalgar Square was already obsolete.

[1] T. Mann, *What a Compulsory Eight Hours Day Means to the Workers.*
[2] *Labour Elector,* Nov. 1888–Mar. 1889.

Consciously and deliberately, Champion and his allies appealed to the workers to form their own political organizations in order to bring about that transformation of society from which, as a class, they had most to gain.

CHAPTER IV

The Challenge to the Caucus: Secession and Permeation

(1)

In September 1887 the comparatively placid flow of business at the Trades Union Congress at Swansea was disturbed by as speech which breathed a new and militant spirit. A young Scottish miner named James Keir Hardie, attending the Congress for the first time, bitterly attacked the respected Henry Broadhurst, M.P., who had for twelve years been the secretary of the Parliamentary Committee and had been an Under-Secretary of State in the Liberal Government. The grounds of the attack were that Broadhurst had supported at a by-election a Liberal candidate who was reputed to be the employer of sweated labour. Broadhurst, thus unexpectedly assailed, defended himself with vigour, and Fenwick, another Liberal M.P. who also took part in the debate, predicted that Hardie's agitation, like Jonah's gourd, would wither as quickly as it had sprung up.

In the event, however, no prophecy could have been more mistaken, sound as it appeared at the time. Hardie's lone protest at the 1887 Congress was the beginning of a movement which in due course transformed not only the Congress itself, but the whole political structure of the country. It was the prelude to the New Unionism and to the changes of political outlook to which New Unionism gave rise.

James Keir Hardie, who was to play the key role in the political developments of the next thirty years, was born in 1856 in Lanarkshire, the illegitimate son of Mary Kerr, a farm servant who later married a ship's carpenter named David Hardie.[1]

---

[1] The birth was registered at Holytown, Lanarkshire, 1 Sept. 1856. The father is described as William Aitken, miner. I am grateful to Mr. J. D. M. Bell of Glasgow University for a copy of the birth certificate. The best life available is W. Stewart, *J. Keir Hardie* (1925), but see also D. Lowe, *From Pit to Parliament* (1923).

The first years of his life form a story of great hardship in circumstances of grinding poverty, for David Hardie was not in
regular employment. Jimmie, as the eldest of the family, was
employed from the age of eight, first as an errand boy and then
as a trapper in a coal-mine. It was before the time of universal
education, and the lad had to learn to read at night school and
with the assistance of his mother. As he grew up, the problem
of poverty worried him, but at first he could see no remedy save
the temperance movement. He threw himself into work for the
Good Templars, the temperance organization, and for the Evangelical Union, which in spite of his secularist upbringing—for
both his mother and David Hardie were free-thinkers—he had
of his own accord decided to join. In 1883 we hear of him
presenting a petition to his local town council to brick up the
side and back entrances of the local licensed houses in order to
prevent any surreptitious offences against the licensing laws.[1]
However, he began to be drawn into trade-union activity: for
although at first a Liberal in politics like most of the miners, he
was more stubborn than most when it came to a clash between
the men and the owners. For his part in organizing the men of
his own pit he was sacked, but he continued the work, eking out
his livelihood as a local journalist. By 1887 he had had some
success in building up an Ayrshire Miners Union and also a
Scottish Miners Federation: but they were weak organizations,
and Hardie became interested in the views of those who were
for using political as well as industrial means to improve the lot
of the workers. Henry George was an influence on his thought;
and when he studied the S.D.F. literature which had begun to
penetrate even to Old Cumnock in Ayrshire where he lived, he
determined to join the S.D.F. when he first visited London.[2]

Hardie visited London with a miners' delegation in 1887, and
he lost no time in making contact with the Socialists, attending
several meetings of the S.D.F. and being introduced to Eleanor
Marx, and by her to Engels himself, who, however, criticized
both the S.D.F. and the Socialist League in his presence.[3] In

---

[1] *Ardrossan and Saltcoats Herald*, 20 Apr. 1883.
[2] J. Neil, 'Memoirs of an Ayrshire Agitator', in *Forward*, 4 July 1914.
[3] *Labour Leader*, 24 Dec. 1898.

the end, he did not join the S.D.F., and the reasons that he subsequently gave for changing his mind are instructive. 'Born and reared as I had been in the country, the whole environment of the clubs, in which beer seemed to be the most dominant influence, and the tone of the speeches, which were full of denunciation of everything, including trade unionism, and containing little constructive thought, repelled me.' These words reveal the strength and weakness of his character and politics. His mind did not run on simple logical lines, above and beyond the comprehension of the people from whom he had sprung. On the contrary, he was of the same stuff as they were, with the same instinctive attitudes, the same religious turn of mind and phraseology, the same inability to distinguish politics from morality, or logic from feeling. His views had already developed by way of Henry George, from Liberalism to Socialism; but these views were assimilated into the background of his own life and experience, which was something that the London Socialist could not share.

As the leader and organizer of a trade union and a federation of unions—weak though these bodies were—Hardie was a valuable recruit to the Socialist ranks, and his adhesion brought a less academic and more homely voice to the advocacy of independent labour policy. At the beginning of 1887 he had started a monthly magazine, the *Miner*, in which he addressed the men in his own blunt style—a style containing all the aggressive spirit of economic discontent without any of the catchwords of Marxism. 'Party be hanged!' he wrote. 'We are miners first and partisans next, at least if we follow the example of our "superiors" the landlords and their allies, we ought to be. . . .'[1]

Such was the stocky, heavily bearded young Scot with the deep, piercing eyes who suddenly broke into the Congress proceedings with a sharp attack on the Secretary. He was the harbinger of the New Unionists; and it was fitting that, although his career was to be primarily a political one, he should make his entry into national prominence as a trade union delegate. Already he had taken part in political work, as a Liberal; but now, in the autumn of 1887, he was adopted

[1] *Miner*, July 1887.

64

miners' Parliamentary candidate for North Ayrshire, and in March 1888, when a vacancy occurred at Mid-Lanark, he was selected as miners' candidate there.

(2)

With the appearance of a labour candidate, the Mid-Lanark by-election at once attracted national attention, and Threlfall, urged on by Champion, came north to assist Hardie on behalf of the Labour Electoral Association. Hardie asked for the Liberal nomination, and followed the usual course suggested by the Labour Electoral Association of promising to abide by the result of a preliminary poll of all Liberals in the constituency. The local Liberal Association would not agree to this 'primary', and they proceeded to select a candidate of their own, a London barrister named J. W. Philipps.[1] Hardie and the miners objected vigorously; and Schnadhorst, secretary of the National Liberal Federation, travelled from London to arrange for Hardie to be offered a seat elsewhere at the next election, with full maintenance as an M.P.[2]

It was characteristic of Hardie that he at once refused this offer, which, though likely to have secured his own future, would have involved the abandonment of the miners' cause in Lanarkshire. Hardie had no quarrel with the Liberal Party programme, so far as it went: his election handbills clinched their appeal with the slogan that 'a vote for Hardie is a vote for Gladstone'. His own programme was not in advance of that of several Radical M.P.s, and the only item of nationalization that he advocated was that of mineral royalties. His quarrel was solely with the local caucus, which was felt to be something apart from and less progressive than the national leaders of the party, as indeed was usually the case. Further, this quarrel hinged on the refusal of the caucus to allow the miners their own choice of member. Hardie was, in any case, a man of stubborn independence; but, as we shall see, his decision to carry on the fight seems to have been justified in the light of the Labour

---

[1] Later Viscount St. Davids.
[2] For Hardie's account of the negotiations, see *Labour Leader*, 12 Mar. 1914.

Electoral Association's subsequent record of unavailing pressure upon local Liberal caucuses in trying to induce them to accept Liberal-Labour candidates. There was, too, an element of sectionalism in his hostility to the 'London lawyer' and his refusal to accept a seat elsewhere at the dictate of the central caucus: it was not for nothing that he styled himself, not just 'Labour', but 'Labour and Home Rule' candidate.

Still, the main principle that Hardie stood for was the universal one that the working class must build up its own political strength, stand on its own feet and fight its own battles. This note of sturdy independence, which he struck repeatedly in the course of the by-election campaign, had not often been heard in the course of the preceding decade. Threlfall had abandoned him to his fate as soon as he refused Schnadhorst's offer; but instead the Socialists, or at least those of them who were trying to rally the labour interest, at once associated themselves with him. Champion had been in touch with him throughout by letter and telegram, and had stiffened his resolution by promises of generous financial support.[1] In view of the strength of the Irish vote in Mid-Lanark, Champion sought to make an alliance with Parnell on behalf of the 'National Labour Party': the terms of the proposed alliance, according to Champion, were to be:

> That on the approach of an election for a seat to which the labour party conceived itself to be entitled, I should confer with Mr. Parnell. If it was agreed that the majority of the electors in the constituency were workmen, the support of the Parnellite party should be given to a labour candidate. If it was agreed that working class electors were in a minority, no labour candidate should be run to divide the Liberal vote. In case of disagreement as to the composition of the electorate, the point should be referred to the final decision of an arbitrator.[2]

But Parnell was no more willing to treat with the Socialists than Chamberlain had been in 1885: the 'National Labour Party' was, after all, so far even less of a political force than the S.D.F.;

---

[1] See Mid-Lanark Correspondence, in possession of Mr. F. Johnson: the extant letters start on 14 Mar. 1888.

[2] *The Times*, 18 Apr. 1888.

and Parnell was afraid of offending the leaders of the Liberal Party with whom he was now in alliance. It was in vain that Michael Davitt, the Irish labour leader, pleaded with him and Schnadhorst on Hardie's behalf.[1]

Nothing daunted, Champion proceeded to the scene of the campaign, and also arranged for Tom Mann, Mahon, Donald and others to assist. Yet other Socialists and extreme Radicals arrived in the constituency of their own accord. It was indeed a remarkable political circus that assembled in support of the independent candidate: Champion himself, the political staff officer from London, with his mysterious supplies of money; Cunninghame Graham, M.P., the aristocratic Scottish laird and Socialist 'hero of Trafalgar Square'; Mann and Mahon, originally working engineers and now professional Socialist agitators; John Murdoch, the old Scottish crofters' leader; a few Irishmen, friends of Davitt, who attempted, largely in vain, to win the Irish voters away from an automatic alliance with the Liberal caucus; and one or two Liberal-Radical M.P.s, rather lukewarm in their hostility to Philipps and inclined to look askance at Champion.[2] The appearance of Champion was a doubtful advantage, for there still hung around him the suspicions that arose from the 'Tory Gold' scandal of 1885, in which he had been so deeply involved. Indeed, the Liberals were soon putting it about that Hardie was, through Champion, in Tory pay, and posters were placarded in the constituency with the following refrain:

> Some Londoner loons, wi' mair siller than sense,
> Ha'e planned to defray a' Keir Hardie's expense;
> Sae if he gets in, we'll be tauld very soon,
> 'Wha pays for the piper can ca' for the tune'.

This, of course, had the effect of neatly reversing Hardie's appeal to Scottish sectionalism. There was also some truth in the accusation that the sources of his finance were irregular. A

---

[1] T. W. Moody, 'Michael Davitt and the British Labour Movement', *Transactions of the Royal Historical Society*, 5th ser., iii (1953), 66.

[2] C. A. V. Conybeare, M.P., to Cunninghame Graham, M.P., 20 Apr. 1888: 'Where do they get the money from? We have a clear right to know. . . . Some of the men who are active in the business are by no means well thought of by our own friends. . . .' (Mid-Lanark Correspondence.)

good deal of it (£100) came from Margaret Harkness, a Socialist novelist[1]; but the rest came from a curious variety of sources that Champion could call upon—as he said in a letter to Hardie, there was 'nothing like quartering on the enemy'.[2]

In the larger towns and where the Irish vote was especially strong, Hardie's supporters met with much opposition, and sometimes at the end of a meeting the vote of confidence in the candidate was defeated. In the villages, however, there was a more favourable response. Hardie would speak on a simple if grandiose theme, defining his programme as 'bread for the hungry, rest for the weary, and hope for the oppressed', and depicting this by-election campaign as 'the beginning of a new era with the democracy, not only of Great Britain but of the world, under which they would draw together and be of one mind, and by which Burns's dream would be realized:

> 'That man to man the world o'er
> Shall brithers be for a' that.'

Graham might then speak, and Champion, who if ever he felt embarrassment must certainly have felt it among these audiences of stern Covenanters, would add a few remarks. Cheers for Gladstone and possibly for Graham and for the candidate himself, would conclude the business, and the village band would then march the campaigners to their next meeting-place.[3]

But vigorous though the canvass was, there was no doubt about the outcome. Hardie was at the bottom with 617 votes out of a total poll of over 7,000. Philipps, the Liberal, was elected, leading the Conservative by a comfortable 900 votes.[4] It was a disappointing result, after all the efforts that had been made, and in view of the fact that Hardie was a local man and a miner. But the power of the existing parties was too strong to be broken at the first onset: it is only in retrospect that the election is seen to have been an important political turning-point. It was generally recognized as in accordance with the British

[1] See her letter (under her literary pseudonym of John Law) in *North British Daily Mail*, 28 June 1888.
[2] Champion to Hardie, 22 Mar. 1888 (Mid-Lanark Correspondence).
[3] *Scottish Leader*, 23 Apr. 1888.
[4] Philipps (Lib.) 3847, Bousfield (C.) 2917, Hardie (Lab.) 617.

political tradition that the Parliamentary parties should not be bound to any definite programme but should change their attitude to particular issues as the issues changed with circumstances, and as the relative strength of the various groups composing each party underwent alteration. There was therefore no reason to suppose that one or other party, Liberal or Conservative, would not allow itself to become the vehicle of the demand for labour representation, being changed in its outlook and composition by a gradual and prolonged process. But the question now was whether the creation of the caucus system had not eliminated this element of flexibility, by putting the choice of members firmly into the hands of the middle class. The Liberal Party's grip on the working-class vote was clearly weakening in the middle eighties: yet its leaders still claimed that it served the interest of the working man. This claim, which still seemed to many to have more validity than the counter-claim of the Conservatives, had yet to be put fully to the test: and for Keir Hardie and the tiny but important nucleus of opinion that he represented, that test was the Mid-Lanark election. Before the election he had said:

> Better split the party now, if there is to be a split, than at the general election; and if the labour party only make their power felt now, terms will not be wanting when the general election comes.[1]

So the split took place, and Hardie and the whole Champion group prepared to take their leave of the Labour Electoral Association. Champion retained for his own purposes the title of Secretary of the Metropolitan Section of the L.E.A., but, with all the audacity of the three tailors of Tooley Street, he emphasized still more strongly his ambitious claim to be the organizer of the 'National Labour Party'; and Hardie with almost equal boldness proceeded without further ado to the formation of the Scottish Labour Party.

(3)

Although there is evidence to show that the possibility of forming a Scottish Labour Party had been mooted as early as

[1] *Miner*, Mar. 1888.

October 1887,[1] it was not until immediately after the Mid-Lanark election that definite action was taken in the matter. Hardie called a preliminary meeting of sympathizers in Glasgow in May 1888, and this group, which met under the chairmanship of John Murdoch, elected a small committee, including Hardie, to arrange the inaugural conference of the party. This was held on 25 August, also in Glasgow, with Cunninghame Graham in the chair.[2] Champion, who was unable to make the journey from London, sent his benediction in the form of an address which was read to the meeting; and a constitution was approved which established as the objects of the party 'to educate the people politically, and to secure the return to Parliament and all local bodies of members pledged to its programme'. The programme consisted of Radical political reforms and labour legislation of a socialistic character, beginning with the statutory limitation of the working day to eight hours. The party was not, however, definitely committed to Socialism as its ultimate object. This was not surprising, for the principal Socialist organization in Scotland, the Scottish Land and Labour League, which now dissolved itself into the new body, was composed of men who recognized the necessity of building a labour party first and making it Socialist at a later stage in its development. The Land and Labour League had been affiliated to the Socialist League, but its organizer, appointed in 1887, was J. L. Mahon, of the 'Parliamentary minority'.[3] Moreover, the new party embraced all those elements which had supported Hardie in his by-election campaign, and included several such as John Ferguson, a Davitt supporter of Glasgow, and Dr. G. B. Clark, the Radical M.P. for Caithness who could not at this time be described as Socialists. Ferguson and Clark were elected Vice-Presidents and Cunninghame Graham President; Keir Hardie, as might have been expected, became Secretary, and the Chairman of the Executive was to be Shaw Maxwell, a former Parliamentary candidate of the Scottish Land Restoration League, a Georgite body.

[1] *Commonweal*, 22 Oct. 1887.
[2] D. Lowe, *Souvenirs of Scottish Labour* (Glasgow, 1919), pp. 2 ff.
[3] Mahon to Engels, 14 Jan. 1888 (Engels Correspondence, Int. Inst. Soc. Hist.). Mahon had by now seceded from the Socialist League and had joined the S.D.F.

J. Keir Hardie
Election photograph 1892

R. B. Cunninghame Graham
Portrait by Sir John Lavery

The First Socialist M.P.s

The new Scottish Labour Party reflected all the weaknesses of the labour movement in Scotland at this time. The Scottish Land and Labour League had had only half a dozen branches, and the additional support that the S.L.P. attracted was heterogeneous and often rather lukewarm. The Irish support for independent labour politics, which had been of some importance in the Scottish Land and Labour League, had largely ebbed away since the Liberal Party took up Home Rule. But there were elements in its organization that indicated positive development. Its name showed that it was designed to be a comprehensive political body, appealing to the whole of the working class; yet it was at the same time quite free from the prejudice of most labour politicians against middle-class sympathizers. Hardie was emphatic on this point, and wrote in the *Miner*:

> If anyone, peasant or peer, is willing to accept the programme, and work with and for the party, his help will be gladly accepted. It would be a strange party, indeed, which would shut out from its ranks such Labour leaders as Cunninghame Graham, Dr. Clark, John Ferguson and Shaw Maxwell have proved themselves to be.

In the same article Hardie went on to describe the tactics the party would employ—the tactics of Champion in England: branches would be formed wherever possible, and by means of lectures and leaflets the problems of labour would be brought into the political limelight; and at elections where neither of the candidates of the existing parties would acknowledge the importance of these problems, labour candidates would be run.[1]

It is interesting to note how Hardie's articles and speeches in these years show him postulating certain axioms which were fundamental to the subsequent development of an independent labour movement—axioms quite in accord with Engels's idea of how an English labour party should grow up. Labour questions, thought Hardie, should take precedence over all other questions, and working men irrespective of party should combine to effect this. Nor was this, he considered, an impossible task: for even without further constitutional reform, working

[1] *Miner*, Sept. 1888.

men could exert a decisive influence at Westminster. But it could only be done if those who were sent to Parliament to represent labour were bound to a definite labour programme. Such representatives, if they were honest men so pledged, need not necessarily be of working-class origin, for the party was to be a catholic one, embracing members of all classes in the community.[1]

Hardie did not at this stage press the first of these points to its logical conclusion. He had not yet abandoned all hope of reforming the Liberal Party, nor did he do so for several years. At the very moment of the foundation of the Scottish Labour Party, in announcing his own resignation from the Liberals, he left the door open for a reconciliation: 'If the Liberal Party desired to prevent a split, let it adopt the programme of the Labour Party.'[2] But the reconciliation would involve a definite advance of policy by the Liberals, and pending that advance, Hardie was conscious of the necessity for going outside the Liberal Party organization and forming a separate nucleus of political strength which, unlike the L.E.A., should be entirely free from Liberal control. The L.E.A. itself could not be won over: the Championites were swept out of it at its conference in October 1888, when a resolution designed to exclude everyone who was not a *bona fide* workman or a representative of a trade union was carried against the opposition of Hardie and the several others of the group who were present.[3]

Hardie hoped also that the T.U.C. could be persuaded as a body to accept his policy. He certainly secured a good deal of the limelight when the Congress met at Bradford in September 1888, and he spoke both on labour representation and on the question of an Eight Hours Bill, on which he carried a resolution to take a referendum of the union memberships. But the Congress was unsympathetic to his criticisms of Broadhurst, which were based on evidence provided by Champion, and Broadhurst played on the current suspicions of the latter by saying that 'Mr. Champion was not his instructor or political director, and had no more to do with him than the man in the

[1] *Miner*, 1887–8.   [2] *Glasgow Herald*, 26 Aug. 1888.
[3] *Report of the Labour Electoral Congress*, 1888.

moon'.[1] As 'the man in the moon' was a common catchphrase for an agent of political bribery, the point of Broadhurst's *ad hominem* reply was not lost on his audience, and the 'independent' amendment on labour representation was accordingly defeated by a large majority (82 votes to 18). It seemed that Broadhurst and his policy of supporting the Liberal Party would be safe for some time from the Championites or any other challengers.

(4)

Meanwhile the majority of the Fabian Society were proceeding with the evolution of a policy very different from that of the Championites—the policy of 'permeation'. Their aim was not to secede from the Liberal Party, but rather to infiltrate its posts of responsibility and influence its Parliamentary programme, so as to bring it round to the acceptance of Socialist measures. It must be remembered that the Fabian Society was a group whose members almost all lived in the London area: and the policy they advocated certainly suited politics in London better than elsewhere. It was difficult for the Birmingham type of caucus, which put control into the hands of the wealthy middle-class members of the locality, to develop in all the metropolitan constituencies, some of which were almost uniformly working class in composition. The Liberal-Radical tradition was strong in London, and there were many Radical workingmen's clubs. Although the Democratic Federation had failed to unite these clubs in an effective challenge to the Chamberlain caucus, they were naturally different in attitude from the less progressive associations of other parts of the country, and were still anxious to find some organization which would press their special claims inside the Liberal Party. For this purpose, the Metropolitan Radical Federation was formed in 1886, and it obtained representation at the annual conferences of the National Liberal Federation, which it sought to influence in the direction of more advanced measures of social legislation.

What the Fabians endeavoured to do, therefore, was to win support for their views in the various clubs which made up the Metropolitan Radical Federation. They assiduously lectured

---

[1] *T.U.C. Report*, 1888, p. 26.

to club audiences in the evenings, and gave the arguments not only for the Socialist state of the future but also for the immediate reforms which they thought practicable from the Radical point of view. They also took an interest in the more bourgeois associations that belonged to the London Liberal and Radical Union.[1] They associated themselves with the Radicals in demanding a reform of London government, and when this was effected by the County Councils Act of 1888, they encouraged the formation on the new London County Council of a Liberal-Radical political group, the Progressive Party. They also fought the London School Board elections in 1888, and achieved some successes, largely because they did not fight simply as Socialists but as members of a Radical coalition. Though Hubert Bland was defeated, both Mrs. Besant and Stewart Headlam were elected, Mrs. Besant being at the top of the poll for the Tower Hamlets division. Another feature of Fabian tactics was to cultivate good relations with the Liberal press, especially the *Daily Chronicle* and the *Star*, which T. P. O'Connor founded in 1888. H. W. Massingham, the assistant editor of the *Star*, was persuaded to join the Fabian Society, and Shaw was for some time the paper's music critic.[2]

The prerequisite of the Fabian policy was mastery of the facts of economics and political science, so that any particular case could be argued on grounds of expediency rather than of principle. In this respect Webb was pre-eminent. His tract, *Facts for Socialists*, was published in January 1887 as No. 5 in the Fabian series. This was the beginning of a remarkable flow of detailed factual information which he maintained in the service of Fabian Socialism. All three of the Fabian tracts published in 1888 were by him, and two of them, *Facts for Londoners* and *Figures for Londoners*, had a direct bearing on the problems of metropolitan government.

But the Fabians were also concerned in the task of formulating long-term Socialist policy for the country as a whole. In the autumn of 1888 they organized a series of lectures on 'The

---

[1] Webb helped to form the Holborn Liberal and Radical Association—see his letter to Secretary, Socialist League, 21 Mar. 1887 (Nettlau Collection).

[2] See Shaw, *The Fabian Society: Its Early History*, for an account (albeit somewhat exaggerated) of the successes of Fabian policy.

Basis and Prospects of Socialism'; edited by Bernard Shaw and published at the end of 1889, these lectures became the famous *Fabian Essays in Socialism*. Providing as they did a distinctive sketch of the political programme of evolutionary Socialism, they were the most important literary product of the society, or for that matter of the indigenous Socialist movement as a whole. They attracted immediate attention, and even the first edition at six shillings sold out rapidly. By early in 1891 altogether over 27,000 copies had been purchased.[1]

The seven Fabian essayists were all members of the Executive of the Society in 1888, and they had repeatedly thrashed out their differences at meetings of the Society and also in smaller groups among themselves.[2] Accordingly the essays, with one exception, approximate to a common point of view. Problems of foreign policy or the balance of overseas trade did not worry them: they considered the future of Britain almost *in vacuo* and assumed that the country would remain as free of external pressures as in the preceding two generations. Within this framework, they offered a reasoned alternative to the revolutionary Socialist programme. In the first essay Shaw, abandoning the Marxian analysis of value, and using the Jevonian theory of Marginal Utility, asserted the social origin of wealth and thereby reversed the conclusions of *laissez-faire* political economy from its own premises. Webb, arguing on historical grounds, suggested that Socialism was already slowly winning the day: and by Socialism he meant the extension of public control, either by the State or by the municipality. William Clarke added a distinctive and less complacent note by pointing to the development, especially in the United States, of trusts and large industrial combinations, though he regarded this phenomenon as likely to ease the transition of property to collective ownership from 'the weak hands of a useless possessing class'.[3] The other essayists, except Bland, pursued the same

---

[1] Pease, *History of the Fabian Society*, p. 88.

[2] Of these smaller groups, the most important was the 'Hampstead Historic', at whose meetings Shaw, Webb, Wallas and Olivier worked out their ideas together. See the memorandum by Wallas of May 1888 (Wallas Papers).

[3] G. B. Shaw, ed., *Fabian Essays in Socialism* (1889), p. 101. Clarke had met Henry Demarest Lloyd, the chief American antagonist of the trusts, and carried on a

theme of moderate evolutionary change. Sydney Olivier, influenced by Comte and Darwin, argued that Socialism was 'merely Individualism rationalized, organized, clothed and in its right mind'.[1] Graham Wallas and Annie Besant both looked forward to a society containing a great deal of decentralization, and attached special importance to municipal Socialism. Dealing in a second essay with the transition to Socialism, Shaw emphasized the importance of the advances towards democracy accomplished by such measures as the County Councils Act of 1888. The extinction of private property could, he thought, be gradual, and each act of expropriation could be accompanied by compensation for the individual property-owner at the expense of all.

Thus nearly all the Fabian essayists postulated a gradual, comparatively even and peaceful evolution of Socialism, which they regarded as already taking place by the extension of political democracy, national and local, and by the progress of 'gas and water' Socialism. They regarded the existing political parties, and especially the Liberal-Radicals, as open to permeation by Socialist ideas, and pointed to the departures which the Radicals had already made from the principles of *laissez-faire*. Judged by the circumstances of their time, the most striking omission of their whole general thesis was the failure to consider the significance of the trade unions and the co-operative societies. As Webb was later to discover, conclusions could be drawn from the working of these institutions which would fit very well with the general theory of what he was later to call 'the inevitability of gradualness'.

Quite discordant from the attitude of the other essayists, however, was the contribution of Hubert Bland, who had never abandoned his original hostility to Liberal-Radicalism. As has been mentioned, he had long been an opponent of the 'catastrophic' Socialism of the S.D.F. and the Socialist League; but this did not lead him to accept Webb's view that the extension

---

brisk correspondence with him. C. Lloyd, *Henry Demarest Lloyd* (New York, 1912), i. 75. Hyndman thought that Clarke's was the best of the essays (H. M. Hyndman, *Further Reminiscences* (1912), p. 212).

[1] Shaw, *Fabian Essays*, p. 105.

of State control was necessarily an indication of advance towards Socialism. Indeed, in the course of his essay, he poked fun at Webb for suggesting that the existence of hawkers' licenses was an example of progress.[1] Pointing to Clarke's evidence of the growth of trusts in the United States and elsewhere, he foresaw an 'intensifying struggle for existence', which would mean that 'Despair will take sides with Hope' on the side of Socialism.[2] In these circumstances, he could not agree that it was possible effectively to permeate the Radical Left: on the contrary, he thought, the Socialist could expect to face the opposition of both the main parties. 'There is a true cleavage being slowly driven through the body politic.'[3] His conclusion from this more fully Marxist analysis was that which he had already expressed in earlier discussions on Socialist tactics, namely, that there was a need for the formation of a 'definitively Socialist Party'.[4]

Bland's point of view was an important one, and in some ways the future was to confirm his ideas rather than those of the other essayists. He was certainly more closely in line with the outlook of the Championite group, some members of which were to play the leading role in the foundation of the Labour Party. Among the Fabian leaders, however, Bland was in a minority of one. The majority, judging national politics by the climate of London, and assuming that the character of Liberalism was the same throughout the country, though that the policy of permeation was the answer not only for the problems of the County Council but also for the wider sphere of Westminster politics. In the following years their association with the Liberals was to be a source of grave mistrust to the leaders of the growing independent labour movement outside London. Consequently, as we shall see, it was not for their immediate political tactics, but for their success in formulating a long-term evolutionary programme, that the Fabians were to be of importance in the eventual foundation of the Labour Party.

[1] Shaw, *Fabian Essays*, p. 212 note.   [2] Ibid. p. 219   [3] Ibid. p. 210.
[4] Ibid. p. 217.

CHAPTER V

The Impact of New Unionism

(1)

MENTION has already been made of the effect of the depression of the 1870's in reducing the membership of the unions and in eliminating the weaker of them. In 1874 the union membership represented at the Trades Union Congress was 594,000; but by the end of the decade it had fallen to 381,000, and the 1874 figure was not exceeded until 1889, even though it amounted to less than 2 per cent of the total population of the country.[1] The union membership was almost entirely concentrated among the more highly skilled workers, for the first attempts to organize the unskilled, such as the Gas Stokers Union, had been killed by the depression. The term 'labour aristocracy', which was used at the time by the Marxists to describe the organized workers, is not inappropriate to point the contrast between the privileges of their position and the weakness of the great mass of the less skilled workers below them. It is true that there were some anomalies: the Lancashire cotton workers, for instance, even if comparatively unskilled, ranked with the 'aristocracy', while the Yorkshire woollen workers, probably owing to the greater diversity of their occupations, were almost devoid of organization. Among the miners, too, the degree of trade unionism varied widely among men of comparable skill in different coalfields—from the well-knit and conservative framework of the Northumberland and Durham unions to the shaky structure of the West of Scotland. About most of the unskilled occupations, however, there was no doubt: the general labourers and the workers in the so-called sweated trades, many of

---

[1] G. D. H. Cole, *Short History of the British Working-Class Movement* (1948), p. 275. There is much uncertainty about the total number of trade unionists in this period: in 1886 one government official suggested 600,000 while another said 1 million (Clapham, *Economic History of Modern Britain*, ii. 155).

whom were female, had no unions, and their miserable conditions of work were at once a cause and a result of their inability to defend themselves. Ignorance and lack of education, together with the weakness of their position *vis-à-vis* their employers, who could so easily replace them from the ranks of the unemployed, were the other principal factors in preventing them from organizing unions.

It was only to be expected, however, that when the years of acute depression had passed and the numbers of the unemployed had dropped, fresh attempts would be made to found unions to cater for the unskilled. The frontier of unionism was a moving frontier, alternately expanding and contracting in response to the changing conditions of the labour market. Yet it is not difficult, in spite of the fluctuations, to discern a long-term trend of improvement in the strength of trade unionism. The rapid growth of British industry in the preceding generation was the basic cause, not only of the general progress of unionism, but also of other closely associated developments such as the extension of working-class education and the progress towards political democracy.

It is remarkable how often in the later 1880's the impulse to this fresh growth of trade unionism was given by Socialist sympathizers. Some of the Socialists, it is true, were altogether impatient with the unions, and made little attempt either to co-operate with those in existence or to help form new ones. The S.D.F., although it took up the demand for an eight-hour day, had been scornful of the effectiveness of trade unionism; and much of the propaganda of the Socialist agitators who visited the Northumberland miners during their strike in 1887 was designed to show that trade unionism was useless and that Socialism was a better alternative.[1] However, some of them, especially those of the Champion group, came to appreciate the significance of trade unionism and began actively to assist the less skilled workers to get their unions going. This help was the more important because of the fact that literacy was still by no means the rule among the lower ranks of labour, and men and

---

[1] Evidence to Royal Commission on Labour, *Parliamentary Papers*, 1892, xxxvi, i, par. 13170.

women who could write and keep accounts had a scarcity value. As early as 1886 Edward Pease of the Fabian Society had started to organize labourers on Tyneside into what was hopefully called the National Federation of Labour.[1] Then in 1888 Champion and Mrs. Besant began to draw attention in the *Labour Elector* and the *Link* respectively, to the plight of the London match girls who worked for Bryant & May's. They did not actually advise a strike, but the match girls were so impressed by having their grievances put down in print that they went on strike of their own accord, and after holding out for a few weeks were successful in obtaining substantial improvements in their conditions of work. They had been supported by a strike fund which their Socialist friends had raised.[2]

Other workers in London took note of this success, comparatively unimportant as it was in itself, and soon the struggle to organize was taken up by the gasworkers, who were working twelve-hour shifts but naturally wanted to change to an eight-hour system, making three shifts a day instead of two. Led in the first place by Will Thorne, one of their own number who was also a member of the S.D.F., by the early summer of 1889 they felt themselves strong enough to make their demand for the eight hours, which, much to their surprise, was conceded throughout London without a struggle. The union was called the Gasworkers and General Labourers Union, and at first it aimed to include all comers within its ranks irrespective of their occupations. It was believed that the unskilled labourers could not be organized in separate industrial groups owing to the mobility of this type of labour: the men who worked in the gasworks in the winter would often drift to different jobs in the summer, and in any case there were no barriers of apprenticeship and craft skill. There was also an element of idealism in the conception of a general union which refused no applicant for membership. In this respect the American Knights of Labor, which had expanded suddenly to over half a million members in 1886–7, was an example to the Gasworkers: in these years it

[1] Pease in *To-day*, June 1887, where he traces the connexion of the N.F.L. with the old Nine Hours League. It was never more than local, and collapsed in 1890, its remnants going into the Gasworkers and General Labourers Union.
[2] For the origin of the strike see *Link*, 14 July 1888.

had actually formed a number of branches in Britain.[1] Eleanor Marx, who had visited America in 1886 with Aveling and Lieb-knecht, and had made a careful study of the labour movement there, exerted a strong influence over Will Thorne, whom she taught to read.[2] She became an officer of the Gasworkers and kept their accounts in order.[3] A Fabian clergyman, Rev. W. A. Morris, became a trustee of the union, and other Socialists such as John Burns and Tom Mann helped in the organizing work. When it began to develop in the provinces its early progress was materially assisted by provincial Socialists: in the West Riding of Yorkshire, for instance, some of the members of the moribund Socialist League busied themselves with forming branches of the Gasworkers Union.[4]

The Gasworkers' success was followed by the great London dock strike of August 1889, in which again the Socialists took a very prominent part. Socialist meetings had been held at the dock gates on many occasions before the strike, but they brought in few recruits from among the dockers, although work at the docks was at that time especially miserable owing to the demor-alizing system of casual labour and poor pay. But the example of the gasworkers in forming a union had an immediate effect on the dockers. A strike broke out more or less spontaneously in August, and it spread to the stevedores and lightermen.[5] At first the secretary of the small Tea Operatives Union, Ben Tillett, was quite unable to cope with the situation. Most of those on strike did not yet belong to any union, and there was no organization to support them. Tillett therefore turned for organizing help to the Socialists, and especially to Tom Mann and John Burns, who had both helped Thorne in starting the Gasworkers Union.

---

[1] H. Pelling, 'Knights of Labor in Britain, 1880–1901', *Economic History Review*, 2nd. ser., vol. ix (1956).
[2] W. Thorne, *My Life's Battles* (1925), pp. 96, 117; Edward and Eleanor Marx Aveling, *Working-Class Movement in America* (1888).   [3] Thorne, op. cit. p. 118.
[4] A. Mattison, Cuttings Book (Mattison Collection, Brotherton Library, Leeds). Mattison was one of a group of working-class Socialists at Leeds and Bradford who worked first for the Socialist League, then for the Fabians, and finally for the I.L.P.
[5] The best accounts of the strike are H. L. Smith and V. Nash, *The Story of the Dockers' Strike* (1890), and H. H. Champion, *The Great Dock Strike* (1890).

In Mann and Burns the dockers secured leaders of quite exceptional ability. Both of them were skilled tradesmen, members of the Amalgamated Society of Engineers. Both had suffered periods of unemployment in earlier years which had stimulated their interest in radical politics. Burns was introduced to Socialism by Victor Delahaye, a French Communard in exile; Tom Mann evolved towards it by reading Henry George, Ruskin, and Thorold Rogers's *Work and Wages*.[1] Mann, now thirty-three, was Burns's senior by two years; but Burns's black beard and sturdy appearance made him appear the elder. By the time Mann joined the Battersea S.D.F. Burns had already become its most prominent member; he was now much more in the public eye than Mann, having been a leader of the Trafalgar Square riots, and having just recently secured election to the London County Council. Exceptional energy, power of personality and rhetorical skill were characteristics that they shared: but Mann was less strong-willed than Burns, and much less arrogant. It was therefore Burns who at once took the lead of the dock strike: he riveted the attention of the men by his showmanship, and his straw hat, used as a symbol of authority, enabled him to dominate and discipline them. He organized daily processions of the strikers through the city, while Mann was responsible for controlling the issue of food-tickets to the needy. Champion was also there to help: he acted as press officer and took a hand in arranging the picketing system. The attention paid to publicity was well worth while, for the strike could not have succeeded without the support of large sections of the public who were impressed by the orderly character of the demonstrations and by the misery of the dockers' conditions of work. The measure of the importance of this outside sympathy is to be found in the contributions to the strike fund. In round figures, £4,600 was contributed by other British trade unions and trades councils, some of which had not fully made up their minds whether such a struggle by a mass of labourers with Socialist leaders was a good thing or not; £13,700 was con-

---

[1] Tom Mann, *Memoirs*, pp. 34 f. According to Katharine Conway, the typical new union leader would possess a copy of Rogers's book (*Weekly Sun*, 21 Jan. 1894). It was a valuable source of historical arguments justifying trade-union action to raise wages.

tributed by the general public, including even some of the dock directors; and no less than £30,000 came from sympathizers in Australia, where radical politics were more advanced than in this country. In the end, after the strike had lasted five weeks, the mediation of Cardinal Manning and others resulted in the acceptance of the strikers' main demands, and John Burns was able to tell the dockers to rejoice in the attainment of what he had prophesied for them—sixpence an hour, or in his own picturesque language, 'the full round orb of the dockers' tanner'.[1] A dockers' union was now set up: Mann became its first president, and Ben Tillett, now rapidly approaching acceptance of the Socialist creed, became its secretary. For some time Champion's *Labour Elector* was the official organ of both the London Dockers and the Gasworkers.

Such a struggle naturally lent inspiration to the whole working class, and the following two years (1889–91) saw many attempts to emulate their success in other fields. Again the Socialists were actively involved. Champion, for instance, with the Fabian De Mattos, helped to found the General Railway Workers Union after failing to persuade the more 'aristocratic' Amalgamated Society of Railway Servants to reduce what he called their 'unnecessarily high subscription of 5*d*. per week', which, he pointed out, prevented the lower grades of railwaymen from joining their society.[2] Not all the work of the Socialists turned out successfully, however: Mahon, Donald and Binning, formerly of the Socialist League and now the sponsors of the Labour Union of Hoxton, tried to form a Postmen's Union, but having no funds and little knowledge of conditions in the postal service they merely succeeded in getting a number of their supporters dismissed from their jobs.[3]

(2)

The Socialists as a whole gained considerably in prestige from their association with New Unionism. The example of devoted leadership that they gave was only rarely spoilt by errors of judgement. It is true, as Champion recognized at the

[1] Smith and Nash, op. cit. p. 147.
[2] *Labour Elector*, 23 Nov. 1889.
[3] H. G. Swift, *History of Postal Agitation* (1929), pp. 198 ff.

time, that it was not for their Socialism that they were respected by the workers, but for their willingness to help in the tasks of organization.[1] Hyndman had wanted John Burns to display a red flag at demonstrations during the dock strike, but Burns had refused, for he knew that it would be impolitic.[2] Champion had been expelled from the S.D.F. in November 1888, and John Burns resigned less than a year later.[3] Nevertheless, he still regarded himself as a Socialist: and the movement was bound to gain in the long run from his popularity and from that of Mann and Thorne who were still in the S.D.F., and who now occupied key positions in trade unionism. Furthermore, the principles of the New Unionism were socialistic in tendency. The belief that their unions could only be based on the welfare of the working class as a whole, which is indicated by their willingness to accept all types of workers for membership, brought the new unionists into sympathy with an important basic conception of Socialism; and their emphasis, owing to a feeling of insecurity, on the value of legislation for the consolidation of their industrial demands made them favourable to the Socialist demand for an independent labour party in Parliament. The new unionists had nothing to lose and a good deal to gain by a policy of political action such as the Socialists were advocating, involving as it did the legislative enforcement of what they were most anxious to win, and, having won, to preserve. It had very soon been made clear to them that their gains by industrial action were not easy to maintain. The gasworkers, for instance, were defeated in a strike at the works of the South Metropolitan Gas Company in the winter of 1889–90, and their members were excluded from the company's employment after a bitter struggle which caused Cardinal Manning to remark: 'There is no justice, mercy, or compassion in the Plutocracy.'[4]

The success of the Championite Socialists in taking the lead of the new unions was undoubtedly largely due to the lukewarm

---

[1] Champion, *Great Dock Strike*, p. 11.
[2] Burns's action was later defended by Engels (*Daily Chronicle*, 1 July 1893).
[3] *Justice*, 28 Sept. 1889.
[4] Thorne, op. cit. pp. 106 ff.; Shane Leslie, *Henry Edward Manning* (1921), p. 376.

The Impact of New Unionism

attitude of the leaders of the established unions, who had always regarded craft and skill as the essential basis of organization. Although the London Trades Council had given the dockers a certain amount of assistance in the course of their strike, Shipton, its secretary, had spoken disparagingly of the new unions as 'mushroom' societies, and Mann and Tillett in their pamphlet, *The New Trades Unionism*, complained that:

> The fact is, the older section represented by Mr. Shipton has no real desire to make trades unionism become the all-powerful instrument for abolishing poverty.[1]

Yet the effect of the events of 1889 and 1890 was to increase the London Trades Council's affiliated membership about threefold, and after a determined struggle between Shipton and Mann, who became a member of the executive in 1889, the policy of the Council was changed and Shipton was forced to agree to a much larger measure of support for new union ventures. Accordingly, in June 1891 the Council gave full backing to the strike of the London bus workers for a day of twelve hours, and it granted £10 for a month's wages to Fred Hammill, one of Mann's supporters who was organizing a union for them.[2] Mann's proposals for the decentralization of the Council into districts were, however, defeated; with the result that the outlying industrial areas set up their own autonomous Trades Councils, and it proved impossible to form a body which could claim to represent all the trade unionists of the growing metropolis.

The echoes of New Unionism were meanwhile resounding throughout the country, and struggles of less importance but sometimes greater intensity and bitterness were waged in provincial towns and ports. The letters of Engels reveal something of the intense excitement of the period as felt by one of the shrewdest observers: he wrote to Sorge in December 1889:

> The people are throwing themselves into the job in quite a different way, are leading far more colossal masses into the fight, are shaking society more deeply, are putting forward much more far-reaching demands: eight hour day, general

[1] T. Mann and B. Tillett, *The New Trades Unionism* (1890), p. 11.
[2] *London Trades Council History* (1950), p. 73.

85

federation of all organizations, complete solidarity. Thanks to Tussy [i.e. Eleanor Marx] women's branches have been formed for the first time—in the Gasworkers and General Labourers Union. Moreover, the people regard their immediate demands only as provisional although they themselves do not know as yet what final aim they are working for. But this dim idea is strongly enough rooted to make them choose only openly declared Socialists as their leaders. Like everyone else they will have to learn by their experiences and the consequences of their own mistakes. But as, unlike the old trade unions, they greet every suggestion of an identity of interest between Capital and Labour with scorn and ridicule, this will not take very long. . . .

Engels's optimism was based not only on the success of the Socialists in capturing the new unions in London, but also on the successful reconstitution of the International in the autumn of 1889. There had been two separate Socialist and Labour congresses held simultaneously in Paris: one was backed by the orthodox followers of Marx and Engels, and also attended by a number of British Socialists including William Morris, Keir Hardie and Cunninghame Graham; the other, summoned by the French Possibilists, who were reformists and opposed to the Engels group, was attended not only by the Fabians and by a number of trade unionists of the old-fashioned pattern but also by Hyndman and other members of the S.D.F.[1] It was because of Engels's hostility that the S.D.F. delegates were forced to consort with the conservative trade-union leaders and the foreign reformists rather than with the Marxists. Fortunately, however, for the future of the movement the two congresses realized the discredit into which their cause was thrown by their disunity, and both groups finally joined to form the Second International. This was a much more real organization than its predecessor of twenty years before, for it embraced strong parties in a number of different countries.

One notable outcome of the foundation of the Second International was the decision to make a demonstration of labour

---

[1] For the Marxist Congress, see *Protokoll des Internationalen Arbeiter-Congresses zu Paris* (Nürnberg, 1890); for the Possibilist Congress, see *Report of the International Workmen's Congress* (1889). The Metropolitan Radical Federation was represented at the Possibilist Congress—a remarkable *tour de force* of Fabian permeation.

solidarity on May Day, 1890. Accordingly, the London Socialists busied themselves with preparations for a great demonstration in Hyde Park on the first Sunday in May, and although in
the course of making the arrangements there was much bickering between the rival groups, the result was a remarkable display of the forces of New Unionism and of the solidarity between its leaders and the Socialists. Even the old unions were
induced to collaborate, although they held what was in effect a
separate demonstration because they were not prepared to
advocate the legislative enactment of the eight-hour day. The
attendance was very large, and Engels, who watched the scene
from the top of a large goods-van, was almost beside himself
with enthusiasm. 'On May 4th, 1890', he proclaimed, 'the
English working class joined up in the great international
army. . . . The grand-children of the old Chartists are entering
the line of battle.'[1]

But this optimism, pardonable under the circumstances, out-
ran the facts. In his more sober moments Engels was well aware
of what he called 'the bourgeois respectability which has grown
deep into the bones of the workers'.[2] Although the new unionists entered the 1890 T.U.C. in force, they were not numerous
enough to outvote the representatives of the craft unions, most
of whom retained their prejudices and their patronizing attitude
towards the new arrivals. John Burns has given us a picture of
the contrasts between the two types of delegate at this Congress:

> The 'old' delegates differed from the 'new' not only physi-
> cally but in dress. A great number of them looked like res-
> pectable city gentlemen; wore very good coats, large watch-
> chains and high hats—and in many cases were of such
> splendid build and proportions that they presented an alder-
> manic, not to say a magisterial, form and dignity.
> Among the 'new' delegates not a single one wore a tall hat.
> They looked workmen. They were workmen. They were not
> such sticklers for formality or Court procedure, but were
> guided more by common sense.[3]

---

[1] Article in Vienna *Arbeiterzeitung*, 23 May 1890, quoted Marx and Engels,
Selected Correspondence, p. 469.
[2] Marx and Engels, op. cit. p. 461.
[3] J. Burns, *The Liverpool Congress* (1890), p. 6.

As the debates proceeded, the two groups clashed not infrequently, and the snobbery of the craftsmen came out strongly at times. Will Thorne tells in his autobiography how he felt obliged to intervene at one point:

> Stung by the boorishness of the old school, I jumped to my feet and hurled this rebuke at them, when they jeered and laughed at one of the general labour representatives: 'A firewood cutter is as good as an engineer. Are you only going to listen to engineers, and not to unskilled workers?' I was wild with rage, but my reprimand went home, and the speaker that I had interceded for was from then onwards given a fairer hearing.[1]

Still, the effect of New Unionism was very noticeable in the decisions of the Congress, although there was no chance of radically transforming its character as an organ of the craft societies. The carpenters, the engineers and most of the miners joined with the new unions to pass a resolution in favour of an eight-hour day by legislative action; and Henry Broadhurst, the secretary of the Parliamentary Committee, who had resisted Hardie's onslaught so easily in 1888 and 1889, now found it convenient to retire on grounds of ill-health. This, however, proved no revolutionary change, for Broadhurst's successor was Charles Fenwick, a miner who was not a Socialist nor even a supporter of the eight-hour day.

This was the high-water mark of New Unionism in its immediate impact on the politics of the trade-union world. It was clear that the movement had had a notable effect on the old unions and trades councils, and had stirred them to a reconsideration of their position *vis-à-vis* their less fortunate brethren. But it was too much to expect them to abandon their cautious sectionalism in favour of the ideas of the general union. For one thing, the officials of the craft unions found it difficult to believe that the newcomers would be able to survive the onset of a depression, which would enable the employers of unskilled men readily to replace their workers if they proved recalcitrant. They were not far wrong, for the general unions suffered severely in the slump of the early nineties. Though they were not

[1] Thorne, op. cit. p. 135.

driven out of existence as they had been in the slump of the seventies, they lost many of their members—a far larger proportion than was lost by the older unions, which had also benefited considerably from the activity of 1889–91. Consequently, they did not bulk very large in the total of trade-union membership. In the years 1892 to 1894 the annual average strength of the principal new unions has been calculated as only 107,000, compared with a total union strength of 1,555,000.[1] Before 1889 the total membership cannot have been much more than about one million: so it is clear that the expansion of the old unions accounted for much the larger part of the retained increase in unionism.

It is not unfair to conclude, therefore, that the permanent organization established as a result of New Unionism did not cover more than a tiny section of the formerly unorganized workers. Take, for instance, the position of female labour. The gasworkers had been very keen, under the influence of Eleanor Marx, to recruit women trade unionists, but in 1908 the total number they had on their books was only 800.[2] All in all, the distribution of strength in the trade-union world had really changed very little. The Webbs, referring to the year 1892, say in their *History of Trade Unionism*:

> The Trade Union world is, therefore, in the main, composed of skilled craftsmen working in densely populated districts, where industry is conducted on a large scale. About 750,000 of its members—one-half of the whole—belong to the three staple trades of coal-mining, cotton manufacture, and engineering, whilst the labourers and the women workers remain, on the whole, non-Unionists.[3]

Moreover, the new unions, as they consolidated their organization, began to resemble the more conservative bodies which previously they had denounced. They discovered that even those workers traditionally classified as unskilled did in fact have a certain scarcity value to their employers by reason of

[1] E. J. Hobsbawm, 'General Labour Unions', *Economic History Review*, 2nd ser., i (1949), 124.

[2] Ibid. p. 135. The total female membership of trade unions at the end of 1900 was 122,047: 89 per cent of this total was in the textile trades (Board of Trade, *Labour Gazette*, 1901, p. 330).

[3] S. and B. Webb, *History of Trade Unionism* (1898), p. 430.

being habituated to their work. But at the same time they found that in order to survive they had to rely, as Dr. Hobsbawm has put it, 'far more on their foothold in certain industries and large works, than on their ability to recruit indiscriminately'.[1] These developments tended to reduce the differences between the new unions and the old, many of which had been just as idealistic in aims when they were founded.

It is in the political field, however, that New Unionism had its most important and lasting influence. There was, to begin with, the enormous access of prestige to the Socialists as a result of their position of leadership in the new unions. Several of them occupied key trade-union posts, and they also had some strength in the trades councils, which had notably increased in numbers and activity since 1889. Many of the Socialist leaders, such as Mann and Burns, had themselves been working members of older craft unions; and the striking development of the nineties was the advance of many of these societies to a more radical political standpoint. The memory of the years of depression and unemployment and the fear of a dilution of their trades by less skilled labour as a result of increasing mechanization were factors of some importance in this change. The Engineers, for instance, yielded to the pressure of an agitation led by Tom Mann and opened their membership to wider sections of employees in their industry.[2] For these reasons it was possible for the Socialists to muster about a quarter of the votes at the annual T.U.C. in the early nineties. They were no longer the tiny group that supported Keir Hardie in 1887 and 1888, but a resolute and determined party always hopeful of capturing the whole Congress for their views.

(3)

The effect of the New Unionism on the Socialist groups was not entirely what might have been expected. It might have been thought that Champion at least would retain his position of leadership in view of his close connexion with the industrial

[1] Hobsbawm, op. cit. (1949), p. 131.
[2] J. B. Jefferys, *Story of the Engineers* (1945), pp. 136 ff.

successes of 1889 and 1890. But the Championites had always been an awkward menage, and Burns and others were suspicious of his Tory associations. The effect of the strikes had been to give the greatest publicity not to Champion himself but to his working-class allies, who began to shape out independent careers for themselves either in trade unionism or in politics. The group finally broke up in 1890 after the publication in the *Labour Elector* of some very indiscreet criticism of Ernest Parke, at that time editor of a Liberal-Labour paper and the defendant in an important libel case.[1] The *Labour Elector*, which was owned and run by Champion, had had a nominal 'Committee of Management' consisting of a number of trade-union Socialists including Burns, Mann and Tillett; some of this group, especially Burns, were strongly averse to alienating progressively minded Liberals. They now withdrew their support from the *Labour Elector*, and its influence and circulation collapsed. Champion went off on a trip to Australia, to examine what he called the 'High Tory state socialism of the young democracies',[2] which was much more to his taste; and while Burns busied himself with Progressive politics, most of the other working-class Socialists devoted themselves to the building up of the new unions.

The success of London Progressivism prevented the emergence in the metropolis of an independent labour movement as a political parallel to the New Unionism. With Sidney Webb as the propagandist of a programme of municipal socialism and with John Burns as its principal labour exponent, the alliance with the Liberals worked smoothly in its early years and the work of the reform went on with little opposition. Owing to the backwardness of London government in the years before 1889 when the L.C.C. was created, there was so much that could be done by Liberals and Socialists together that a politically independent labour movement seemed to be unnecessary. This accounted for the distinct difference of political attitude between the new unionist of London and his counterpart in the provinces. As Katharine Conway put it a few years later: 'In

---

[1] Engels to Sorge, 8 Dec. 1890 (*Labour Monthly*, 1934, p. 252).
[2] H. H. Champion, 'A Labour Enquiry', *Nineteenth Century*, July 1891.

London he listens to the persuasive reasoning of the Progressives: in the provinces, face to face with Liberals of the Illingworth, Kitson and Pease type, he is doggedly Independent.'[1]

In any case, in London the divisions inside the working class
were more acute than in the more fully industrialized North.
The old-fashioned craft unions which controlled the London
Trades Council—tailors, bookbinders, builders and cabinet-
makers—seemed hardly to have felt the impact of the industrial
revolution: it was no wonder that, like their predecessors in the
Chartist movement, they tried to keep aloof from the wider
industrial struggles of the time. In many parts of the north of
England, on the other hand, large-scale industry was much
commoner, even if most of the textile firms were still family
businesses. Lancashire, West Yorkshire and the North-East were
areas in which one would expect a labour organization to secure
the widest success. The seed of the Socialist gospel was late in
finding its way to provincial soil; but when it came it was the
more fruitful. The S.D.F. foothold in Lancashire was a precarious one in the eighties, especially as the Lancashire cotton
unions were well-established societies whose members were
for the most part fairly satisfied with the wages and conditions
which their leaders had won for them. But the failure of the
S.D.F. to expand rapidly might be put down in part to the dogmatic and sectarian character of their propaganda.[2] Only at the
end of the eighties was Socialism being voiced by advocates of
less strident and more appealing tone. The Radical *Sunday
Chronicle* of Manchester became the vehicle of the increasingly
socialistic utterances of Robert Blatchford, a powerful popular
journalist, who was later to acquire a great reputation as editor
of his own newspaper, the *Clarion*. While Blatchford was on the
Sunday Chronicle he exposed the misery of the Manchester slums,

---

[1] *Weekly Sun*, 21 Jan. 1894. Alfred Illingworth was M.P. for Bradford, 1880–95,
and owner of a worsted-spinning firm; Sir Joseph Pease was M.P. for Barnard
Castle, 1885–1903, and Chairman of the N.E. Railway Co. and of Pease & Partners,
Ltd., iron masters; James Kitson, first Baron Airedale, was M.P. for Colne Valley,
1892–1907, and an iron and steel manufacurer. Pease was succeeded in his constituency by Arthur Henderson, Kitson by Victor Grayson, and Illingworth—eleven
years afterwards—by Fred Jowett. Thus by 1907 Labour and Socialist representatives had replaced the industrialists in all three constituencies.

[2] In 1888 the S.D.F. had six branches in Lancashire with a total of 96 members
(*Justice*, 13 May 1893).

and, more than that, he drew his own political conclusions, and early in 1890 announced to his readers his acceptance of Fabian Socialism.[1]

The miners of Northumberland and Durham could not be expected to be favourable to the general Eight Hours Day agitation which the Socialists were working up, for they were working a seven-hour day which they knew would be prejudiced by the legal enforcement of a longer period as the maximum. The momentary popularity of Socialism during the Northumberland strike of 1887 was therefore not likely to be repeated in the near future. West Yorkshire, however, was much more suitable for the acceptance of the new idea. There appeared to be a real opening for new unionist activity in the woollen and worsted industries, which were closely concentrated in West Yorkshire but so far indifferently organized. In the winter of 1889–90 Thorne and Curran of the Gasworkers visited Yorkshire to establish their union, not only among those employed in the gas industry but among the unskilled workers of all trades. They found help among the little Socialist League groups of Bradford and Leeds, members of which were prepared to take over local secretarial duties. The Leeds gas strike of 1890 was one of the most formidable struggles of the time, and Engels himself, acting as a sort of revolutionary generalissimo, rewarded Will Thorne with an inscribed copy of *Capital* for his part in the affair.[2]

A further important influence was the *Yorkshire Factory Times*, a weekly founded in 1889 by John Andrew, the proprietor of the *Cotton Factory Times* of Lancashire, and designed to appeal to trade unionists in the woollen and worsted industries. Andrew's policy, based on his success with the Lancashire paper, was to employ the union organizers in the localities as his correspondents, relying on them not only to forward local news but also to push the sales of the paper. But the contrast between the two types of union organizers, in Lancashire well established and conservative, in Yorkshire precarious and politically advanced, made all the difference between the politics of

[1] *Sunday Chronicle*, 23 Mar. 1890.
[2] Thorne, op. cit. pp. 131 f.

93

the two papers. Moreover, the editor of the Yorkshire paper was Joseph Burgess, formerly a Lancashire cotton piecer, but already a pioneer of independent labour representation.[1] Ben Turner, of the General Union of Textile Workers, was one of the Yorkshire union organizers who worked for the paper, and he realized that the paper in turn was responsible for what success the union contrived to win: 'The establishment of that paper', he wrote some years later, 'made our union prosper.'[2]

By this time, too, the Fabian Society's educational propaganda was well under way, and *Fabian Essays* was attracting widespread attention. In the autumn of 1890 the Society, having received a donation from a generous member, H. H. Hutchinson, undertook a lecturing campaign in Lancashire and Yorkshire, and as a result there suddenly appeared a constellation of local Fabian Societies in the northern counties. Some of these were helped into existence by members of branches of the Socialist League, whose central organization was now in the process of dissolution. The social composition of these local Fabian Societies was often in striking contrast to that of the parent body, for in many cases the membership was almost entirely drawn from the working class.[3]

(4)

But a movement of even greater importance was set in motion by an external event. The closing years of the eighties had been generally fairly good from the point of view of trade, but in 1890 the Yorkshire textile industry received a sudden blow from the United States in the imposition of the McKinley tariff. One immediate result was an attempt by employers to reduce wages. At Christmas the work-people of the great worsted factory of Manningham Mills at Bradford were notified by placard of large cuts in their wages. Although they were not organized in a union, the workers struck in a body, and the

[1] In 1885 he had edited a *Nottingham Operative* in support of John Burns's candidature at the General Election. See his *John Burns*, pp. 5 ff.
[2] B. Turner, *Rise and Progress of the Heavy Woollen Branch, G.U. of Textile Workers* (Huddersfield, 1917), p. 66.
[3] Pease, *History of the Fabian Society*, p. 95; Fabian Society, *Annual Report* 1891.

conflict, which was a prolonged one, led to much bitterness between employer and labour in the neighbourhood. In April 1891 the authorities threatened to prohibit the open-air meetings held by the strike committee; and one of these meetings was broken up by the police. A very similar series of events had taken place during the 1887 engineers' strike at Bolton, and there the result had been that eight labour candidates were elected to the town council: but after a short time they failed to retain their unity and independence from the other parties.[1] Now in Bradford, however, with the backing of the *Yorkshire Factory Times* and the growing stimulus to political independence provided by Socialist tracts and lectures, a permanent political body was established. At the end of April a little group met to discuss the formation of a Bradford Labour Union, and the organization was launched in May with W. H. Drew, strike leader and correspondent of the *Yorkshire Factory Times*, as its first president. Several former members of the Bradford branch of the Socialist League were at once attracted to the new body: they included Fred Jowett, a future Labour cabinet minister, at this time helping to manage a small woollen firm.[2] The constitution of the Labour Union specifically stated that 'its operations shall be carried on irrespective of the convenience of any political party', and this attitude of rigid independence made it the pioneer of a new type of local political organization.[3] Candidates were adopted for two of the three Parliamentary constituencies of Bradford: one of them was Robert Blatchford, the Manchester Socialist journalist; the other was Ben Tillett, the London Dockers' leader. In November 1891 the Labour Union put up two local candidates for the town council, but both were defeated. This initial failure did not divert the Union from the path of strict independence, for it rejected outright a Liberal offer of a political agreement for Parliamentary purposes, whereby Tillett would have had a straight fight with

---

[1] *Bolton Weekly Journal*, 5 Nov. 1887; Bolton and District United Trades Council, *Jubilee Souvenir* (1916).
[2] A. F. Brockway, *Socialism over Sixty Years* (1946), p. 37; Bartley in *Labour Leader*, 13 Apr. 1901.
[3] The same phrase occurred in the constitution of the L.E.A. as approved at its 1888 Congress; but it lost all significance as a result of the expulsion of the Championites.

the Conservative in one division provided Blatchford was with-drawn from the other.[1] Later, Blatchford did withdraw, but this was for personal reasons. Partly, no doubt, it was because he was conscious of his limitations as a speaker: but he was really much too busy in a new journalistic venture to find time for nursing the constituency.

The firm establishment of the Bradford Labour Union was largely due to the newspaper support that it received. In the first place, the success of the *Yorkshire Factory Times* encouraged the proprietor to cover a still wider field, by establishing the *Workman's Times*, to which Joseph Burgess's editorial activities were transferred. In the autumn of 1891 both these papers were running a series of Socialist articles by Robert Blatchford, who had by now been ejected from the *Sunday Chronicle* on account of his views. The result was the establishment of Labour Unions on the Bradford model in other northern centres: the Colne Valley Labour Union dates from July 1891, when it was found-ed by the members of a Social Democratic club at Slaithwaite; and in August a Salford Labour Electoral Association was formed by members of the local S.D.F.

As further reinforcement to the growing movement came Blatchford's establishment of the *Clarion*, published weekly at Manchester from December 1891 onwards. This was an openly Socialist journal, but it combined plenty of entertainment with its serious political purpose. Blatchford's journalistic appren-ticeship had been spent on a sporting paper, and he had learnt the art of vigorous and gay writing. He read the pamphlets of the S.D.F. and the Fabians, and he came to accept Socialism as a way of bringing back happiness into a miserable world. He and several others of the staff of the *Sunday Chronicle* had formed a friendly and jovial team; with them he founded Cinderella Clubs to provide poor children with an occasional treat; with them he left the *Sunday Chronicle* when at last its proprietor, Edward Hulton, forbade him to continue preaching Socialism; with them he built up the *Clarion* as a new and independent journal. Having served as a regular soldier for several years, he

---

[1] J. Burgess, *Will Lloyd George Supplant Ramsay MacDonald?* (Ilford, 1926), p. 38.

had a due sense of the responsibilities of national defence, and a respect for the comradeship of army life. He thus avoided the excesses of pacifist sentiment achieved by many of the 'Little England' school. He was never a Radical in the old-fashioned Cobdenite sense, and he did not hold with the gloom of Sunday observance and teetotalism. To the Manchester School he was an enemy in their very midst: and all the more effective because of the vivid style and spontaneous zest of his writings. Hyndman, in March 1892, spoke of Blatchford having given the cause of Socialism 'a tremendous push forward in the North of England. . . . I find his converts in every direction.'[1]

Fundamentally, Blatchford was not interested in politics— that is, in the humdrum work of organizing elections and obtaining members and support for local electoral clubs and societies. However, on his own doorstep in Manchester, there was an obvious opportunity for him to help form an independent labour union, and to systematize the existing jumble of local labour and Socialist bodies—the Fabian Society (of which he was the President), the Trades Council, the Labour Electoral Associations, the S.D.F., and the Labour Church which John Trevor, a Unitarian minister, had founded.[2] In May 1892 Trevor, Blatchford and a few others formed an Independent Labour Party for the Manchester District, committed to Socialism, and with an even more rigid policy of independence than that of the Bradford Labour Union. The fourth clause of its constitution read as follows: 'That all members of this party pledge themselves to abstain from voting for any candidate for election to any representative body who is in any way a nominee of the Liberal, Liberal-Unionist, or Conservative parties.' The difference of name—'Independent Labour Party' instead of 'Labour Union'—is also significant of an increasing awareness of the purpose of the new movement in the national political scene.

By this time, it is clear, the independent labour movement was catching on in a big way in the North of England. Here was a widespread agitation, supported by important weekly

[1] *Clarion*, 5 Mar. 1892.
[2] For the Labour Churches, see below, Chapter VII.

newspapers with considerable circulation among the working class, building up a network of working-men's political clubs, which in turn had little broadsheets of their own for local purposes. Socialism was now more than the fad of a few London intellectuals: thousands of ordinary humble folk were turning towards it as offering the hope of redress for their pressing grievances. The intellectuals had performed their main task well: they had provided a unique range of propagandist literature, ranging from Carpenter's visions of a fuller democracy to Hyndman's prophecies of economic collapse, and from the brilliant theorizing of *Fabian Essays* to the imaginative Utopian romance of Morris's *News from Nowhere*, first published in book form in 1891.[1] But the time had now come for the establishment of a national party which would be more representative of the new converts than the sectional societies of the metropolis could ever become; and for this purpose there had to be a fresh start in political organization.

[1] *News from Nowhere* was published in instalments in *Commonweal* in 1890, and appeared in an unauthorized edition in America in the same year.

CHAPTER VI

The Emergence of the National I.L.P.

(1)

IT was widely felt that the success of the Socialist and independent labour propaganda in the North of England justified the formation of a new party. The movement was getting too large for any existing structure: and the Socialist groups of London were suspect, either because they were too revolutionary or, in the case of the Fabians, because of too close association with the Liberals, who tended to be much less radical in the provinces than they were in London. Between permeation and revolution, it was felt, there was another and more reliable approach to political power. The way the wind was blowing was clearly shown by a resolution carried unanimously at a conference of Fabian Societies held in London in February 1892: 'That this meeting, being of opinion that the best way to forward the Labour cause is by the workers acting independently of both political parties, hails with satisfaction the formation of an independent labour party, and heartily wishes success to the movement.'[1] The 'party' did not exist yet, but the sentiment evidently did: and Sidney Webb, sensing the feeling of the meeting, which was largely composed of working-class Fabians from the north of England, discreetly accepted the motion. The London Fabians were still doubtful of the necessity of independent political action, but the Northerners had made up their minds, and their anxiety to translate their convictions into political structure was very evident.

Things did not move swiftly enough for the national organization to be in existence in time for the General Election of 1892. Many changes had indeed taken place in the general political situation since the previous election. The Unionist government

---

[1] *Workman's Times*, 13 Feb. 1892.

99

which had taken office in 1886 had been responsible for some important reforms—the County Councils Act of 1888 being notable among them. But Gladstone and the Liberals had been consolidating the forces left at their disposal after the split with the Liberal Unionists. The Liberal Party had lost many of its great Whig supporters, and had thus begun to evolve once more in the Radical direction, in spite of the loss of Chamberlain. At the conference of the National Liberal Federation at Newcastle in 1891, a long list of reforms was accepted as the programme of the party. This 'Newcastle Programme' included various phrases designed to attract the labour vote: there were hints about the limitation of the hours of labour and about the payment of members of parliament; but the more direct appeal was to the Celtic fringe, with Irish Home Rule and Church Disestablishment in Wales and Scotland, and to the agricultural vote, with reforms in the land laws and rural local government. Nevertheless, the fact that the Liberal Party was more Radical than it had been before induced many to take this programme at its full face value, and the London Fabians, who had been partly responsible for suggesting some of the details of the programme, by means of their influence in the London Radical associations, were anxious to see a Liberal victory at the election. If the trade unions were to back an attempt to form a national labour party with their accumulated funds, then, the Fabians argued, there would be a real chance of success; but efforts by individuals and by tiny political societies were, they thought, doomed to failure. In 1892 they urged that the T.U.C. should be induced to finance labour candidates[1]; but they must have realized that this advice was not likely to be acted upon, for when Hardie at the 1891 Congress had moved a resolution for a penny levy on trade union members to establish a Parliamentary fund for labour candidates, he had been defeated by 200 votes to 93.

The trades councils were generally more responsive to the militant spirit of the Socialists but not uniformly so. We have already seen how in London Mann and his supporters who had tried to make a radical reform of the London Trades Council

---

[1] *Fabian Election Manifesto* (Tract No. 40, 1892).

had been forced to compromise with the established leaders. One outcome of Mann's campaign was a London Trades Council Representation League formed as a voluntary body in December 1891, but its official sponsors gave it a very half-hearted backing, and its members, who numbered only a few hundreds, were divided on the issue of independence from the Liberals.[1] London was indeed stony ground for the seed of the new idea. The new unionist boom had led to a similar boom in 'advanced' political journalism in London, but little success attended the many new ventures published for the first time in this period. Weekly newspapers were continually being produced with a flourish, only to fade away quietly after a few months' existence: Frank Smith's *Workers' Cry*, for instance, which attempted to rally a 'Labour Army' somewhat on the lines of the Salvation Army in which he had served; the *Labor Leader*, with which the former Socialist Leaguer Fred Henderson was associated; the *North London Press*, later the *People's Press*, sponsored in part by members of the Fabian Society and edited by Shaw Maxwell, a member of the Scottish Labour Party who had migrated from Glasgow[2]; Tom Mann's *Trade Unionist*, whose objects included the co-ordination of all trades council activities, and also the reform of the London Trades Council[3]; and the *Nationalisation News*, founded as the organ of the short-lived Nationalization of Labour Society which was established 'to carry into effect the principles of Bellamy's *Looking Backward*'.[4] The rapid failure of all these London papers, contrasted with the success in the North of the *Clarion* and the *Workman's Times*, gives an indication of the weakness of the enthusiasm aroused among Londoners for the idea of an independent labour party.

In Scotland, too, the political situation was not maturing as was hoped by those who had welcomed the foundation of the

---

[1] *Workman's Times*, 11 and 18 June 1892.
[2] *Fabian Society Annual Report*, 1890, p. 11.
[3] See Mann's letter to Alf Mattison, 2 Mar. 1891: letter-book of Mattison, in possession of Mrs. Mattison, Leeds.
[4] Edward Bellamy was the American author of a Utopian romance entitled *Looking Backward, 2000–1887*, which foresaw a state of society in which all industry was nationalized. At least seven branches of the (British) Nationalization of Labour Society were founded, but they did not last long. The enthusiasm for Bellamy's ideas was much more widespread in the United States (N. Hillquit, *History of Socialism in the United States* (New York, 1903), p. 318).

Scottish Labour Party. The party had made little progress since its foundation in 1888; and Hardie, who had in 1889 changed the title of his paper the *Miner* to the *Labour Leader* in order that it might serve as the official organ of the party, soon found it impossible to keep the paper going, and in August of the same year he allowed it to be absorbed into Champion's *Labour Elector*, of which he became the Scottish correspondent. As we have seen, this paper, in turn, disappeared early in 1890. The growth of the Scottish party was chequered by disagreements of a partly personal and partly political nature: for instance, Chisholm Robertson, the miners' leader, made a bitter attack on Hardie at the 1889 T.U.C. at Dundee. Similar dissensions were partly responsible for the weakening of the Scottish miners' unions at this time.[1] The Scottish Labour Party was apparently not yet a homogeneous body with a clearly decided policy. Many of its members hoped that it would be able to make an electoral pact with the Liberals, and indeed Cunninghame Graham was foremost in negotiations to this end, which only fell through owing to the usual difficulty of bringing the local Liberal caucuses into line with the attitude of the national organization of the Liberal Party.[2]

The Scottish Labour Party consisted not only of subordinate branches, but also of many affiliated but independent bodies—Radical Associations, Ruskin Societies, Single-Taxers and so on.[3] Under the test of a General Election in which the party attempted to fight independently, its lack of political solidarity became evident. Davitt's friend John Ferguson, for instance, who was a vice-president, was to be found supporting the Liberal opponents of labour candidates, in accordance with the Irish Nationalist policy[4]; and C. A. V. Conybeare, another vice-president and a Radical M.P., stood as the official Liberal candidate for his Cornish constituency. Their names had to be removed from the list of the officers of the party. This was not a

[1] Hardie's evidence to Royal Commission on Labour, *Parliamentary Papers* (1892), xxxvi. i, par. 13164.
[2] *Labour Elector*, 22 Mar. 1890.
[3] Even at the 5th Annual Conference of the party, held in Jan. 1894, a year before it dissolved, out of a total of 88 bodies represented only 24 were entitled branches of the party (Lowe, *Souvenirs*, pp. 160 ff.).
[4] *Labour Elector*, 11 Feb. 1893.

step that the party could undertake without embarrassment, for two Liberal M.P.s, one of whom was Conybeare, had between them contributed £500 to the Special Election Fund, which was well over one-third of the total.[1] However, the election was fought by five Scottish Labour Party candidates, in all cases against Liberal opposition, which prevented them from coming anywhere near success. The party also showed some activity in municipal affairs and produced a number of pamphlets and leaflets from its Glasgow printers, the Labour Literature Society.

In England there was no central organization at all. The S.D.F. had had ambitious plans for up to a dozen candidates, Hyndman having promised to find the money, but when the time came he could not honour his obligation, having suffered in the Barings financial crisis of 1890–1; and so the whole S.D.F. campaign plan collapsed in sympathy with the stock markets.[2] Aveling had been trying hard to boost the idea of an independent labour party through his Legal Eight Hours League, which was sponsored by the committee which organized the May Day demonstration.[3] Shaw Maxwell's *People's Press* acted as official organ of the League and strongly backed Aveling's agitation; but the bodies forming the League were mostly trade-union branches and Radical clubs, and they were lukewarm in their support.

The consequence was that individual labour leaders had to put up as Parliamentary candidates without the backing of any national organization, but in the hope that local factors would give them a chance of success. Hardie had been adopted early in 1890 by the Radical Association of West Ham South, by an arrangement sponsored by Dr. John Moir, a Radical friend of his, and with Champion's approval at the time.[4] The constituency was a favourable one, for it was outside the L.C.C. area and full of new-unionist dockers and labourers. Hardie was active in the district, and the unexpected death of the official Liberal candidate left him with a straight fight against the

---

[1] *Labour Leader*, Jan. 1893.
[2] Hyndman, *Further Reminiscences*, pp. 197 ff.; *Justice*, 9 Aug. 1890 and 6 Aug. 1892.
[3] Its foundation conference was reported in *People's Press*, 19 July 1890.
[4] *Labour Elector*, 8 Mar. 1890.

Conservative. In order fully to devote himself to political work, he resigned his post as a paid trade-union official at the end of 1891.[1] But personal success at the General Election was not his only interest. He was well aware of the need to set the movement on a national basis, and now that Champion's influence was in eclipse he did his best to persuade John Burns to take the lead in a campaign for the co-ordination of the various independent labour candidates throughout the country. This was no new departure for Hardie, as from the time of the Dock Strike he had been attempting to identify Burns with the movement nationally, to arrange a speaking tour for him in Scotland under the auspices of the Scottish Labour Party, and to induce him to call a conference of all independent labour elements in the country.[2] For the elections, Burns was strongly placed in Battersea, where, to the disgust of the S.D.F., he had organized the Battersea Labour League as a private concern of his own. Hardie's letters to Burns in these years reveal his willingness to serve as Burns's subordinate in any attempts he might be prepared to make to rally the 'independents', and they also betray some anxiety about Burns's present position *vis-à-vis* the Liberals, with whom, as a Progressive on the L.C.C., he was already in close collaboration. In May 1891 Hardie wrote to Burns:

> Now is the time to realize your idea of a conference of those, as far as known, who have not sold themselves to the party managers. The farce enacted during Whit week of the Electoral Association would give point to such a gathering. A congress of workers and no mention of the Eight Hours Bill—what a monstrosity! Schnadhorst has got hold of the gang and hence the omission.
> Desperate efforts are being made by Schnadhorst and Co. to entrap every man worth having, and it is important that those of us who are not entangled in the party net should be guarded in our utterances. Should the Liberals get into power at next election their neglect of the Labour question will compel some plain talking, and the fewer ghosts of former utterances there are to rise in judgment against us the better it will be. Like yourself I believe we have more to hope for from that party than from the other, but this applies to the

[1] Hardie in *Labour Leader*, 28 Dec. 1901.
[2] See letters from Hardie in Burns Collection, B.M. Add. MSS. 46288.

rank and file only, and not to the leaders, and to prevent mis-
understanding, the less said about this 'hope' the better.
I will be glad to learn what you think of doing. I mean to be
in London during June, but might be preparing the way for
a contingent being sent from Scotland to the conference
should you think of calling it.[1]

Burns did nothing, however, in spite of Hardie's persistent
exhortations. He was not interested in the wider movements
now that he was sure of Battersea, and he was happy to devote
himself to the tactic of exerting the same friendly pressure on
the Liberals at Westminster as he was already exerting on the
Progressives at Spring Gardens. There was, in fact, no one of
sufficient stature to act as leader of the independent movement
in England. Cunninghame Graham had already sponsored a
conference in London to discuss labour representation, but it
was rendered abortive by the fact that the Scottish Labour
Party was the only body of the slightest importance prepared to
back it.[2] Graham was well aware of the difficulties of his own
position as the only Socialist in Parliament. This Scottish aris-
tocrat, for all the mordant wit of his speeches which revealed
the promise of his literary future, was really quite unsuited to
the political life. His years of adventure in the wilds of Spanish
America had given him a taste for the politics of revolt: but he
represented nobody—not even, now, his own constituency—
and it was natural for him to be dismissed as a mere 'cowboy
dandy', as *The Times* put it.[3] He admitted his weakness to
Burns, and urged him to consult with Hardie on the subject.
'The House', he said, 'is beginning to find out that there is
nothing and nobody behind me. Anyone but the idiots in
Parliament would have seen this long ago. . . .'[4]

Champion, meanwhile, was staging a come-back to the political arena. His already tarnished reputation had suffered further
from the news of his intervention in Australian politics and
opposition to the Shearers' strike then in progress. On his return
to Britain he secured appointment as assistant editor of the

[1] B.M. Add. MSS. 46288.
[2] *People's Press*, 10 Jan. 1891.
[3] Quoted Tschiffely, *Don Roberto*, p. 212.
[4] Graham to Burns, 22 Oct. 1891 (Burns Correspondence).

influential monthly review, the *Nineteenth Century*. He arranged
to put up for Parliament at Aberdeen, where he had strong
local ties and was on good terms with the leaders of the local
Labour Party, for whose existence he was largely responsible.
He further endeavoured to get the Newcastle Labour Party,
which he had also helped to form, to promote the candidature
of Fred Hammill, though this fell through in the end. More important than this, he arranged through the *Workman's Time*
donations of £100 each to the election funds of four London
labour candidates including Hardie, Burns and H. R. Taylor,
an S.D.F. member who was on the executive of the London
Trades Council. The source of the money was not revealed, but
all the candidates managed to pocket their political pride, and
without such assistance Taylor at least would not have been
able to go to the poll.[1]

It was the foregone conclusion of the election that independent candidates, lacking finance and proper organization,
were in general doomed to failure. With the exception of J.
Havelock Wilson, the seamen's leader, who won a three-
cornered fight at Middlesbrough, they very rarely polled well
save where the Liberals left them straight fights with the Conservatives; and the readiness of Havelock Wilson to come to
terms with the Liberals after the election showed that he could
not be regarded as a true independent. Hardie, at West Ham
South, refused Schnadhorst's offer of assistance in running his
campaign, though he was as conciliatory as he could be to the
Liberal voters in the constituency. 'Generally speaking', he
said in his manifesto, 'I am in agreement with the present programme of the Liberal Party so far as it goes, but I reserve to
myself the absolute and unconditional right to take such action
irrespective of the exigencies of party welfare, as may to me
seem needful in the interest of the workers.'[2] Hardie duly
secured the support of the Liberal voters, and was elected by a
majority of over a thousand; and Burns secured a similar success
at Battersea.

---

[1] *Justice*, 6 Aug. 1892. The only other S.D.F. candidate was W. K. Hall at
Salford, who received the support of various independent bodies.
[2] Stewart, *Keir Hardie*, p. 71.

All the other independent candidates were defeated: but one of the defeats was a remarkable moral victory. This was at West Bradford, where Ben Tillett, although at the bottom of the poll in a three-cornered contest, secured 2,749 votes, which was less than 600 short of the Liberal victor. His funds came partly from the Fabian Society of which he was a member[1]: but the reason for his high poll was the strength of active workers and supporters belonging to the Bradford Labour Union. This Bradford election induced some of the Liberals to appreciate at last the significance of the independent movement and to realize that it drew its support from both the existing parties. The *Bradford Observer*, a Liberal paper, made an analysis of the voting which led to the conclusion that the Labour supporters were drawn in almost equal proportions from the Liberals and the Conservatives.[2] This was surprising to the Liberal pundits, who had always proceeded on the assumption that the politically conscious working man invariably voted Liberal, and had consequently not realized how many working-class voters, especially in industrial areas, had already gone over to the Unionists. If this had not been so, there would have been very little basis for attempting to form an independent party: but since it was so, and was shown to be so, the policy of independence first carried into practice by the Bradford Labour Union could be regarded as having some justification.

But Tillett, the Bradford candidate, had not secured election. Cunninghame Graham had been defeated, and the only nominally independent members of the new House were Havelock Wilson, Burns and Hardie. Discounting Wilson, the leadership of the independent movement rested with Burns and Hardie. The Parliamentary limelight was on them, and the development of a national organization in time for the next election depended on their initiative. The question was: could they work together for this object, and could they give the now widespread independent labour supporters the national leadership that they lacked and required? Could they make it clear that they had a policy which was an alternative not only to that of the Conservatives, but

---

[1] *Fabian Society Annual Report*, 1893.
[2] *Bradford Observer*, 5 July 1892.

also to that of the Liberals, who, pledged to all sorts of reforms as they were, now took over the responsibility of government?

(2)

The first preparations for the new Parliament indicated that Burns was doubtful on the issue of complete independence. Hardie had already announced his intention of sitting on the opposition benches, whatever government came to power: but Burns was unwilling to commit himself to this, and the reason for his attitude, given in a letter to Cunninghame Graham, is interesting: 'On the L.C.C. the wobbling Progressives have been kept to their work by candid and independent friends in their midst: they would have laughed at them if they had joined the Moderates. People stand more from their friends than from their enemies. . . .'[1] Arguments like these did not augur well for the future, and although Burns did in the end consent to sit in opposition with Hardie, his attitude to the Liberals continued to be based on the conception that 'people stand more from their friends'. It gradually became clear that it was Hardie alone who stood for the principle of independence. Burns in any case was temperamentally unsuited to work in harmony with Hardie or any other working-class leader: for his early success as an agitator and his present great popularity had made him intolerant and arrogant. Although his political attitude was by no means unprincipled, it was subject to the powerful influences of the personal hostilities and feuds which were conjured up in his mind by his own vanity. In short, the only reliable Parliamentary asset of independent labour was Keir Hardie.

This unique position of Hardie's in Parliament was a difficult one, but it presented him with a great opportunity for publicizing his cause. He was often hampered by his ignorance of the rules of the House—an ignorance which his political isolation rendered difficult to remedy. He was not a man who made friends easily—his upbringing and early life had been too bitter for that—but there was a depth of human feeling behind his

<hr>

[1] Burns to Graham, 29 July 1892 (B.M. Add. MSS. 46285).

rough exterior that made those who were initially sympathetic all the more loyal in their friendship; and his simple, clear manner of expression, combined with his early experience of poverty and suffering, made him very effective in the role he assumed as the crusader of the working class and the antagonist of Capital. Alone of labour M.P.s up to that time, Hardie became more independent instead of less so after his election—a tendency that was to work to his disadvantage when he had to face the electorate again.

When the House met, he caused a sensation by arriving at Westminster in a cloth cap and tweed jacket, conveyed on a two-horse break with a trumpeter on the box. The incident, which arose from the extempore enthusiasm of his supporters, was elaborated in the press into a deliberate insult to the House by the new M.P.[1] On 18 August he raised the question of an autumn session 'for the consideration of measures designed to improve the condition of the people', but the Speaker ruled that the question could not be raised until a new government had been formed; and so the House adjourned for the long recess until February 1893.

Meanwhile Burgess, now editor of the weekly *Workman's Times* which he had directed on an independent policy since early in 1891, had already launched what was to prove a successful campaign for a national organization to be called the Independent Labour Party. On 30 April 1892 he invited all readers who wished to join to send him their names and addresses. The names, he promised, would be sorted by constituencies, and local sympathizers would be put in touch with one another with a view to the formation of branches. By the middle of September over 2,000 names had been sent in, and the process of forming local branches was well advanced.

The idea of forming a labour party in this simple way was not a new one. Champion's *Labour Elector* had tried much the same procedure in 1889, and so had the London *Labor Leader* two years later. But the *Workman's Times* was a bigger paper, and the movement was more mature than before. Moreover, Burgess was, even to excess, a man of dogged perseverance. He

---

[1] For Hardie's account of the incident, see *Manchester Guardian*, 18 Apr. 1914.

hammered away continually at his scheme of building up local branches and then forming a national I.L.P., until in the end success crowned his efforts. When his campaign began, the only independent labour organizations in England and Wales were those at Bradford, Colne Valley, and Swinton and Pendlebury near Manchester, together with Blatchford's own Manchester and Salford I.L.P. and Champion's Newcastle Labour Party. But the campaign had an immediate effect. In June branches were founded at Plymouth, Stafford, Mansfield, Bolton, Hull, Liverpool and Birmingham, and possibly in other towns as well; and thereafter the catalogue of organization continued without ceasing for the rest of the year. It was a remarkable illustration of the power of the press in crystallizing popular sentiment into widespread political activity.

The creation of the local branches had turned out to be un-expectedly easy. The problem of how to link them together was more difficult. Burgess suggested that a provisional London committee be set up to consist of—the choice is significant—Cunninghame Graham, Mann, Tillett, Quelch of the S.D.F., and Fay, the London representative of the *Clarion*.[1] This sug-gestion aroused the wrath of Drew of Bradford who wrote to Burgess: 'Depend upon it no executive will suit the provincials that they have had no hand in forming. What you should set your face towards is a conference of provincial men and Lon-doners, and you cockneys ought to unbend and come, say to Bradford, a central town, where you will find plenty of food for reflection. . . .'[2]

Burgess, who was now editing the *Workman's Times* from Lon-don, had personally presided over the formation of the London I.L.P., which took place on 13 June at a meeting at the Demo-cratic Club in Essex Street, just off the Strand, where journal-ists and others of labour sympathies were wont to meet. A pro-visional executive was elected with Shaw Maxwell as its secre-tary and Burgess himself, H. A. Barker of the Labour Union, and the Dockers' leader Tom McCarthy among its members. The body was entitled 'National Independent Labour Party

---

[1] *Workman's Times*, 30 July, 1892.
[2] Ibid. 13 Aug. 1892.

(London District)', with a view to linking up with a national organization as soon as it was created: but Drew's letter had shown that the arrangements could not be fixed up by the Londoners alone, or imposed by them upon the rest of the country. Shaw Maxwell, writing on behalf of the London I.L.P. to the *Workman's Times*, put the case cautiously:

> . . . It is of infinite importance that the organization shall be national, having branches, if possible, in every constituency. It would, of course, be a *sine qua non* that every branch of the party should have a perfect autonomy in regard to local matters while subscribing to a central fund for general purposes. Thus it is believed that the sinews of war could be at the disposal of a democratically-elected directing body to carry out the objects of the party wherever in the judgement of the central executive an attack would be most effectual. . . . The London Council . . . hope to be able to join with delegates from other constituencies in a conference, where a programme may be agreed upon and the foundations of a United National Independent Labour Party may be solidly and truly laid.

It is noteworthy that Hardie was present at the Council meeting which decided to send this letter, and that it reflected very closely his own views on the question.[1] The Council was throughout giving him the fullest assistance in his Parliamentary work, even to the extent of sending out a 'whip' to every M.P. asking support for his proposal for an autumn session.[2]

At this point, however, the arguments in favour of using London as the centre of the movement lost force with the refusal of the S.D.F. to co-operate. At the annual conference of the Federation in August a resolution advising members 'to render every assistance in the formation of the Independent Labour Party' was rejected in favour of an amendment recommending 'benevolent neutrality'.[3] The amendment was carried by 20 votes to 10, and the sponsors of the I.L.P. therefore had reason to hope that the dissentient minority in the provinces might still force the hand of the S.D.F. leaders by throwing in their lot with the new party. 'It is simply the official attitude that is

---

[1] Minutes, London District, I.L.P., 15 Aug. 1892.
[2] Ibid.
[3] *Justice*, 13 Aug. 1892.

unchanged,' wrote Burgess, 'and I have not lost hope that we may yet see the S.D.F. officially represented on the Central Executive of the National I.L.P.'[1] The Fabian Society at the same time refused to take the initiative in attempting to form a United Socialist Party, Shaw urging that it was an impossible task 'until the S.D.F. decisively turns its back on the schoolboy make-belief of waving a red flag and pretending to be a revolutionary committee'.[2]

At Drew's suggestion, the Trades Union Congress at Glasgow in September was made the opportunity for a preliminary conference of independent labour representatives. Burns was invited to attend, but did not do so[3]; and Hardie, who had been instructed to act on behalf of the London Council, was elected to the chair. It was decided to organize a conference of 'authorized delegates from the Independent Labour Party' at an early date, and an Arrangements Committee was appointed consisting of Drew, of the Bradford Labour Union; William Johnson, of the Shop Assistants Union and the Manchester I.L.P.; Pete Curran, formerly in Champion's Metropolitan L.E.A. and now an organizer of the Gasworkers; James Macdonald of the London Tailors, a member of the S.D.F. who fought Dundee at the General Election for the Scottish Labour Party[4]; George Carson, chairman of the Executive of the Scottish Labour Party; and, by way of flavouring for this group of trade union leaders, Katharine Conway, a young Newnham graduate and Fabian lecturer. Carson acted as secretary to the Committee and at once issued a circular letter addressed 'To the Independent Labour Parties in Great Britain'.[5] At a meeting of the Committee early in November it was finally decided to hold the conference at Bradford on 13 and 14 January 1893.[6]

Thus the national conference was at last arranged, principally as the result of the work of Burgess, Hardie, and Drew. Although

---

[1] *Workman's Times*, 6 Aug. 1892.

[2] *Workman's Times*, 26 Nov. 1892; Fabian Society Executive Minutes, 17 and 28 Oct. 1892.

[3] Graham to Burns, 18 Aug. 1892 (B.M. Add. MSS. 46285).

[4] Not to be confused with James Ramsay MacDonald, the future Prime Minister, for whose early career see below, pp. 175f.

[5] Published in *Workman's Times*, 17 Sept. 1892.

[6] *Bradford Labour Journal*, 11 Nov. 1892.

Membership card of the Socialist
League, Hammersmith Branch

Cartoon for May Day, 1896, and
for the International Socialist
Congress of the same year, held
in London

Membership card of the Independent Labour Party

Art in the Service of Socialism: 2
Three designs by Walter Crane

The Emergence of the National I.L.P.

Hardie had no direct part in the work of the provisional committee, his views were given full weight, and the structure of the party was largely built on the lines that he envisaged. In an article in the *Workman's Times* in October he argued that it should be built on the model of the T.U.C.: there should be a National Executive, to correspond to the T.U.C. Parliamentary Committee, and charged with the duty of carrying out the decisions of the conference. This system would at first leave a great deal of autonomy to the local bodies, whose financial contributions to the National Executive, Hardie maintained, should, to start with, be purely voluntary. The executive would, however, assist in running elections and in finding candidates, and in due course the satisfactory working of the system would automatically endow it with greater authority and would lead to a more centralized national organization.[1] Hardie's forecast was not far wrong: as it turned out, the organization as actually set up only differed from this outline in that the financial contributions were made compulsory—though many branches neglected their duty in this respect for some of the time.

Two men who had done much for the independent labour movement stood outside all the arrangements: Burns and Champion. Champion had secured a good poll of almost a thousand votes at Aberdeen at the General Election, and he had found funds, as we have seen, for several of the London labour candidates, including Hardie and Burns. But since then he had attacked Hardie for 'betraying the interests of his class to latter-day Liberalism', and this attack was resented by the London District Council, which had previously been negotiating with him.[2] However, the promoters of the conference were most anxious that both he and Burns should attend, and they were making efforts to secure their presence at Bradford until the very last moment.[3] Burns apparently made no effort to be present; Champion was delegated to attend by the Aberdeen I.L.P., but illness prevented him travelling to Bradford.[4]

[1] *Workman's Times*, 15 Oct. 1892.
[2] *National Observer* (Glasgow), 8 Oct. 1892; Minutes, London District I.L.P., 17 Oct. 1892.
[3] *Workman's Times*, 24 Dec. 1892; Burns's Diary, 18 Dec. 1892 (B.M. Add. MSS. 46312).   [4] *Labour Elector*, 14 Jan. 1893.

As for the London Fabians, they were willing enough to attend, and desirous of seeing a labour party formed; but they were pessimistic about this particular attempt to form a party which they believed to be premature. Shaw expressed their point of view when, in the autumn of 1892, he wrote to the *Workman's Times*:

> What can we do but laugh at your folly? . . . The only vital difference between the Fabian Society and the S.D.F. is that the Fabian wants to grow the plums first and make the pies afterwards, whilst the Federation wants to make the pies first and find the plums afterwards. This is also the idea of the Independent Labour Party, which thus turns out to be nothing but an attempt to begin the S.D.F. over again. . . . Can you show me any differences between the Independent Labour Party of the early nineties and the Democratic Federation of the early eighties?[1]

Bradford gave the answer to Shaw's question by showing the country that it was not merely a convenient geographical centre for a political conference, but also the home of an enthusiasm which far transcended anything that the propaganda of the S.D.F. had ever produced. There was in these days something of a mass movement among a considerable section of the local workers, and this is revealed in the pages of the *Bradford Labour Journal*, a weekly paper published by the Labour Union. The number of societies and local clubs in Bradford whose activities are recorded is very remarkable. Apart from the Fabian Society, the Labour Church, the Trades Council and the local trade union branches, there were at the end of 1892 twenty-three local labour clubs, all of them concentrating on the instruction rather than on the entertainment of their members, who in total numbered about three thousand.[2] One of the clubs, not the largest, ran three lectures, an orchestral performance, and a shorthand class in a typical week. The subscription was nor-

---

[1] *Workman's Times*, 8 Oct. 1892. Cf. his remark in a letter to Wallas of 20 Sept. 1892: 'this N. I. Labor Party . . . is nothing but a new S.D.F. with Champion instead of Hyndman' (Wallas Papers).
[2] The number of clubs is mentioned in a letter from Carpenter to Mattison (Mattison letter-book); the membership figure is given in *Workman's Times*, 24 Dec. 1892; other details are from *Bradford Labour Journal*.

mally a penny a week, with an entrance fee of sixpence, and the clubroom would be open every evening and at the week-ends with newspapers and games provided but in most cases only tee-total drinks for sale. It was not surprising that all this organiza-tion began to bring success in municipal politics: after the elections of 1892 there were two independent labour councillors, one of them being Fred Jowett. The independent labour move-ment had other municipal successes this year: Halifax elected three councillors, and secured an alderman as well; Stockton elected two councillors, and several other towns one each. But to crown the Bradford achievement and to confirm its leader-ship of the movement, the inaugural conference of the national party was, by Drew's invitation, to be held in the newly ac-quired Bradford Labour Institute, which was prepared for the occasion in the brief interval between its acquisition and the opening of the conference.

(3)

The Bradford Labour Institute was not new. Its history was symbolical: it passed from the hands of one crusading cause to another. It had first of all been a Wesleyan Reform Chapel, and later it had been used by the Salvation Army. It stood just near the spot where the Manningham strikers had demonstrated against their employers, and it was surrounded by the mills and warehouses on which the trade of Bradford depended. Re-decorated hastily by members of the Bradford Labour Union, and furnished with benches and tables decked out in scarlet cotton cloth, it was just ready in time for the inaugural confer-ence of the I.L.P. on 13 January 1893.[1]

The opening of the conference presented a scene novel in British political history.[2] Certainly there were many faces to be seen which were already familiar to those in contact with labour politics. Among the veterans of the Socialist stage army were Mahon, Donald, and Aveling, the latter representing the modest

---

[1] *Methodist Times*, 12 Jan. 1893; Katharine Conway, quoted Brockway, *Socialism over Sixty Years*, p. 43.

[2] The best accounts of the conference are, beside the official *Report*, the *Bradford Observer*, 14 and 16 Jan. 1893, and Shaw's account in *Workman's Times*, 28 Jan. 1893.

membership of the Legal Eight Hours League. Joseph Burgess, garrulous as ever and proud of his personal success, was there; and Keir Hardie, the only M.P. to be present, who had spent the autumn publicizing the conference up and down the country, arrived in his famous cloth cap and tweeds; Ben Tillett, now an alderman of the L.C.C., was again in Bradford, the scene of his great Parliamentary contest of the previous year; and among others who attended were John Trevor of the Manchester Labour Church, and Bernard Shaw, his tall thin figure and red beard making him conspicuous. Champion was away ill, and Blatchford arrived only after the proceedings had begun. But the most interesting feature of the gathering was the presence of a new type of political delegate—the intelligent, respectable, working trade unionist of the new labour clubs. Men of this type, young and friendly, their countenances gleaming with good humour above their loose red ties, dominated the scene. They were not politicians for politics' sake; they were the working class in earnest, the product of the new education and the widening franchise. Their enthusiasm and discipline impressed the observers in the gallery and the reporters who crowded at the press table. They were the tangible evidence of a new factor in British politics.

A study of the representation in more detail reveals the geographical strength and weakness of the new movement. The delegates numbered about 120, and of these the overwhelming majority came from the industrial north of England or from Scotland. There was not a single representative from Wales, Ireland or any part of southern England save London, Chatham and Plymouth.[1] Altogether over one-third of the delegates came from Yorkshire Labour Parties and Clubs, nearly all being from the woollen area—a large proportion, even allowing for the fact that the conference was held close to their homes. There were, too, eleven representatives of northern Fabian Societies, and six of S.D.F. branches in Lancashire. This preponderance of Northerners reflected the recent phenomenal growth of the movement and the shift of its centre of gravity.

[1] There would have been one from South Wales if S. G. Hobson had not missed his train. See his *Pilgrim to the Left* (1938), p. 35.

The London political leadership, on the other hand, was not represented even in accordance with its strength. The London S.D.F. leaders would not come, and Burns and Mann were notable absentees. Of the eleven nominal delegates from London several, for instance Katharine Conway, had few real ties with the capital. In the words of Shaw, 'London was practically out of the Conference'.[1]

The proceedings were opened, appropriately, by Drew, the local leader, who had been so largely responsible for the success of the preliminary arrangements. Unfortunately he was less capable as a conference chairman than as an organizer, and consequently Hardie, who was, with the exception of Tillett, the only labour leader of national importance present, was elected to the chair.[2] The conference at once ran into difficulties over the question of whether to admit the two London Fabian delegates, of whom Shaw was one. The 'permeation' tactics of the London Fabians were unpopular among the rank and file of independent labour, especially as it was known that they had no intention of abandoning their positions of influence inside the Liberal Party. On the night before the conference, Shaw had addressed a meeting of provincial Fabian delegates, and had suggested that the whole idea of immediately establishing an independent party was premature.[3] Rumour flew round overnight, and so it was not surprising that the credentials of these two delegates were disputed and finally only approved by the narrow margin of two votes. As it turned out, Shaw's contribution to the discussion of the serious problems before the conference was of considerable value.

The principal questions with which the conference had to deal were the choice of name for the party, the drafting of a constitution and programme, and the election of an executive.

The choice of name was a foregone conclusion so far as most of the English delegates were concerned, but Carson and Smillie, acting on behalf of the Scottish Labour Party, suggested the title of 'Socialist Labour Party'.[4] Burgess and Katharine

---

[1] *Workman's Times*, 28 Jan. 1893.   [2] Hardie in *Labour Leader*, 2 Apr. 1914.
[3] See Curran's letter in *Workman's Times*, 4 Feb. 1893.
[4] Under instructions from the conference of the Scottish Labour Party held earlier in the month. See *Workman's Times*, 14 Jan. 1893.

Conway made the significant reply that Socialism in the title would limit the development of the party. 'The new party', said Miss Conway, 'has to appeal to an electorate which has as yet no full understanding of Socialism.' Tillett underlined the point by saying that 'He wished to capture the trade unionists of this country, a body of men well organized, who paid their money, and were Socialists at their work every day and not merely on the platform, who did not shout for blood-red revolution, and when it came to revolution, sneaked under the nearest bed.' He followed up this oblique reference to the Hyndmanites with a gratuitous attack on 'hare-brained chatterers and magpies of Continental revolutionists'—a remark which was not calculated to please the one fraternal delegate present, Eduard Bernstein, the able London correspondent of the German Social-Democratic paper *Vorwärts*, who was later given an opportunity to reply.

The decision to leave the title as 'Independent Labour Party' reflected an awareness of the origins and roots of the party in the local labour unions and parties, some of which were not explicitly committed to Socialism. The primary object of these bodies was to build a Parliamentary party on the basis of a programme of labour reform, and the principal allies of this party were to be, not the existing Socialist societies, which were insignificant, but the trade unions, whose leaders were in most cases still to be converted to the independent policy. In this decision the fundamental differences between the I.L.P. and the earlier Socialist societies **is** revealed: the means of political action are regarded as of primary importance, and the theoretical approach gives way to the practical.

But this does not mean that the party was not to be a Socialist party. The proposal to define its object as 'to secure the collective ownership of the means of production, distribution and exchange' was carried as a substantive motion by an almost unanimous vote.[1] The conference was evidently strongly Socialist; and this impression was confirmed when the programme came

---

[1] A limiting amendment moved by J. L. Mahon and supported by A. K. Donald to make the object of the party 'to secure the separate representation and protection of labour on public bodies', thus omitting all reference to Socialism, was defeated by 91 votes to 16.

to be discussed. A strong committee including Blatchford, Aveling and Drew was appointed to prepare a programme, and their report, presented by Aveling, was taken on the second day of the conference.

The first section of the programme was not political but economic, and the first point was 'the restriction by law of the working day to eight hours'—the main issue of all contemporary labour agitation. Next came various other economic reforms of a palliative nature—the abolition of overtime and piecework, the prohibition of the employment of children under fourteen, and provision for the sick, disabled, aged, widows and orphans; and finally, the Socialist objective, collective ownership of the land and all means of production, distribution and exchange. Two other points were added by the conference: one was 'free, un-sectarian, primary, secondary and university education' (an amendment to substitute 'secular' for 'unsectarian' received no support); the other was 'provision for properly remunerated work for the unemployed'—a vague formula which, on the advice of Shaw and Aveling, took the place of a suggestion for the organization of Home Colonies, a hobbyhorse of Hardie's.[1]

Aveling's committee had prepared a list of political reforms of the usual Radical character, but it was decided to substitute a single clause which read, 'The Independent Labour Party is in favour of every proposal for extending electoral rights and democratizing the system of government'. This formula was significant: while reserving the party's interest in constitutional reform, it emphasized its determination to put economic questions before political ones in its propaganda and policy.

Finally, there were two fiscal points proposed—abolition of indirect taxation and a graduated income tax. To the former, one of the delegates, still no doubt under Radical influences, proposed to add 'the taxation of ground values', but Shaw, ever on the look-out for theoretical weaknesses, pointed out that thereby they made the 'very undesirable distinction between incomes arising out of Rent and those coming from Interest,

---

[1] Home Colonies were advocated by the Scottish Labour Party (Lowe, *Souvenirs*, p. 83), and Hardie recommended them to the Royal Commission on Labour as a remedy for unemployment (*Parliamentary Papers*, 1892, xxxvi. i, par. 13119).

which, he thought, they ought to have grown out of by now'. This, indeed, had been the whole burden of the Socialist criticism of Henry George. Shaw moved that the first point read, 'Abolition of indirect taxation, and taxation, to extinction, of unearned income'; and this was carried with one dissentient.

Thus the conference, with the help of Aveling and Shaw, the Marxist and the Fabian, provided the party with a concise and clear-cut programme without inconsistency or divergence from basic Socialist doctrine. The constitution, on the other hand, was not without faults in its machinery. As was natural in a movement consisting of a large number of autonomous local bodies, there was considerable unwillingness on the part of the delegates to lose the identity of their own organizations. Drew moved a resolution in favour of a 'federation', and this was carried *nem. con.* after the delegates of S.D.F. branches and of the London Fabian Society had stated that they would be unable to join. The conference then proceeded, quite inconsistently, to declare that 'the supreme and governing body of the Independent Labour Party shall be the Conference of Branch Delegates' and that 'the Conference of Branch Delegates shall elect an Executive, their term of office to be until the ensuing Conference'. This was on the normal trade-union pattern, as also was the decision, made in spite of Shaw, that the secretary should be elected by the whole body of delegates. The executive —which, as if to indicate the limitations of its powers, was entitled the National Administrative Council—was to be an unwieldy body of fifteen, elected on a geographical basis. Having no power to initiate policy, it was merely to carry out the instructions of the Annual Conference, electing one of its members at each of its meetings to act as temporary chairman. It was pointed out that meetings of so large and so scattered a body would be expensive, but the conference was determined not to allow the executive to degenerate into a London clique, and it refused to modify the arrangement, considering that it would be worth the expense.

Shaw Maxwell was elected secretary. A former chairman of the Scottish Labour Party, he was a lithographer by trade but had become engaged in London journalism and was now the secretary of the London Council of the I.L.P. He had therefore the support of both the Scottish and the London delegates. The chosen members of the executive included all the members of the arrangements committee except James Macdonald, who remained loyal to the S.D.F.; and in addition, Burgess and Aveling for London; two miners' officials, William Small and Chisholm Robertson, for Scotland[1]; and among the representatives of provincial England, John Lister, member of an old Yorkshire family and squire of Shibden Hall, near Halifax. Lister became treasurer of the party.

Some discussion took place on restrictions of membership, in the course of which Shaw exemplified the doctrine of permeation by admitting that he '. . . was on the Executive of a Liberal Association, and had taken some trouble to get the position in order to push labour interests there. He intended to stick to it, and most of the energetic men whom he knew in London had done the same thing, and had found that there was a great deal of good to be done thereby.' A very vague clause proposed by Aveling that 'No person opposed to the principles of the party shall be eligible for membership', was accepted by a large majority, but the chairman pointed out that local parties could make what further restrictions they thought fit.

A severe tussle followed over an attempt by the Manchester delegation to impose upon the party the Fourth Clause of their own constitution. This would have bound all members of the party to abstain from voting at all elections in which no Socialist candidate was standing. A Bradford delegate moved an amendment that in such cases members should vote in accordance with the decision of the local branch. Blatchford spoke out uncompromisingly for the Fourth Clause, but without avail, and the Bradford amendment was adopted. This was not so much a victory for local autonomy as a defeat for dogmatism.

Finally there was the question of finance. It was decided that all branches should pay an affiliation fee of three pence a year for each member to a fund 'which shall be used at the discretion

---

[1] Small had been Secretary of the Lanarkshire Miners and Vice-President of the Scottish Labour Party. Chisholm Robertson had been President of the Scottish Miners National Federation.

of the Central Executive'. To give the executive some control over Parliamentary candidatures, and to prevent irresponsible candidatures financed from outside, Burgess proposed a resolution 'to establish a central Election Fund, to be disbursed by the Executive, and to decline all contributions to the said Fund, whether large or small, the donors of which stipulate that the contributions shall be assigned to any given candidate, or make any other stipulation which interferes with the discretion of the Executive in Parliamentary Candidates'. The resolution was opposed by J. L. Mahon and A. K. Donald, probably acting for Champion, whose unorthodox methods of financing candidatures were well known; however, it was carried, and the executive was thereby established as master in its own house so far as finance was concerned.[1]

Further resolutions defining the powers of the executive were dealt with, and it was instructed to issue a manifesto explaining the party programme and 'pointing out the international character of the Labour Question'.[2] The conference closed peaceably with a tribute to Hardie's chairmanship, and Shaw Maxwell presented him with the conference bell as a memento of the occasion. The official record closes as follows: 'Mr. Hardie slowly gave out the first two verses of "Auld Lang Syne" twice, started it himself on a judiciously-pitched low note, and then the delegates, all joining hands, sang the two verses with considerable precision and much heartiness, following it with three cheers for the Independent Labour Party. This was the end of the Conference.'

The very choice of 'Auld Lang Syne', a regular favourite at the end of Trades Union Congresses, was in a way symbolic of the character of the new party.[3] The members of the I.L.P. recognized the necessity of working in close alliance with the

[1] 'The Tory money move', said Shaw, 'was . . . checkmated, so far as the power of the Conference went, by the resolution that all donations must be given *unconditionally*, to be applied as the party thinks fit; and the stand by J. L. Mahon and A. K. Donald only increased the determination of the Conference to carry it' (*Workman's Times*, 28 Jan. 1893).
[2] The initiative for this resolution came from a German member in London. See Minutes, London District I.L.P., 24 Dec. 1892. The manifesto was not issued until November; it was reprinted in full in *Economic Journal*, June 1894.
[3] The S. D.F. usually concluded its conferences with 'The Marseillaise'—equally characteristic.

trade-union movement, and of organizing on a similar pattern. They were Socialists: indeed a majority of the new Council were members either of the London Fabian Society or of one of its provincial satellites. But their Socialism, arrived at empirically through experience of the failings of earlier labour agitations, did not blind them to the immediate practical issues of policy. The first essential was political independence, with a platform of economic reform. 'We maun gang oor ain gait', as Hardie summed it up in his address from the chair. 'The demand of the Labour Party is for economic freedom. It is the natural outcome of political enfranchisement.'

The national press was surprised and a little worried by the smoothness and concord of the proceedings. There was, indeed, no precedent for such a conference. For the first time working men were attempting on a national scale to take over the control of Parliament and thus fully to exploit the advantages given them by the franchise acts. For the first time, too, trade-union democracy was extended to a political party, whose inspiration was to come from below rather than above. Engels, who had frequently demanded the formation of a political party of precisely this character, now saw his demand realized. In a letter to Sorge he gave the Bradford Conference the stamp of his approval:

> The rush to Socialism, especially in the Industrial centres of the North, has become so great that this new party right at this first congress has appeared stronger than S.D.F. or Fabians, if not stronger than both together. And since the *masses* of the members make good decisions, since the weight lies in the provinces and not in London, the centre of cliques, since the programme in its main points is ours, Aveling has done right to join and to take a seat on the Executive.[1]

Even Shaw was prepared to admit that the conference 'might have done worse', and was claiming credit for its achievements.[2]

---

[1] To Sorge, 18 Jan. 1893 (*Labour Monthly*, 1934, pp. 749 f.). Engels was also quite prepared to commend the I.L.P. in public: at a meeting to commemorate the anniversary of the Paris Commune he spoke of it as 'the very party which the old members of the International desired to see formed' (*Workman's Times*, 25 Mar. 1893).

[2] *Workman's Times*, 28 Jan. 1893. Shaw often subsequently claimed to have been largely responsible for the successful establishment of the I.L.P.: but the absurdity

William Morris was silent now, doubtful of the case he had made in the eighties against Parliamentary action. The *Labour Elector's* enthusiasm, on the other hand, was embarrassingly possessive: 'The first Conference of the Independent Labour Party has been a great and unqualified success. . . . These results are due, principally and originally, to our work.'[1] Of the Socialists, only the S.D.F. struck a completely pessimistic note, taking the view that in not emphasizing the Socialist objective in the name of the party the conference had doomed it to lose its independence: 'We recognise, and recognise heartily, the perfectly honest and disinterested attempt on the part of many of the promoters of the I.L.P. to help forward the emancipation of the workers. But we know that the attempt will fail. . . .'[2]

Whatever the future might hold, the very birth of the I.L.P., the creation of this institutional form, was an event of primary importance not only in labour history but also in the general political and constitutional evolution of the country.

---

of this claim is revealed by his letter to Pease of 11 Jan. 1893, just before the conference: 'My present intention is to go uncompromisingly for Permeation, for non-centralised local organisation of the Labour Party, and for the bringing up of the country to the London mark by the supplanting of Liberalism by Progressivism' (Fabian Society collection).

[1] *Labour Elector*, 21 Jan. 1893.
[2] H. W. Lee, Secretary of the S.D.F., in *Justice*, 21 Jan. 1893.

CHAPTER VII

Labour and the Churches

(1)

ALTHOUGH the Christian Socialist tradition played an important part in the relations between the established church and the
labour movement in the nineteenth century, it is probably the
existence of Nonconformist churches, many of them more
closely in touch with the working class than the Establishment
was, which determined the attitude of the majority of Socialists
and Radicals to religion and prevented the emergence of a
strong anti-clerical tradition as in France. The Chartists, for
instance, found that the churches most sympathetic to their cause
were the recently formed societies which had split off from the
Wesleyan Methodist Connexion, and which associated a desire
for democratic organization in their ecclesiastical government
with a leaning towards radicalism in politics.[1]

Towards the end of the nineteenth century, however, this
distinction between the churches is less reliable than before.
The great movements of revolt in the Methodist tradition had
come to an end, and with the enlistment of Nonconformity as a
whole behind the banner of the Liberal Party many of the older
distinctions were beginning to disappear. All churches, whether
Nonconformist or not, were influenced by contemporary discussion of the social problem, and in many cases it was the
Anglican clergyman who was boldest in support of the Socialist
cause, for he was more independent of his congregation than
many members of Nonconformist ministries, and could act
more freely as his conscience moved him. Moreover, the Catholic Church, which had many adherents among the most
depressed labouring class, many of whom were Irish immigrants, was especially aware of the gravity of the social problem:

---

[1] H. U. Faulkner, *Chartism and the Churches* (New York, 1916), gives the general
picture of the attitude of the churches to the Chartists.

Cardinal Manning, who played an important part in the settlement of the London dock strike in 1889, once wrote that it was necessary to 'engineer a slope', meaning thereby that means must be found to raise the standards of the poor by a process that should be steady, if gradual. He advised and encouraged the new unionists, agreeing with them, as he told Tom Mann, that 'the public authorities ought to find work for those who want work, or relief for those who cannot'.[1]

In the Church of England the tradition of Christian Socialism was revived by Stewart Headlam. In 1877, as curate of St. Matthew's Bethnal Green, Headlam founded the Guild of St. Matthew, which became a Socialist organization. Its original purpose was to combat the preachers of secularism, then especially vigorous in East London under the lead of Charles Bradlaugh.[2] Early in the 1880's, however, Headlam found a new interest after reading Henry George, and later he joined the Fabian Society. But his object was always primarily religious, to combine the tradition of Christian Socialism which he took from F. D. Maurice and Charles Kingsley with the sacramental doctrine of high Anglicanism. It was significant that the title of the monthly magazine which Headlam edited as the organ of the Guild was called the *Church Reformer*.

Headlam wrote a tract on Christian Socialism for the Fabian Society, but he was in fact a Georgite rather than a Socialist all his life.[3] He was, however, a vigorous controversialist, and gave the impression of being much more extreme in his politics than he really was. He had equally vigorous colleagues in the cause: Thomas Hancock, for instance, being much impressed by the church parades that the Socialists organized in the eighties, preached a sermon entitled 'The Banner of Christ in the Hands of the Socialists', in the course of which he declared that 'the thing which economists, politicians, scholars—in hatred or in love—call "Socialism" is itself "Christian".'[4] Indeed, in September 1884 the Guild established itself as a very 'advanced' body by passing the following resolution, which is remarkable for a

[1] Leslie, *Manning*, pp. 367 f.
[2] Bettany, *Headlam*, p. 79.
[3] Ibid. pp. 137 ff.
[4] M. B. Reckitt, *Maurice to Temple* (1947), pp. 132 f.

society consisting, as to a third of its members, of Anglican parsons:

> That whereas the present contrast between the condition of the great body of workers who produce much and consume little and of those classes who produce little and consume much is contrary to the Christian doctrines of Brotherhood and Justice, this meeting urges on all Churchmen the duty of supporting such measures as will tend—
>
> (*a*) To restore to the people the value which they give to the land;
> (*b*) To bring about a better distribution of the wealth created by labour;
> (*c*) To give the whole body of the people a voice in their own government; and
> (*d*) To abolish false standards of worth and dignity.[1]

But the Guild of St. Matthew, which never had more than 400 members, by no means represented the sum total of churchmen deeply interested in social questions and anxious to take action with others of their faith.[2] There were, for instance, those who summoned the upper classes to provide direct practical assistance for the poor of the East End: Samuel Barnett, vicar of St. Jude's, Whitechapel, founded Toynbee Hall in 1884 in memory of Arnold Toynbee, and Canon Scott Holland founded Oxford House in the same year: and many similar institution were later founded in London and in the provincial towns. The emergence of the political Socialist movement interested the clergy, and Champion was invited to address the Church Congress of 1887.[3] In the following year the Lambeth Conference appointed a committee on Socialism, and its report declared that 'No more important problems can well occupy the attention—whether of clergy or laity—than such as are connected with what is popularly called Socialism'.[4] There was also at least one vigorous local society, the Clifton and Bristol

[1] Bettany, op. cit. p. 81.
[2] For G.S.M. membership see A. V. Woodworth, *Christian Socialism in England* (1903), p. 123. For a fuller treatment of the Church of England's attitude, see D. O. Wagner, *Church of England and Social Reform since 1854* (New York, 1930).
[3] Champion's address is reprinted in *Common Sense*, 15 Oct. 1887; for a summary included in the proceedings of the Church Congress see *The Times*, 6 Oct. 1887.
[4] S. Webb, *Socialism in England* (1893), p. 65.

Christian Socialists, who elected a member to the Bristol School Board in 1889.[1]

In the same year Scott Holland formed the Christian Social Union, on the whole a much less controversial body than the Guild of St. Matthew and consequently much more influential within the Church. Scott Holland was an intellectual and had been a pupil of T. H. Green. Under his leadership the C.S.U. sought to influence the high circles of the ecclesiastical polity rather as the Fabians later sought to influence cabinet ministers and bureaucrats. Its journal, the *Economic Review*, which was edited in Oxford, had rather a Fabian air. But the C.S.U. differed from the Fabian Society in that it was much more successful so far as immediate influence was concerned. It had 2,600 members by 1895, and was thus seven times as large as the Guild of St. Matthew; and between 1889 and 1913, out of fifty-three episcopal appointments, not less than sixteen went to members of the C.S.U.[2] But it was not a Socialist body even in the sense that the Guild of St. Matthew was. Scott Holland spoke in the language of Socialism at times: for instance, he advocated permeating the Liberal Party, and getting it, as he said, to 'overthrow the Nonconformist capitalist, and come into close touch with Labour'[3]; but as time went on, the distinctive vigour of the C.S.U. seemed to weaken as its ranks opened to more and more members, and this fact was recognized by those who in the new century set up a new and separate body, the Christian Socialist League.

It becomes difficult, therefore, to draw a distinction between the attitude of the Nonconformist ministry and that of the Establishment, and to argue that the former was notably more sympathetic to the special interests of labour. It is true that the

---

[1] S. Bryher, *An Account of the Labour and Socialist Movement in Bristol* (1929), pp. 42 ff. Although the Christian Socialist tradition was by origin Anglican, the term was widely used, e.g. by the Christian Socialist Society founded by W. H. P. Campbell and others, which took over the management of the *Christian Socialist* magazine from the Land Reform Union. The society as later reconstituted as the Christian Socialist League: its president was Dr. John Clifford, the prominent Baptist leader; its vice-president, J. Bruce Wallace, a former Congregationalist minister and founder of the Brotherhood Church. Not to be confused with the (Anglican) Christian Socialist League founded in 1906.

[2] S. Paget, *Henry Scott Holland* (1921), p. 204; Reckitt, op. cit. p. 138.

[3] Paget, op. cit. p. 211.

Labour and the Churches

old sects, the Unitarians, the Quakers and the Congregational-
ists had strong democratic and humanitarian traditions; and
orthodox Methodism, though politically conservative at first,
had always been in a real sense the religion of the poor. Methodist class meetings and lectures had been a training ground for
political radicals and early trade union organizers in the technique of popular organization.[1] But the Nonconformist ministers
were often hampered by dependence on the direct support of
their congregations, and this frequently meant dependence on
the most generous laymen. Many Nonconformist churches thus
bore an unfortunate resemblance to the Liberal associations
with which they were often closely connected: nominally democratic, they tended to become oligarchies of local wealth. Thus
it was not unusual for Nonconformist churches to establish pew
rents like those of the Anglican churches. Keir Hardie was
among those who drew attention to this abuse:

> . . . They would often find even the churches marked off
> in sections, one part for those who did not care to associate
> with the common herd, the seats luxuriously cushioned and
> the kneeling-stools well upholstered, in striking contrast to
> the accommodation for the poorer classes. . . . They were
> sometimes asked why the working man did not attend church,
> but was it to be wondered at?[2]

A special difficulty for the Methodists was their association
with the rising classes who had made good during the growth of
industrialism. Individualism was usually the distinguishing
feature of their creed, much more so than Wesley himself would
have liked, and those who practised it most successfully were
often the churches' most influential members.

There is plenty of evidence that towards the end of the century the more far-sighted Nonconformist leaders realized the
danger of the situation that had been created in this way. In
1892 Hugh Price Hughes, leader of the 'Forward Movement' in
the Methodist Church, warned his readers in the *Methodist
Times* that:

[1] R. F. Wearmouth, *Methodism and the Working Class Movements of England 1800–
1850* (1937), pp. 216 f., 249 f.
[2] *Workman's Times*, 27 Jan. 1894.

Middle-class, well-dressed and well-fed Dissenters are in great danger of assuming an attitude of more or less conscious antagonism to the New Democracy. . . . Very rarely indeed are the arrangements of Methodist churches adapted to the tastes and preferences of the working classes. Office and authority are almost everywhere in the hands of tradesmen and professional men. It is the rarest thing to find a genuine representative working man on any of the governing bodies of our Church. All this is more or less assumed as a matter of course, or is utterly unrecognized by our official leaders. But it presents itself in a different light to the working classes themselves.[1]

Yet at a time when even the Nonconformists were losing touch with the members of the working class and acquiring a respectability which indicated a loss of the old enthusiasm and moral fervour, we look in vain for signs of a vigorous religious revolt from below. The earlier nineteenth century had seen a constant effervescence of radical groups in passionate rebellion against the domination of the Connexion, the result being the division of Methodism into numerous fragmentary sects. Later, however, this spontaneous reaction seemed to come to an end, and the working classes presented an appearance of comparative indifference to intense religious fervour.[2] The attraction of the Salvation Army was largely due to the material benefits offered by its propagandists—a method of recruitment which set the pattern for a competition of the churches in providing welfare facilities to secure favour with the down-and-out.[3]

Why was it that religion seemed to be departing from the life of the lower classes? It could hardly be the case yet that improved material conditions had removed the longing for a

---

[1] *Methodist Times*, 20 Oct. 1892.

[2] The success of Primitive Methodist missions among the agricultural labourer, and the help they gave to Arch's National Agricultural Labourers Union, provide an exception to this generalization. In certain localities religious feeling remained very strong. See C. R. Williams, 'The Welsh Religious Revival 1904–5', *British Journal of Sociology*, 1952, which, however, confirms the general thesis.

[3] C. F. G. Masterman, in an essay discussing the *Daily News* religious census of 1902–3, concludes that 'In London the poor (except the Roman Catholic poor) do not attend service on Sunday, though there are a few churches and missions which gather some, and forlorn groups can be gathered by a liberal granting of relief' (Masterman, *In Peril of Change* (1905), p. 274). See also G. Haw (ed.), *Christianity and the Working Classes* (1906), especially the chapters by Canon Barnett, Arthur Henderson and George Lansbury.

spiritual life and the hope of salvation to come. A more plausible explanation would be that the work of Darwin and Huxley had converted the more literate to secularism or at least led them to doubt and indifference. It is true that Bradlaugh's National Secular Society had branches in nearly all industrial towns, and exerted a strong appeal to working men who were seeking to educate themselves. The publicity that the S.D.F. obtained through the N.S.S. was, as we have seen, a factor of some importance in the first phase of Socialist propaganda. But this does not seem to provide an adequate explanation of the much more widespread religious apathy of the common people.[1]

The main reasons may be found in a different direction. Town populations engaged in mechanical industry were, as Veblen has suggested, hostile to the discipline of devoutness. Consequently, as the industrial towns developed, churchgoing declined. Moreover, the co-operative and trade-union movements, and the working-class political organizations, all of which largely developed after the middle of the century, provided an alternative outlet for social energy. Once these bodies had been established, they provided a distraction from the work of the churches. New types of voluntary organizations were gaining support at the expense of the old.

This profound social change did not escape notice at the time. Joseph Chamberlain, himself a leading Unitarian and for some time the chief organizer of the Nonconformist political pressure group, once said: 'I have always had a grudge against religion for absorbing the passion in men's nature.' Mrs. Webb who recorded the remark, paid careful attention to the method of Chamberlain's political campaigning, and after living for some time among working-class folk in Lancashire she concluded that 'that part of the Englishman's nature which has found gratification in religion is now drifting into political life'.[2] It was not merely that the same methods of organization were used—for, as already indicated, the Methodist class meetings, the itinerant lecturers, the conferences all had their parallel in

---

[1] The N.S.S. was not in fact, very large. In 1884, at the height of its influence, it only had seventy-two branches. See Annual Report published in *National Reformer*, 8 June 1884.

[2] B. Webb, *My Apprenticeship* (1926), p. 140.

the political sphere—but, more than that, there was the same apocalyptic spirit of faith and hope animating the secular cause. The new heaven was brought down to earth, but it was none the less remote for that—and none the less real.

(2)

In this transfer of social energy from religion to politics, the Labour Church movement deserves attention as a significant transitional stage. It grew up by the side of the political movement for an independent labour party, and it was supported by the same people. Yet in its early days it satisfied a need that could not be met in a purely political body. To understand this it is necessary to examine its history, and first briefly to trace the career of John Trevor, its founder.

Trevor's spiritual travail was typical of many of his age. Born in 1855 and orphaned while still a child, he grew up under the care of Puritan grandparents at Wisbech, Cambridgeshire, where he was taught to believe in the reality of eternal damnation and the wrath of God. 'How to escape Hell—that was the one absorbing problem of my early years', he says in his autobiography.[1] The misery of his early life was due not to poverty but to the severity of school discipline and religious training, which wore hardly on one whose physique was by no means strong. At the age of twenty-two his faith collapsed and he rejected the truth of the New Testament. But Trevor could not live without religion, and in due course he found a new faith from which the traditional conventions of orthodoxy had disappeared, and where there remained only the simplest elements of religious belief. He became a Unitarian minister, and was appointed assistant to the Rev. P. H. Wicksteed at a church in London.

Of all the members of the Unitarian ministry Wicksteed was probably the ablest and certainly the most congenial to Trevor. He was a brilliant mathematician with a wide interest in economic and social problems. Henry George, Jevons and Comte formed the background to Wicksteed's attitude on these

[1] J. Trevor, *My Quest for God* (Manchester, 1897), p. 5.

questions, which in turn helped to shape the economic theory of
the early Fabians through the 'Economic Circle' to which he and
they belonged.[1] He was for some time the Warden of University
Hall, which was founded by Mrs. Humphrey Ward to propa-
gate the 'New Theology of Modernism'. The eighteen months
which Trevor spent as Wicksteed's assistant had a profound
effect upon him, and when in June 1890 he was appointed
minister of a church of his own in Manchester his mind was
already favourably inclined to Socialist ideas, and he was
acutely aware, as he says, of the 'frightful gulf between the
Churches and the world'.

Trevor could at first see no solution of the difficulties of the
Church. He studied the work of various organizations, especially the Salvation Army, without satisfaction.[2] In April 1891
he attended a Unitarian Conference in London, and heard
Ben Tillett, the dockers' leader, asserting that the working
classes were not irreligious, and making a plea for churches
'where the people could get what they needed'. Shortly afterwards, in conversation with a working man who had formerly
been a member of his congregation but who now no longer
came to the services, he became conscious that even the atmosphere of his own church was unsatisfactory, and he determined
to found a new church where no one would feel out of place
because of the lowliness of his social standing.

The first service of the Labour Church, as he decided to call
it, was not held until October. In the meantime Trevor had
sought and obtained help from members of his former congregation, and had set about the work of organization and propaganda. His speaker at the second Sunday service was Robert
Blatchford, who drew an audience far too large to be housed in
a hall with 400 seats. Trevor now set about enrolling members
and discussing the constitutional basis of the church. Other
visiting speakers were obtained—Tillett, Wicksteed, Tom
Mann and Dr. Stanton Coit of the South Place Ethical Society
in London all spoke at Sunday services in the early days of the
Manchester church. A newspaper account of the service at

---

[1] C. H. Herford, *Philip Henry Wicksteed* (1931), pp. 206 ff.
[2] Trevor, in *New Era*, Feb. 1892.

which Tillett spoke tells us that the lesson was taken from Bellamy's *Looking Backward*, and that 'undoubtedly the most touching incident of the afternoon was the loud burst of applause which greeted the name of Christ, when it was first mentioned in the afternoon service by Tillett'.[1] Trevor also visited London and sought to establish a church there, but without success at first: though the Brotherhood Church established by J. Bruce Wallace, a former Congregational minister, was somewhat similar. It was principally in Lancashire and Yorkshire that the idea caught on in something like its original form: and there too there was a good deal of variety in each particular case. At Bolton, for instance, the Rev. B. J. Harker made his church a Labour Church 'so far as their constitution as a Congregational Church would allow',[2] while at Bradford a Labour Church was established by the action of Nonconformist churchgoers who were dissatisfied with the attitude of their ministers to the social problem and annoyed by the support they gave at the General Election of 1892 to Tillett's Liberal opponent.[3]

The minutes of the Bradford Labour Church, which survive, provide interesting reading. The church was run by a committee on which there were several prominent members of the Labour Union as well as some women. The president elected at the opening meeting was Fred Jowett, who had led the revolt against the platform at the meeting of Nonconformists held in support of the Liberal candidate opposing Tillett.[4] The new church started without premises or properties, but these were gradually acquired and a start was made at the first meeting by an order for twenty-four collecting bags. In conjunction with the Labour Union and the local Fabian Society, a disused chapel was rented as a permanent Labour Institute: this was where the inaugural conference of the I.L.P. met. Then a music committee was formed, and lamps, seats and chairs were obtained, and arrangements made for the singing of hymns at the meetings. The finances of the church were raised painfully by small contributions from its members, nearly all of whom were

[1] *British Weekly*, 5 Nov. 1891.
[2] *Labour Prophet*, May 1892.
[3] Brockway, *Socialism over Sixty Years*, pp. 40 f.
[4] Ibid. p. 41.

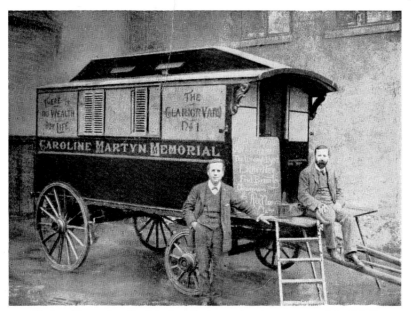

Clarion Van, subscribed for by *Clarion* readers in memory of the I.L.P.
propagandist Caroline Martyn, who died in 1896 at the age of 29

Manchester Labour Church leaflet
announcing first anniversary service,
October 1892

Cover of the first edition of Robert
Blatchford's *Merrie England*, 1894

Forms of Labour Propaganda

working men and their families, and the minutes record the successful application of one of the members for the return of a florin put in the collection by mistake for a penny.[1]

The Bradford Labour Church is but one example of many Labour Churches formed in the early nineties. It is difficult at times to distinguish between their activities and those of the I.L.P., and between the political and the religious, for they were closely connected. Both bodies had similar memberships, and both obtained the same type of speakers. Even the form of the meeting differed very little, the Sunday service being marked only by a hymn and a brief prayer and a 'reading from some Religious or Democratic Book', as well as an address.[2] In some towns, it must be admitted, the establishment of a Labour Church was little more than a convenient device for securing meeting halls from proprietors who were unwilling to let to political organizations on Sundays.[3] Usually, however, there was more to it than this. Trevor himself believed that the Labour Churches should form a national organization of their own, and in January 1892 he founded a monthly magazine called the *Labour Prophet* to further this aim. A full-time general secretary was appointed, but this was found to be an expense that the churches could not afford. A Labour Church Union was established in 1893, and at its greatest extent some twenty-five local churches belonged to it, nearly all of them being in Lancashire and Yorkshire. The Union held an annual conference but had no other central organization apart from Trevor's propagandist enthusiasm. He drew up the following principles as the basis of the Union, and they were endorsed by the conference:

1. That the Labour Movement is a Religious Movement.
2. That the Religion of the Labour Movement is not a class Religion, but unites Members of all classes working for the abolition of commercial slavery.
3. That the Religion of the Labour Movement is not Sectarian or Dogmatic, but Free Religion. leaving each man free

---

[1] Minutes, Bradford Labour Church, 12 Aug. 1892.
[2] Blatchford in Andrew Reid (ed.), *The New Party* (1894), p. 15.
[3] S. G. Hobson, *Pilgrim to the Left*, p. 41. The Dundee Labour Church 'kept the religious element in the cause robust, and it allowed lecturers to obtain a hearing on Sundays' (Lowe, *Souvenirs*, p. 97).

to develop his relations with the Power that brought him into being.

4. That the Emancipation of Labour can only be realized as far as men learn both the Economic and Moral Laws of God and heartily endeavour to obey them.

5. That the development of Personal Character and the improvement of Social Conditions are both essential to man's emancipation from moral and social bondage.

The activities of the Labour Churches were publicized in the monthly *Labour Prophet*, which Trevor edited. There was also a Labour Church hymn-book, in which Longfellow and Tennyson find a place beside the Socialist songs of William Morris and Edward Carpenter. Further, both Trevor and Wicksteed published tracts explaining the principles of the movement. The churches were encouraged to expand their activities in the educational sphere, and to run adult classes for the study of ethics, economics, social history and religion. Cinderella clubs were formed to give poor children an occasional treat, and gradually a regular children's Sunday School movement grew up under Labour Church auspices.[1]

(3)

The subsequent history of the Labour Churches does not take very long in the telling. The number of churches, including those which did not affiliate to the Church Union, did not expand much beyond fifty,[2] and already at the turn of the century there were signs of decay among many of them. Attempts were made to establish an affinity with the Ethical Societies of the London area, whose leaders were in many cases favourably inclined to the labour movement. At least six Labour Churches were affiliated with the Ethical Union at one time or another.[3] But the Ethical Societies were less directly political and more highbrow than the Labour Churches. Ramsay MacDonald

---

[1] Not all the Cinderella Clubs and Socialist Sunday Schools owed their inspiration to the Labour Churches, but it was easy to run such activities in conjunction with a Church. Seventeen Socialist Sunday Schools are listed in the *Labour Annual* of 1898, p. 86.

[2] The maximum number in existence at one time was fifty-four in 1895. D. F. Summers, ' The Labour Church and Allied Movements', Ph.D. thesis, Edinburgh, 1958, p. 311.

[3] G. Spiller, *Ethical Movement in Great Britain* (1934), p. 114.

was a stalwart of the Ethical movement, and devoted a good deal of his efforts to it after the collapse of the Fellowship of the New Life, the parent of the Fabian Society. But he did not feel much enthusiasm for the Labour Churches, which as early as 1898 he regarded as having become merely a cover for ordinary political propaganda.[1]

This criticism, as we have seen, was certainly true in part even in the early years. Later, too, we find the Birmingham Labour Church, for instance, in affiliation with the local Labour Representation Committee along with the Socialist branches and trade union lodges, and helping to fight elections in the early years of the new century. The same church actually absorbed a local Fabian Society, the terms of the amalgamation being that the Labour Church would provide in the centre of the city a regular course of lectures on social problems.[2] No doubt such an institutional link between a Fabian Society and a Labour Church must have been exceptional, for one does not expect to find any compatibility between the intellectualism of the Fabians and the popular religious sentiment of the typical Labour Church: there is a report of an attempt in the early 1890's to form a Hampstead Fabian Church, whose object was to be 'a level-headed enthusiasm': but it is not surprising to find that nothing came of this.[3]

So far as links with the I.L.P. are concerned, however, there is a different story to tell. Trevor had not merely helped to form the I.L.P., first of all by persuading Blatchford to establish a local organization in Manchester, and then by helping to sponsor the Bradford Conference[4]; he went further, and as a *quid pro quo* he obtained a recommendation of the Council of the party to all its local branches to found Labour Churches.[5] It is not surprising, therefore, that the churches became mixed up in sectional politics at times. However, they did not entirely share

---

[1] *Ethical World*, 24 Dec. 1898.
[2] Minutes, Birmingham Labour Church.
[3] *Workman's Times*, 2 Sept. 1893.
[4] 'Although Blatchford did the writing, much of the inspiration came from John Trevor', said H. A. Atkinson, who, like them, was in the group of seven men who formed the provisional committee of the Manchester I.L.P. (Herford, *Wicksteed*, p. 227).
[5] I.L.P. Council Minutes, 28 May 1894.

the fortunes of the party. With the encouragement and financial support of Philip Wicksteed, Trevor kept his *Labour Prophet* going until 1898, but it was then replaced by a smaller *Labour Church Record* which was only published quarterly.[1] Trevor himself was a chronic invalid, and without his enthusiasm the movement began to disintegrate. We hear of several of the churches sending petitions to Parliament in 1900 praying for an early conclusion to the South African War; but in the new century, even while the I.L.P. was rapidly expanding, the Labour Churches decayed. Very few of them appear to have survived the 1914 War. The most notable remnant of their influence was to be found in the continued existence of a number of Socialist Sunday Schools for children, normally run in conjunction with branches of the I.L.P. or S.D.F.

The decline of the Labour Churches is to be attributed partly to the success of the more convivial Clarion Fellowship and the other forms of social organization that Blatchford sponsored, for instance the Clarion Cycling Clubs that became the rage in the North of England. The progress of sport and entertainment at the expense of religion and serious political discussion is a phenomenon of the twentieth century, and we can see one aspect of its beginnings in the simultaneous success of the Clarion Cycling Clubs and the failure of the Labour Churches.[2] It was also partly due to Blatchford's ostentatious abandonment of religious faith in the early years of the present century, and his publication of *God and My Neighbour* (1903), which caused much controversy in Socialist circles. Again, a reason for the decline of the Labour Churches may be found in the steadily changing attitude of the denominational churches to the social problem. Keir Hardie had said in 1893, 'The first duty of the Church to the social problem is to understand it'.[3] Many of the existing churches were not attending to this duty at that time, and so the Labour Churches had a real function in the first few years of their life. This was recognized by some sympathetic

---

[1] 'The Labour Church, rested on Wicksteed's broad shoulders as long as I was connected with it', wrote Trevor subsequently (Herford, op. cit. pp. 220, 226).
[2] The first Clarion Cycling Club was formed at a meeting held in Birmingham Labour Church in 1894. See below, p. 162.
[3] *Labour Leader*, 15 Mar. 1893.

Labour and the Churches

churchmen: for instance, in 1894 the Chairman of the Congregational Union, Dr. G. B. Barrett, speaking of the Labour Churches, said that 'This attempt of Labour to vindicate its right to a place in the Church of God' was 'a rebuke as well as a warning to us'.[1] As the years passed, the proportion of the clergy and ministers who were aware of the social problem greatly increased, while at the same time the religious apathy of the working class continued to grow: so that the special factors which led to the appearance of the Labour Church movement were no longer in existence.

The career of the Labour Churches was brief and, if one judges by the paucity of allusion to them in subsequent literature, unimportant. One come across only an occasional reference to them in the records of the twentieth century.[2] Not infrequently they are mentioned in biography, such as that of William Temple, who said of a Labour Church service at Leicester in 1907: 'I have never felt so near the real presence of true religion'—a remarkable tribute, this, at a time when most of the Labour Churches were in decline.[3] In the same year, the Fifth Annual Congress of the Russian Social-Democratic Party was held in a London Brotherhood Church, which Maxim Gorki described as 'unadorned to the point of absurdity'.[4]

One reason for the lack of attention paid to the Labour Churches is that neither churchman nor agnostic knew quite what to make of them. In part, it is true, they were indicative of the strength of religious feeling among those who took part in the new political movement. The attitude of Keir Hardie and of the other leaders thrown up by the movement in Scotland and the north of England was very different from that of the London Socialists. Hyndman went so far as to declare, on one occasion: '6I have no prejudice against any religion. . . . We interfere with no man's private belief.'[5] But his personal hostility to the churches was well known. It was with more credibility that the Fabians asserted their neutrality, stating that they had 'no

[1] Quoted *Labour Prophet*, Nov. 1894.
[2] E.g. C. B. Hawkins, *Norwich: a Social Study* (1910), pp. 288 f., on Norwich Labour Church, which continued to flourish.
[3] F. A. Iremonger, *William Temple* (1948), p. 332.
[4] *Days with Lenin* (1932), p. 5. I owe this reference to Mr. M. L. Pearl.
[5] H. M. Hyndman, *Social Democracy* (1904), p. 7.

distinctive opinions on religion'.[1] Hardie, on the other hand, regarded religion as the essential basis of a Socialist faith. 'I claim for Socialism', he said, 'that it is the embodiment of Christianity in our industrial system.'[2] For him, religion and politics were not merely complementary: they were aspects of an identity. His own attitude was Arminian rather than Calvinistic, and so it was compatible with the latitudinarianism of the Labour Churches. To one who, like Hardie, had been a champion of the Evangelical Union and the Good Templars even longer than he had been interested in politics, the atmosphere of the Labour Churches with their blend of politics and religion was entirely congenial. Hardie was always the most popular of the speakers of the Labour Church, just as he was the most popular of the political leaders. 'For a time', he once wrote,

it seemed as if the labour movement would founder on the rocks of materialism. Bread and butter politics were in the ascendant, and men spoke and wrote as if bread and butter were the end and the means. This, however, was only the surface aspect of the movement. The teachers and prophets of the nineteenth century—Thomas Carlyle, Joseph Mazzini, Walt Whitman, John Ruskin, Alfred Tennyson, and William Morris—taught far otherwise, and their influence has been silently, yet forcefully, leavening the minds of men. The great message of their deliverance has been the elevation of the spiritual side of man's being, showing how all material things are but useful in so far as they serve to aid in developing character.[3]

With or without the Labour Church as his platform, Hardie's oratory always had a religious flavour. We read, for instance, in a report from the I.L.P.'s Welsh organizer in 1898: 'Sunday morning we had a good meeting on Pen y Darren "Tips" between Merthyr and Dowlais. The meeting was of a religious character, opened by Hymn, Lesson and Prayer, and Keir preached the sermon to a large and attentive audience.'[4] The spiritual quality of Hardie's propaganda was something that not all the other leaders of the I.L.P. could achieve without

---

[1] *Report on Fabian Policy* (Fabian Tract No. 70, 1896).
[2] *British Weekly*, 18 Jan. 1894.
[3] *Labour Leader*, Jan. 1893.
[4] I.L.P. Council Report from Head Office, July–Aug. 1898.

striking a false note, but Snowden's success was based on a very similar appeal, and he was noted for what was called the 'Come to Jesus' of his speeches.[1]

We can find a parallel for this association of political and religious aspiration in the Chartist Churches which accompanied the Chartist movement, though they were too transient for there to be much surviving evidence of their character. Trevor had not heard of them until after he had founded his first Labour Church. There were also a few contemporary bodies of a similar type in America and in Australasia: in 1896 Trevor was in contact with two churches in the U.S.A. at Lynn, Massachusetts, and Providence, Rhode Island; and he reported a move to found one in Australia. 'The Anglo-Saxon in England and America', he observed, 'has shown himself able, more than any other race, to throw off the husks of religion without losing the kernel.'[2]

But although it is impossible to deny the strong religious faith of many of the I.L.P. leaders and members, we can hardly regard the Labour Churches as being fully in the Nonconformist tradition, as Trevor suggested. This time, it might rather be said, the kernel of religious faith was thrown off as well as the husk of religious formality. Trevor himself had declared that 'The Labour Church demands no acceptance of a religious belief from its members. . . . It makes life and work the basis of union, rather than a confession of faith.'[3] It was difficult to see what was left of religion after every doctrine of Christianity, had been thrown overboard. What could be said, for instance of the William Morris Labour Church set up in Leek in Staffordshire to perpetuate the memory of one who was certainly a distinguished Socialist, but who did not believe in God at all?

It is true, of course, that the Labour Church movement had some elements of resemblance to the religious revolts of earlier years. Nor can it be doubted that to join its ranks, or for that

[1] P. Snowden, *Autobiography* (1934), ii. 82.
[2] *Labour Prophet*, Aug. 1896. Eighteen months later he heard of another church at Boston, Mass., and of a Socialist Church at Christchurch, New Zealand (*Labour Prophet*, Jan. 1898).
[3] J. Trevor, *Labour's First Principle* (Labour Prophet Tract No. 3, n.d. ? 1892, p. 13).

matter to join the political party wherever it was filled with the same spirit, was to be associated in a generous comradeship which encouraged all its members to forget old differences in the comprehension of a new gospel. Essentially, however, this gospel was one of social amelioration and not of religious salvation. It must accordingly be considered not as a purely religious manifestation, but rather as a symptom of religious decline, of the transference of religious enthusiasm to the political sphere.

It would be untrue to suggest that the labour movement in general or the Labour Churches in particular were responsible for hastening the decline of religious feeling in this country. If they had deliberately tried to do so they would have failed, as the Secularists discovered. The essential fact was that organized religion was on the ebb anyway, and although the labour leaders were not as a rule aware of it, their activity reflects this, for they were engaged in pointing the way to alternative outlets for social energy. Consciousness of sin existed, certainly, but under the influence of the new political teaching it was no longer accompanied by a sense of personal responsibility.[1] It came to be believed that the major causes of poverty and environmental ugliness were social in origin, for they were the by-products of an unsatisfactory, but remediable, industrial system. If the remedy were only applied, then the Brotherhood of Man would come to pass, and as the Labour Churches implied, the Brotherhood of Man was more important than the Fatherhood of God. Nothing remained of religion, except an ethical approach to politics of the type that we find in the work of Edward Carpenter, who was one of the most popular speakers at Labour Church meetings. Carpenter's renunciation of established religion, industrial civilization and middle-class morality was as complete as it could be. At one time a clerical Fellow of Trinity Hall, Cambridge, he had retired to a cottage in the country near Sheffield where he practised sandal-making, and wrote his various works in criticism of existing civilization. However, his type of anarchic ethics, though it suited the new intelligentsia of Socialism such as Ramsay MacDonald and the Glasiers, proved

---

[1] Beatrice Webb makes this point in her interesting Chapter iv, 'The Field of Controversy', in *My Apprenticeship*.

to be of no more permanent value to the working class as a whole than the Positivism of a generation earlier, or the Theophilanthropy of the French Revolution. It was too subtle, amorphous and intangible for the ordinary mind to grasp.

At least, then, we can say of the labour movement before the turn of the century that it was not a purely materialistic agitation. To those brought up in a religious atmosphere it offered not merely an ethical background but also something of the outward forms of religion to which they were accustomed. Except in the case of the teaching of the S.D.F., it offered its new faith not as a substitute for, but as a complement to, any belief that its audience entertained in the life beyond. Where religious feeling was still comparatively strong, Socialism took on most completely the guise of religion: in the industrial centres of Nonconformity—West Yorkshire, parts of Lancashire, parts of Scotland and South Wales. One of the concomitants of Nonconformity in the late nineteenth century was temperance propaganda—in itself, one might argue, an interesting deviation of real religious activity. It was not purely accidental, therefore, that the first Independent Labour Union was born in a coffee 'tavern' in Bradford, one of the most strongly Nonconformist towns in the country. Nor was it accidental that the I.L.P. leaders were always anxious to promote teetotalism within the party—as Keir Hardie said, no doubt quoting a slogan of his days with the Good Templars, 'Labour and liquor don't mix'.

But the Labour Churches themselves gained support merely as a short-lived protest against the link which the Nonconformist churches had established with the middle class, and in particular against the alliance with the Liberal Party. A purely negative protest of this sort could not last. It was not at all the same thing as the Christian Socialism 'from above' that animated the Guild of St. Matthew and the Christian Social Union. It was 'untheological and even anti-theological, and non-ecclesiastical and even contemptuous of any external organization or expression of religion'.[1] Its origin was political, and, as we see it exemplified in the teaching of John Trevor and Keir

[1] G. C. Binyon, *The Christian Socialist Movement* (1931), p. 181.

Hardie, it could not but help to further the process which Mrs. Webb describes as 'the flight of emotion away from the service of God to the service of Man'[1]—a process which seems to have been continuous from the later decades of the last century to the present day.

[1] B. Webb, *My Apprenticeship*, p. 130.

CHAPTER VIII

Early Years of the I.L.P.

(1)

THE Bradford Conference had raised high hopes of the new Independent Labour Party, which was intended to rival the Liberals and Conservatives in the fight for Parliamentary power. But the reality of its position fell far short of what its supporters at first imagined was possible. The position of its National Administrative Council was at first clearly a difficult one. The reason for its size was, as we have seen, to prevent a local clique securing domination of the party, but the advantage gained thereby was largely offset by the fact that, owing to the extra cost, meetings had to be few and far between. Frequent claims for the expenses of its fifteen members were not likely to be popular. In spite of these disadvantages, the Council had somehow to assert its claim to control, although it did not include among its members the most prominent advocates of its cause. Keir Hardie did not stand for election to the Council, partly because he would have preferred to be President, as the Scottish Labour Party had originally proposed[1]; partly perhaps because he thought that his absence would make Burns and others more amenable to its discipline. Blatchford also remained outside: he did not like serving on political committees, and in any case he was busy writing. These two leaders were at any rate pledged to support the Council. But there was the risk of positive hostility not only from the S.D.F. but also from other Socialist leaders such as Burns and Mann, who were both involved in London Progressivism. The I.L.P. was able to rely on many of the remnants of the Socialist League, especially in Yorkshire; but the S.D.F. had strengthened itself at the expense of the League in London, and had also rapidly extended its

[1] *Workman's Times*, 14 Jan. 1893.

hold in Lancashire.[1] Although henceforth it was never as large as the I.L.P. it was always a formidable competitor. Moreover, Champion was manoeuvring his way back into the political limelight, having the revived *Labour Elector* at his command and, so it was believed, unlimited funds at his disposal.[2] Associated with him as before was Maltman Barry, that 'most Marxian of Tories and Toryest of Marxians' as Cunninghame Graham described him,[3] now openly boasting his connexion with the Conservative Party—indeed a sinister influence to the purists of independent politics.[4] Finally, the national press was overwhelmingly hostile to the I.L.P. and anxious to misinterpret any indiscretion or sign of weakness; and the agents of both the great parties were seeking to break down the policy of independence by offers of financial assistance or by promises designed to satisfy personal ambition.

The I.L.P. Council had no office at its disposal and no machinery for the collection of capitation fees. Having been elected on a territorial basis, it was inevitably an ill-assorted company, and the London members represented virtually nobody but themselves. The erratic Aveling, the loquacious and egotistical Burgess, the tactless, dandified Shaw Maxwell could not be expected to get on either amongst themselves or with more stolid and respectable colleagues from the North—still less to attract outside sympathizers to the new party. It was not surprising, therefore, that the result was a demonstration of weakness. Because of the financial situation, the National Administrative Council met only twice in the year following the Bradford Conference, in March and in November. A meeting in London in May was cancelled, and in October the secretary of the London District Council was actually instructed to withhold the capitation fees and to enquire from John Lister

---

[1] In June 1893 the S.D.F. claimed 62 branches, a total larger than ever before except for the boom during the strikes of 1887; in August 1894 the official total was 91 (*Justice*, 24 June 1893 and 11 Aug. 1894). For the growth of its Lancashire branches see *Justice*, 13 May 1893.

[2] The first issue of the revived *Labour Elector* was dated 7 Jan. 1893. In May it became a monthly instead of a weekly. In June it assumed the sub-title 'The Organ of the Independent Labour Party'.

[3] *People's Press*, 13 Sept. 1890.

[4] Barry admitted himself to be a paid agent of the Conservative Party in a letter to the *Workman's Times*, 3 Sept. 1892.

'whether there was any truth in the rumour that the N.A.C. had been virtually dissolved'.[1]

Fortunately, political factors tended to strengthen the position of the party. Hardie's vigorous propaganda, up and down the country as well as in Parliament, had its effect, and stiffened the members' attitude on the issue of strict independence. The political situation was one that he could well take advantage of. The Liberals were in office, but they were showing no signs of dealing with the relief of the unemployed or of accomplishing the important reforms enumerated in the Newcastle Programme. The problem of the unemployed was very serious: the distress was on a national scale, and Hardie calculated, with good reason, that there were over a million out of work. Throughout the country local I.L.P.s took the initiative in forming distress committees to provide food and shelter for the needy and to press public bodies to assist by offering relief work. The S.D.F. methods of organizing demonstrations of the unemployed were revived, and many an industrial town echoed to the tramp of their marching feet and the pathetic sound of their song, 'The Starving Poor of Old England'. In February, Hardie moved an amendment to the Address from the Throne, deploring the absence of any measures to deal with unemployment. From this time onwards, whenever Parliament was in session, he made full use of question-time to ventilate labour questions, especially during the Hull dock strike in April and May. Even the London Fabians, still so proud of their success in playing 'such bewildering conjuring tricks with the Liberal thimbles and the Fabian peas',[2] now made a *volte-face* and heartily denounced the Government in their manifesto of November, 'To Your Tents, O Israel'—a document whose literary freshness goes far to conceal the fact that they were simply accepting, albeit temporarily and hesitantly, what the independent labour leaders had been advocating for years.[3]

---

[1] Minutes, London District Council I.L.P., 2 Oct. 1893.
[2] G. B. Shaw, *The Fabian Society*, p. 19.
[3] The manifesto was published as an article in the *Fortnightly Review*, Nov. 1893. For its origin as a concession to 'the more ardent spirits' in the Society, especially the 'Democratic Club connexion', see Shaw to Wallas, 8 Sept. 1893 (Wallas Papers).

One important question of organization remained to which the Bradford Conference had given no definite answer. Was the I.L.P. to be a federation or a centralized party? At the Conference, the S.D.F. delegates and the London Fabians had announced that they would be unable to affiliate; and though the London Fabians did not represent the feeling of their provincial societies, the problem found a simple solution by the transformation of many of the latter into local I.L.P. branches.[1] Apart from the Scottish Labour Party, which was in a class by itself, only Aveling's Eight Hours League and Bloomsbury Socialist Society remained to claim affiliation, and the strength of these bodies was not such as to induce the I.L.P. Council to allow them to disturb the emerging pattern of the party. The Eight Hours League contained Radical clubs, and to accept this affiliation, it was felt, would have seriously compromised the principle of political independence. The Bloomsbury Socialist Society was rejected because the London Council had refused to accept it—a technical ground probably concealing the suspicions widely held about Aveling's character. It was decided that for the next annual conference no invitations were to be sent to any organization which was not a 'branch' of the I.L.P. Thus the I.L.P. transformed itself into a more centralized organization and avoided that lack of homogeneity which had been a constant source of weakness in the Scottish Labour Party; and the Scottish Labour Party itself was dissolved at the end of 1894.[2]

But the real test of the I.L.P. Council's authority was its electoral policy: and from the start it encountered difficulty with those who should have been its supporters. There was a by-election at Grimsby, where Broadhurst, defeated in 1892, sought re-election as a 'Lib-Lab'. The I.L.P. representatives who were sent to the scene to speak against him met with unexpected competition, for Champion intervened and, although working on the same side, was clearly running a campaign of

---

[1] In 1893 the Fabian *Annual Report* mentioned the formation of 72 provincial societies. But by 1896 there were only 18 in existence, and in 1900 only 4 local and 4 university societies. Not all of them had merged with the I.L.P. Many faded away by the desertion of their members; a few joined the S.D.F.

[2] Lowe, *Souvenirs*, p. 170.

his own. The situation was tricky: everything that Champion said could not be countenanced by the I.L.P., and, as Hardie pointed out, 'the work of the free-lance is accomplished when the main body of the army comes up'.[1] The I.L.P. leaders decided, in view of Champion's connexion with Maltman Barry, that they could only preserve their reputation for independence by dissociating themselves entirely from both. At their meeting in March they passed a resolution disclaiming responsibility for candidatures which they had not formally endorsed; but this was not enough, and later on Shaw Maxwell arranged to obtain the signatures of most of the Council members to a letter repudiating Champion, which was published in the press at the end of April.[2]

The trouble was that the Council was not entirely united against Champion, who proceeded to rally the dissident elements in the party, pointing out that Hardie's position was as irresponsible as his own. With the aid of Chisholm Robertson, the Scottish miners' leader, with whom Hardie had been at odds for some time, and with the support of his own personal following in Aberdeen, Champion attempted to revive the Scottish Trades Councils Labour Party, a somewhat amorphous body formed in 1891 in order to give the Trades Councils an opportunity of concerting policy at the General Election.[3] The attempt was unsuccessful, for, faced by a choice between Hardie and Champion, most I.L.P. supporters preferred Hardie and were as suspicious of Champion's condescending attitude as they were doubtful of his integrity. In September Champion attended the T.U.C. at Belfast, and tried with little success to win over some of the delegates who were I.L.P. members. In October he held a conference of the dissident elements at Dundee, but no more support was forthcoming and the conference achieved nothing.[4] Only the Aberdeen I.L.P. could be described as enthusiastically in his favour. He was, in any case,

[1] *Labour Leader*, 15 Mar. 1893. Broadhurst was defeated at the polls by his Conservative opponent, though it is doubtful whether this was the result of the intervention of the I.L.P. and Champion.
[2] *Workman's Times*, 29 Apr. 1893.
[3] For an account of its origin and early dissolution see *Annual Reports* of the Aberdeen Trades Council, 1891-3.
[4] *Dundee Weekly News*, 14 Oct. 1893; *Labour Leader*, Feb. 1894.

a sick man at the time, and for the sake of his health he was advised to go overseas again. Early 1894 saw the end—his final departure to Australia, the demise of the *Labour Elector*, and Maltman Barry's virtual disappearance from labour politics. Champion's last public appearance before he sailed was as a visitor to the second annual conference of the I.L.P. at Manchester in February 1894, when from the gallery of the conference room he saw the Council's disapproval of himself receiving the hearty applause of the delegates.[1]

Champion's exit meant the end of a real threat to the future of the party. Yet his 'Tory Socialism' represented an intelligible point of view, and the British labour movement was the poorer without it. There was a lot to be said, for instance, for his policy of accompanying protective legislation for labour with a cautious programme of tariff reform.[2] A man of intellect, energy and courage, he had aspired to be the Parnell of the new party, but his *de haut en bas* attitude to working men made him unpopular with them. He was obsessed with the idea that money was the key to all political problems. In his view it was, as he said, 'like faith in religion, the substance of things hoped for and the evidence of things not seen'.[3] Some of the money he provided had come from the most impeccable sources, for instance the £100 subscribed to Hardie's Mid-Lanark election by Margaret Harkness, the Socialist novelist[4]; but much of it came from persons whose generosity was provoked by other political interests. Champion's fatal error was his association with Maltman Barry, and it is possible that this was a connexion from which he would have liked to withdraw but could not, owing to Barry's being able to threaten him with exposure. Another 'Tory Gold' scandal like that of 1885, for which Champion had been largely responsible, would have finally ruined him: so he continued in collaboration with Barry until his position became obviously untenable. Once in Australia, he set up as a journalist and

[1] In spite of an eirenicon which he had just issued to the local press (*Manchester Guardian*, 2 Feb. 1894).
[2] For his views, see his various articles in the *Nineteenth Century*—altogether nine were published between 1888 and 1892. See also his book, *The Root of the Matter* (Melbourne, 1895).
[3] *Aberdeen Standard*, 5 Oct. 1893.
[4] See above, p. 68.

bookseller, and did valuable work for the Socialist movement in that country: showing thereby what most of his opponents in Britain recognized, that his convictions were at least sincerely held. 'For all his faults', said Keir Hardie at a later date, 'there is no denying the sacrifices which Mr. Champion made for Socialism'[1]: and these words of recognition from one not given exaggerated praise may serve to sum up his career in British to politics.

It was hoped that the exclusion of Champion would induce the Labour leaders who were still outside the I.L.P. to make up their minds to join. Burns appeared to be as reluctant as ever, and he showed his antipathy to the I.L.P. by a speech at the Belfast T.U.C., denouncing 'the arrant frauds that in the name of Independent Labour and Socialism were going about the country doing everything to disintegrate Labour and trade unionism'.[2] Perhaps as a result of this display of hostility he was elected Chairman of the T.U.C.'s Parliamentary Committee. Other prominent trade unionists, however, proved less perverse. Already before the annual conference met in Manchester in February 1894 plans were on foot to secure a new Council whose membership would meet with general trade-union approval. The greatest gain was Tom Mann's consent to stand for the secretaryship, and his election to that post. His temporary excursion into London Progressivism as secretary of the London Reform Union was now at an end. He had toyed with the idea of entering the Church, but had finally decided that his vocation did not lie in that direction.[3] His capacity for getting on with others would be of great value to the I.L.P. Shaw Maxwell had done his best, but he was too aggressive and open in his dislikes to be universally popular, and his propensity for loudness of attire tended to alienate working-class sympathizers.[4]

A number of other changes in organization were made at the Manchester conference. The previous year's accounts showed a loss of £80, although the total expenditure was only £217, £100 of which was the secretary's salary. Capitation fees

[1] *Labour Leader*, 23 Apr. 1898. [2] *T.U.C. Report*, 1893, p. 48.
[3] Mann, *Memoirs*, pp. 120 f.
[4] For Shaw Maxwell, see Glasier in *Labour Prophet*, Apr. 1893; also, more briefly, Shaw in *Workman's Times*, 28 Jan. 1893.

amounted to only £56, enough to cover a membership of 4,500. Since it was claimed at the conference that there were about 400 'branches' now in existence, and that the number had doubled in the course of the year, it was reasonable to hope for an increase of income from this source. An obvious economy was effected by cutting down the size of the Council to nine members including the officers. It was also decided to appoint a president as well as a secretary and a treasurer, for Hardie had changed his mind about taking office, wishing to act as a counterweight to Mann's 'mercurial temperament' as he later put it.[1] 'The time has come', he said at the conference, 'when it is imperative that men shall show without doubt on whose side they are. I am on the side of the I.L.P.'

Hardie's prestige throughout the country was now considerable; he was on the point of establishing the *Labour Leader* as a weekly newspaper based on London as well as on Glasgow; and to work with him for the party he had not only the dynamic personality of Tom Mann, but also a Council which was chosen by ballot of all the delegates instead of on a geographical basis. The new Council was stronger and more homogeneous than its predecessor, and consisted almost exclusively of representatives of the north of England. Curran, now prospective Parliamentary candidate for Barrow, and G. S. Christie of Nottingham, the *Labour Leader* cartoonist, alone survived from the old Council —all the others who stood for re-election were defeated. The new-comers were Aldermen Ben Tillett, again the prospective candidate for Bradford; Alderman Tattersall of Halifax; and two Manchester men, Leonard Hall, Navvies' organizer, and Fred Brocklehurst, a Cambridge graduate and secretary of the Labour Church Union. Burgess, who did not stand for re-election, deplored the lobbying that went on to determine the election, which was all too similar to the elections of the T.U.C. Parliamentary Committee. 'Lancashire and Yorkshire', he pointed out, 'practically determined the whole of the allotment of seats.'[2] In view of the party's strength in these areas and its weakness elsewhere, this was really to be expected. The Council was instructed to meet at least once in three months in future;

[1] *Labour Leader*, 21 Apr. 1905.   [2] *Workman's Times*, 10 Feb. 1894.

and representing as it did the real strength of the movement in the Northern industrial centres, it was reasonable to suppose that it would provide a more powerful lead than before.

The keynote of the conference was the necessity for an appeal to trade unionists. No less than four of the resolutions had a bearing on this question. One of them asserted that nobody should be an officer or candidate of the party if he was not a member of his appropriate trade union, or 'being other than a workman, fails to conform with Trade Union principles'. Other distracting proposals were all defeated: the Lancashire men, who had strong local S.D.F. branches to contend with, were all for an amalgamation with the S.D.F. in order to form a national Socialist party, but the rest of the conference had no intention of sacrificing the party's identity, especially as the S.D.F. was very weak outside London and Lancashire.[1] There was also a suggestion that the name should be changed to 'Socialist Labour Party', but after Hardie's speech from the chair appealing to the 'memories and associations' of the old name, there was virtually no support for the proposal. Finally, the Manchester delegates revived their campaign for the Fourth Clause: but although there was a real difference of opinion on this question the majority was not in favour, and an amendment was accepted giving the local branches the power to decide what action should be taken at by-elections, and laying down that General Election policy was to be decided for all the branches by a national conference specially summoned for the purpose.

Thus the Manchester conference corrected some of the faults of the party's administration and gave additional emphasis to the basic principles of its policy. Progress in the first year had been a little uncertain, but the good feeling and enthusiasm of the second conference indicated, as Hardie said at the time, that 'the Independent Labour Party had come to stay'.

(2)

The development of a stronger national control of the party must not lead us to suppose that the 'branches' were not still

---

[1] The S.D.F. was not in favour of fusion at this time. See below, p. 174.

From W. Hill, Socialism and Sense (*1895*)

'Politicians of the Balloon' by F. Carruthers Gould.

very much their own masters in matters of local policy, organization and finance. It is easy to over-stress the degree of centralization that took place; indeed it was only in 1895 that a single room was acquired for a national office, and an assistant to the secretary appointed.[1] The party remained for some years to come a collection of virtually autonomous bodies, absorbed in their own local affairs, hearing of each other's activities and of the events in the wider sphere of national politics only through the newspapers and by the agency of the little band of Socialist lecturers who circulated throughout the country like itinerant Methodist preachers.

The lecturers were devoted enthusiasts who gave much to the cause in which they believed and took little in return. If they had income from other sources, or if they were lecturing only part of their time, they would be content to speak without fee, but if they were full-time lecturers with no other income they had to make some charge for their services in order to keep themselves alive. Several of them were well-educated women, still in their twenties: for instance, the austere Caroline Martyn, and the vigorous and persuasive Enid Stacy, and Katharine Conway, who married Bruce Glasier, a Scottish disciple of William Morris, and brought him into the I.L.P. Indeed, the 'new woman' was almost as important an element in the leadership as the new unionist. Then there were a few perennial propagandists such as Edward Carpenter, who spoke for all sorts of Socialist organizations as well as the I.L.P. Finally, there were the members of the Council, including the vigorous Tom Mann and—greatest draw of all—Keir Hardie, 'Member for the Unemployed', shouldering the burden of the 'Labour Question' in the House of Commons, but careful never to let slip an opportunity of building up the movement in the country. All these speakers would come prepared to address either a branch meeting or a congregation of the Labour Church, or, more likely still, both: for their oratory, however political it was, was fervent and apocalyptic in tone and hardly needed adaptation for the requirements of the Labour Church. A visit from a national speaker such as one of these was a highlight in the life

[1] Minutes I.L.P. Council, Apr. and Aug. 1895.

of an I.L.P. club: the sentimental appeal of a woman speaker, the fiery venom of Tom Mann, or the slow rugged oratory of Hardie would leave its mark on the audience; the enthusiasm of the local officers would be redoubled, and new members would be recruited from those who had been attracted to the meeting.

A picture of the local societies in the Yorkshire villages, where there was much activity at this time, is given by a sympathetic journalist who had visited the area on a short tour from London:

> Nothing is too hard for the members in their virgin enthusiasm to do. They run their little prints, they sell their stock of pamphlets, they drop their pennies into the collecting box, they buy their I.L.P. tea and cocoa etc. as though they were members of an idealistic Communist society. Their poverty is nothing. I know of one Labour Association that conducted the registration of a town of 40,000 inhabitants for the sum of 14s. 6d. The same work used to cost the Liberals £40 to £50, and it now costs the Conservatives three times that much.[1]

Although some of the local societies kept their news-sheets going for many years, the schemes for the co-operative sale of various commodities were usually short-lived: for one thing, the existing co-operative societies regarded it as competition within their own sphere. The political work, however, did not depend upon the success or failure of these money-raising ventures. We have seen how the local labour clubs were organized in Bradford, and we must imagine the same interest in lectures and classes developing throughout the Yorkshire textile area and in many other industrial centres as well. For example, the Lockwood Labour Club, Huddersfield, in 1894 began to run a weekly *Merrie England* class. A chapter of Blatchford's work of that name was read each week, and then carefully examined and discussed by the members. This is typical of the earnest educational activity of the clubs.[2]

---

[1] *Seedtime*, July 1894. The writer was Ramsay Macdonald, now on the point of joining the I.L.P.

[2] *Huddersfield and Colne Valley Labour News*, 10 Feb. 1894.

Local politics provided the best opportunity for practical work and experience, and for the first time attempts to gain municipal representation in the labour interest were put on a systematic basis in many towns, and linked to a comprehensive policy to extend municipal powers and services and to improve the conditions of municipal employees. Local government was especially important to minority parties such as the I.L.P. and the S.D.F., for it provided a sphere where those unable to enter Parliamentary politics could gain experience of government and responsibility. The Socialists did not control any local authority in these early years; but since every minority was given a place on the governing committees and a real voice in the proceedings of the councils, their influence could be felt as soon as their representatives were elected. On the School Boards, moreover, minorities could soon obtain representation by 'plumping' for their candidates. This activity by a small but determined element led to an increased general interest in local elections, and new awareness of the scope and importance of local government. The Labour councillors, fortified by Fabian tracts which explained what their councils could legitimately do, pressed for the construction of 'artisan dwellings', for public baths, better sanitation, and many other reforms. They appealed to the trade-union vote by demanding better wages and conditions for municipal labour, and the provision of work for the unemployed. In many cases they were elected by joint action between the Socialist societies and the trades councils—the local pattern of a development that was not yet possible on the national scale. And so the Labour groups slowly became a permanent feature of many town councils.

Although the London Fabians thought the I.L.P. had been formed prematurely, and could not fully appreciate its enthusiasm for independent action, they were pleased to see how the local Labour groups relied on Fabian instruction, and there was a good deal of practical co-operation. The Fabian leaders accepted with a good grace the disappearance of their local societies in the North in the great wave of I.L.P. activity, and did everything they could to provide the local candidates with ammunition for their municipal campaigns. They issued tracts and pamphlets on subjects of importance in local politics, such as education, housing, public health, the provision of allotments and so on. Then, for the instruction of provincial Socialists, the Fabian Society offered boxes of chosen books which were circulated to the branches on the payment of a small fee.[1] In spite of differences over tactics, the I.L.P. was at one with the Fabians in the belief that it was necessary to make use of existing political institutions in order to further economic and social change, without paying further attention to constitutional reform. In this respect they disagreed with the S.D.F., and when the latter demonstrated in London for universal suffrage, Keir Hardie, who had been asked to speak, refused and added his regret at finding the S.D.F. 'placing itself in line with mere Radicalism'.[2] The I.L.P., like the Fabians, recognized that there was much to be done on the basis of the existing franchise, and it settled down to do it—often, be it noted, in co-operation with the provincial branches of the S.D.F., which were less dogmatic than the London Executive.

But the I.L.P. was still not a national body in the sense of acquiring a certain minimum of strength all over the country. It was failing to become a mass movement as its founders had intended, and as was essential in order to establish an effective Parliamentary party. If the London Fabians judged the strength of the I.L.P. nationally by its strength in London, it is not surprising that they were sometimes contemptuous of its works, and considered it a 'wrecking party'.[3] The I.L.P. leaders realized how little support they had in the metropolis, and in September 1894 they ran a campaign designed to improve their tenuous hold. The campaign was not a success, through no lack of effort on the part of Hardie, Mann and others. At the L.C.C. election in March 1895 the I.L.P. candidates made a very poor showing, and Hardie was very disappointed. The fact was that the political and social climate was not encouraging, and the seed of the I.L.P. idea could not flourish there. Some of the reasons for this

[1] Out of a total of 100 subscriptions for Fabian book-boxes in the year 1896–7, 46 were from I.L.P. branches and clubs, 11 from Fabian Societies, 10 from trade unions and trades councils, and 22 from other Socialist bodies and reading societies (Fabian *Annual Report*, 1897).
[2] *Justice*, 7 Oct. 1893.   [3] B. Webb, *Our Partnership* (1948), p. 171.

have already been indicated: notably, the fact that large-scale industry had not developed very far in London, and that the Progressive Party was a successful alliance of Liberal and Labour on the L.C.C. Again, it was in London that the S.D.F. was most strongly rooted. In addition, part of the trouble was that by now the I.L.P. had acquired the Nonconformist sentiments of the North of England, which did not go down well in London. Devout, hymn-singing fervour did not square with the requirements of London audiences, so much more cosmopolitan and secular, and so much less friendly to the sentimental radicalism of the North. Hardie was aware of the difference. In 1894 he remarked in the *Labour Leader*: 'Hitherto no I.L.P. club has been opened in London, which is something to be thankful for, as club influence in the metropolis seems to have a distinctly deteriorating effect.'[1] At the end of 1895 he admitted that the I.L.P. in London was 'still in the chrysalis stage',[2] and two years later, after more set-backs at the School Board elections, he said: 'The I.L.P. spirit of breadth and strength has never been shown in London. The movement has not an individuality of its own. It is but a bad reflection of something else.'[3] It is certainly true that the minutes of the London District Council present a dismal record of internal dissension and bickering over constitutional niceties. It was not surprising that Aveling was expelled on grounds of political irresponsibility: if there was one thing on which all British Socialists agreed, it was on the iniquity of Eleanor Marx's lover.[4] He had already been defeated in the elections for the second I.L.P. Council early in 1894. But he was only one of many victims dispatched by a body which could ill afford any reduction in the quality or quantity of its membership. Clearly, the London I.L.P. was no improvement on the rudimentary Socialist organizations of the eighties.

The differences of political and social background which separated London and the North accounted for many of the

---

[1] *Labour Leader*, 15 Sept. 1894.
[2] Ibid. 23 Dec. 1895.   [3] Ibid. 4 Dec. 1897.
[4] Aveling rejoined the S.D.F. later, but the revelation of his part in causing Eleanor Marx's suicide in 1898 united all the Socialists against him. He died a few months later. *Justice*, 30 July and 13 Aug. 1898.

misunderstandings which occurred between the leaders of the
I.L.P. and the London Fabians. Shaw's revision of 'To Your
Tents, O Israel' had been published early in 1894 as *A Plan of
Campaign for Labor*, incorporating detailed proposals for arrang-
ing fifty labour candidates with the support of the trade unions
and trades councils.[1] But as the trade unions failed to act, and
as the I.L.P.'s propaganda in London proved such a failure, the
Fabians reconsidered their attitude to the coming election.
Some of them had always been doubtful of the policy of 'To
Your Tents, O Israel': Beatrice Webb, for instance, had noted
in her diary as early as Christmas 1893: 'I am not sure whether
after the event I altogether approve of it. There is some truth in
Graham Wallas's original observation that we were rushed into
it by fear of being thought complacent and apathetic by the
Independent Labour Party.'[2] It did not need very much to
persuade the Fabians to change round once more and to re-
assert their alliance with the Liberals. The I.L.P., they were
convinced, could not succeed without official trade-union support. It was in vain that Hardie attempted to explain to them
the fighting attitude of the local I.L.P. branches in the north of
England. He took part, with Mann, in an informal Fabian-
I.L.P. conference in January 1895,[3] and also lectured to the
Society in London. 'To reach the masses of the people', he told
them, 'something more than academic education and discussion
on abstract propositions is necessary. The workers will only
rally to a fighting policy.'[4] If the Fabians thought otherwise on
the basis of their local observations, it was not necessary to
remind them, as Curran did in the course of the discussion after
Hardie's lecture, that 'London is not England'—a reminder
that, for all their claims of intellectual superiority, they often
seemed incapable of fully appreciating.

Moreover, in the North the tremendous power of Blatchford's journalism, which had played such a large part in calling
the movement into existence, was still at work invigorating and
developing it. The *Workman's Times* died in October 1894, very
largely because the effort of organizing the I.L.P. had deprived

[1] Published as Fabian Tract No. 49. [2] B. Webb, *Our Partnership*, p. 110.
[3] Ibid. pp. 121 ff. [4] *Labour Leader*, 26 Jan. 1895.

the paper of what wider public it had. The *Clarion*, on the other hand, had a widespread appeal because of the brilliant journalism of Blatchford's team. His series of articles inviting John Smith, the typical working man, to join the ranks of the Socialists was published as *Merrie England*, and the penny edition issued in 1894 sold three-quarters of a million copies in a year. This gave a great lift to the circulation of the *Clarion*, and freed it temporarily from the urgent financial embarrassments that normally beset Labour papers.[1]

The features of *Merrie England* that made it so popular were its simplicity and directness of style, and its engaging enthusiasm for the ordinary pleasures of life that had been submerged by industrial civilization. 'I would stop the smoke nuisance. . . . I would have the towns rebuilt with wide streets, with detached houses, with gardens and fountains and avenues. . . . I would have public parks, public theatres, music halls, gymnasiums, football and cricket fields, public halls and public gardens for recreation and music and refreshment. . . .'[2] How could all this be done? Blatchford demonstrated that the working class, who were seven-eighths of the population, received little more than a third of the national income. He also argued, principally on the basis of an article by Kropotkin, that Great Britain and Ireland could be self-sufficient in agricultural production. The whole problem, therefore, he maintained, could be solved by nationalizing the land, industry and commerce, and by limiting industrial production to the extent actually required for the supply of the people in Britain. Thus the doctrines of Marxian Socialism, as transmitted to Blatchford through the agency of Hyndman and the Fabians, were transformed into a policy of national autarky which, at the time it was propounded, could hardly be taken seriously by those who knew anything about Britain's position in world trade.

But the economic arguments in the book did not really matter. Blatchford was not equipped to deal with the practical problems of political administration. He was, however, in his element as a popular journalist who could stir the public

---

[1] *Clarion*, 15 Dec. 1894.
[2] R. Blatchford, *Merrie England* (1894), pp. 43 f.

imagination with his vivid writings. He found other ways, too, of exploiting the interest in Socialism. In 1894 he founded the Clarion Scouts—bodies of young Socialist pioneers who were to spread the faith by such original methods as leaflet raids by bicyclists. This activity was sometimes misdirected, and the I.L.P. leadership, seeing the diffusion of energy it involved, regarded it with somewhat mixed feelings. Even the organizers became a little alarmed at times when the Scouts were to be found sticking labels advertising Socialism on every object that they came across, private and public property alike.[1] But Blatchford had hit upon a method of propaganda that fitted in with the trend of the times—the development of sport as a social activity—and it improved the *Clarion* circulation at the same time as it spread the idea of Socialism in directions where it had not previously penetrated. It also enabled a lot of young people to enjoy themselves, and Blatchford attached a lot of importance to that. He encouraged the formation of a Glee Club, of a Camera Club, and of a Field Club, and for a time ran a special supplementary paper, the *Scout*, to support their activity and that of the more numerous cycling clubs.[2]

One reason for the establishment of the Clarion Scouts had been to find a way of bringing Socialism to the agricultural areas. It was felt at the time that Socialism should appeal strongly there, especially as the whole basis of Blatchford's conception of Socialism was a policy of agricultural self-sufficiency. In 1895 the I.L.P. at its annual conference followed his lead by accepting a long and detailed list of agricultural reforms including the nationalization of land values, and placed these prominently at the head of its programme, in the hope of catching the eye of the rural voter. It was all to very little purpose: the general picture of the party's activity in the first year of its existence remained one of considerable vigour in the industrial North of England, especially in the woollen area, with

[1] *Scout*, June 1895.
[2] The first Cycling Club was formed in Mar. 1894. Two years later there were 120 clubs and within three years a membership of over 7,000 was claimed. Clarion Club Houses were also set up, forerunners of the present-day Youth Hostels. See the *Scout*, 1895–6; T. Groom, *National Clarion Cycling Clubs Jubilee Souvenir* (Halifax, 1944).

pockets of strength in parts of Scotland and the Midlands; but weakness in London and other southern towns, and complete absence of interest in virtually all the rural areas.

This picture is confirmed by an examination of the *I.L.P. Directory* published early in 1895, shortly after the Scottish Labour Party had dissolved itself into the I.L.P. Out of just over 300 branches listed, 100 were in Yorkshire (mostly in the West Riding), over seventy in Lancashire and Cheshire, forty in Scotland (mostly in or near Glasgow) and thirty in the London area. Of the sixty remaining branches, the bulk were in the Midlands or in the north-eastern counties of England, which left Wales, Ireland and the eastern and southern counties virtually without representation. The party had its upper- and middle-class members, who might belong to any part of the country; but primarily it was an industrial party with a definite local bias—first of all in the woollen areas, then in the cotton towns, and thirdly to some extent in the more scattered engineering districts of England. In order to replace the cosmopolitan Socialism of the eighties, the I.L.P. leaders had sought to found a national party: but that party, in the first few years after its birth, seemed to have become restricted to the merely provincial.

(3)

After Gladstone retired from the premiership in 1894, the Liberal government seemed doomed to early collapse, and rumours of a General Election were already in the air. The hopes of the I.L.P., under the leadership of Hardie and Mann, were very high and quite out of proportion to the membership of the party. This was partly because of the tendency to judge the strength of the party by its strength in its strongest centres, such as Bradford or Halifax; partly because, for a variety of reasons, the candidates it put up at by-elections did unexpectedly well; mostly out of sheer inexperience and because the leaders of the party had very little idea how many members the party actually had. It was clear that the fees paid by the branches to the Head Office did not give any idea of the real number of their members, but what that number was nobody knew. Fees were paid on about 10,000 members in 1894–5, and on about two-thirds of that number in 1895–6 after Mann had persuaded the conference to increase the annual capitation fee from threepence to a shilling. The real membership of the party may perhaps have been several times this figure, as its leaders claimed, but if their fees were not reaching Head Office, this was hardly a matter for satisfaction. In any case, the I.L.P. propaganda appealed most successfully to the young, and it was not known how many of these recruits were still unqualified to vote, either by age or for some other reason. These were considerations which did not occur to the leadership of a party which had not yet been put to the test of a General Election.[1]

The by-election record had been a remarkable one. Within a few weeks of the Bradford conference Lister had secured over a quarter of the total vote at a three-cornered election at Halifax; and considerable polls, though not as substantial as this, had been achieved with little preparation at the contests at Attercliffe and Leicester in the summer of 1894. Finally, at East Bristol in March 1895, H. H. Gore, a Christian Socialist fighting alone against a Liberal, had missed victory by only 183 votes in a total poll of over 7,000. These were portentous results, and it was not surprising that political observers generally, including members of the I.L.P., read into them rather more than the event of the 1895 General Election was to justify.

The Attercliffe election, furthermore, had given the working class some idea of how far a Liberal caucus would go in order to avoid a Liberal-Labour candidate. The proposed working-man Liberal candidate was treated much as Hardie had been treated at Mid-Lanark in 1888—and much as Arthur Henderson was to be treated at Newcastle in 1895.[2] The victim at Attercliffe was Charles Hobson, a well-known local trade unionist and a prominent figure in the Labour Electoral Association. The constituency consisted predominantly of working-class voters, but the Liberal Association would have nothing to do with Hobson and chose instead one Alderman Langley, an employer. Hobson retired, and the I.L.P. to avoid letting the

[1] See e.g. Hardie's very optimistic article in *Nineteenth Century*, Jan. 1895, in which he claims a total membership of over 50,000.
[2] *National Review*, Aug. 1894; M. A. Hamilton, *Arthur Henderson* (1938), p. 30.

matter go by default decided to run Hardie's friend, the London journalist Frank Smith. In a three-cornered contest Smith got over a thousand votes, which was a good result in view of the fact that before the election there was no I.L.P. branch in the constituency. In any case, a contest of this character was well worth while to draw national attention to the new party, and to the attitude of the Liberals to a labour candidate. Attercliffe, indeed, was the incident that led Ramsay Macdonald to leave the Liberals, whom he had served as a paid party agent, and link his future with the I.L.P. 'Liberalism,' he wrote, 'and more particularly local Liberal Associations, have definitely declared against Labour, and so I must accept the facts of the situation and candidly admit that the prophecies of the I.L.P. relating to Liberalism have been amply justified.'[1]

As a result the I.L.P. was in good heart for the General Election, and great things were hoped for from the constituencies which were to be fought. A more carefully controlled and planned campaign would perhaps have reduced the number of candidates to a small number of seats where the best chances existed: but this, after all, was the first election since the birth of the party, and there were few precedents to go on and little means of being sure which constituencies offered the best chances; and in any case all the local parties were spoiling for a fight and it would have been no easy task to hold them back.

The difficulties the candidates had to face, and the importance of their efforts as propaganda for their cause, is well illustrated by Bruce Glasier's account of part of his campaign with Tom Mann in the latter's constituency, the Colne Valley:

> At Crosslands we held a short meeting at 6.30 which had been previously announced. It was with difficulty we got the crowd around us. Men and women hung round the houses and the walls but seemed afraid to form part of the meeting. When I had said a few words of introduction Mann rose and requested the people to come forward as he could not afford

---

[1] Letter to Hardie, published in *Labour Leader*, 28 July 1894; quoted Stewart, *Keir Hardie*, p. 91. MacDonald himself had had the experience of being rejected by the Liberal Association ('The 350') of Southampton: but he had little claim on the constituency, not being a local man. See *Southampton Times*, 28 Apr. 1894 and 9 June 1894.

to strain his voice. Still they would not move, and I went over and called upon the women to show the men an example of courage, and with a kind of cheer brought the greater portion forward. . . .

In those days it was dangerous, even in the Colne Valley, to have anything to do with the Socialists. Mann was a vigorous candidate, and he carried on his activity until long after the summer night had fallen. Glasier gives a vivid picture of him:

> . . . with his hair matted upon his forehead, perching out of the gloom, revealed by the flickering light of a farthing candle which a supporter held under the shelter of his jacket. The sweat was rolling down Tom's face as he sent a torrent of impassioned argument down upon his hearers, hammering and riveting his statements with hands and fists. . . .

It was late in the evening when the weary campaigners were able to call at the I.L.P. club at Golcar and have 'an hour's attempted jollity on "hop non-intoxicating ale" ' as the reward of their efforts.[1]

Altogether the I.L.P. fought twenty-eight constituencies, and in all but four of them the candidates faced opposition from both the other parties. None obtained the success that might have attended one or two of them had a more limited and concentrated strategy been employed. It was true that, with the help of the *Clarion* and the *Labour Leader*, the money was found to run all the contests, and that the Parliamentary fund of the I.L.P. was £200 in credit when the election was over.[2] The great misfortune, however, was that Hardie lost West Ham South, partly because, owing to his national campaigns, he spent comparatively little time in the constituency, and partly because his attitude of rigid independence in the Commons had lost him the support of many Liberal and Irish voters.

There was, indeed, no love lost between the I.L.P. and the Liberals at this election. The National Liberal Club greeted the news of Hardie's defeat with great enthusiasm, and the victory

---

[1] Glasier, Diary Fragment.

[2] The election expenses of the I.L.P. candidates were sometimes less than a quarter and always less than a half of those of any of their Liberal and Conservative opponents (*Labour Leader*, 19 Aug. 1899, quoting official returns).

of the Conservative candidate was displayed as a Liberal gain. Hardie ventured the angry remark that 'The Labour and Socialist Parties will heceforth vote so as to sweep away the only obstacle in their path—the historic Liberal Party',[1] and this tactless statement lost votes for I.L.P. candidates in other parts of the country where the election was still going on. Dr. Pankhurst, the former Radical, who had a straight fight with a Conservative at Manchester, found his constituency placarded with the quotation[2]: and the young Ramsay MacDonald, in these early days a stern critic of the leadership, had this to say to a Liberal friend in explanation of his own heavy defeat at Southampton: 'Hardie by his own incapacity lost his seat and none of us—being scapegoats—got in. . . . The party of progressive ideas is so badly led that it is almost suicide to join it.'[3]

Yet in spite of all mistakes and misfortunes the Socialist poll was generally a high one: 44,000 votes for thirty-two candidates (including the four run by the S.D.F.) was not an unsatisfactory total. The only really disappointing results were those of the Scottish candidates. No less than seven seats were fought in Scotland, including five in Glasgow—far too many, taking into account that the Scottish branches had recently been rent by the Hardie-Champion discord, and that even more recently a most unseemly dispute had arisen between Hardie and the Glasgow Labour Literature Society and was actually taken to the law courts.[4] None of the Scottish candidates secured a poll of over 500.

Outside observers naturally made the most of the failure of the Socialists to elect a single member. John Burns spoke of the I.L.P. campaign and the money raised for fighting it as 'the most costly funeral since Napoleon'[5]; and Mrs. Webb confided to her diary the opinion that 'The I.L.P. has completed its suicide. Its policy of abstention and deliberate wrecking has

---

[1] *Daily Chronicle*, 19 July 1895.

[2] E. S. Pankhurst, *The Suffragette Movement* (1931), p. 134.

[3] Letter to Herbert Samuel, 16 Aug. 1895, quoted in the latter's *Memoirs* (1945), p. 26.

[4] Hardie's dispute with the Labour Literature Society was a complicated one: Glasier thought he was in the wrong (Diary Fragment, 19 May 1895). See Hardie's article in *Labour Leader*, 17 Aug. 1895; the Society's pamphlet, *Mr. J. Keir Hardie versus Labour Literature Society Ltd.* (Glasgow, 1895).

[5] Loe, *From Pit to Parliament*, p. 86.

proved to be futile and absurd.'[1] Others more penetrating or less prejudiced thought differently. Bernard Shaw took the view that a party which had on the average polled so well had justified its campaign[2]; and the shrewd journalist J. L. Garvin, writing in the *Fortnightly Review*, argued that the results pointed 'not to the elimination of the Independent Labour Party from practical politics, but to its permanence as an increasingly powerful and disturbing factor'.[3]

This General Election, the first that the I.L.P. had fought, marked the end of the first stage of its history. It became clear for the first time how long and hard was the path to political power: but, inside the party at least, there was little excuse for recriminations against Hardie and Mann for the way the campaign had gone. These two leaders had set a fine example of devotion to the party's interests. Their tactics had been simple and straightforward: to fight the political battle on every front, in order to measure their own strength, to rally their friends and to discover new sources of support. This was the first and most purely propagandist phase of the party's existence. The Conservatives had secured a large majority, and it did not look as if there would be another General Election for some time. At least, however, the I.L.P. could take credit for having done its best to the limits of its members' strength. The S.D.F. had been quite outclassed by such a performance: with only one-seventh the number of candidates it failed to secure a higher average poll. Keir Hardie summed up in his usual dogged fashion: 'Despondency? No, no, rather proud, savage elation. Half the battle won the first time, and that, too, the most difficult half But we must learn how to fight elections.'[4]

[1] 10 July 1895 (B Webb, *Our Partnership*, pp. 126 f.).
[2] *Daily Chronicle*, 22 July 1895.
[3] *Fortnightly Review*, Sept. 1895.
[4] *Labour Leader*, 27 July 1895.

CHAPTER IX

The Consolidation of Sectionalism

(1)

It is very difficult to get a clear picture of the activities of the S.D.F. in this period, but it is unlikely, at any rate after 1892, that any real challenge to Hyndman's authority took place. The Federation had always been a conspiratorial organization, and it rarely declared in any detail the sources of its finance of the total number of its members. After the foundation of the I.L.P. it was even more reluctant to provide information, for fear of a comparison with the larger party. Consequently, a good deal of what can be found out about the S.D.F. must be derived from hostile comment, and especially from the revelations of former members who had been expelled.

Nevertheless, it is clear that the competition of the I.L.P. did not cause a decline in the membership of the older body. The great wave of Socialist recruitment after 1889 seems to have increased its numbers steadily until about 1896; and already in 1893 its leaders were boasting a membership of over 1,000 in Lancashire alone.[1] In 1894 the Secretary claimed that there were altogether 4,500 members,[2] but judged by regular financial payments to the national organization, this was probably an overestimate of at least 50 per cent. Central office total income figures are available for the years 1893 to 1900, and they show that the S.D.F. was normally in a much stronger financial position than the I.L.P.: this enabled it to pay for a full-time organizer much more regularly than the I.L.P. could, and it often had more than one. Fuller figures would no doubt reveal how far the organization depended upon the resources of Hyndman's

[1] *Justice*, 13 May 1893. In February 1894 it was stated that out of a total of 82 branches there were 27 in Lancashire and 30 in London: but the total of members in Lancashire was considered to be larger than that of the London branches (*Justice*, 3 Feb. 1894).
[2] *S.D.F. Conference Report*, 1894, p. 16. See below, Appendix A.

own pocket or those of other wealthy supporters.¹ Mention has
already been made of the collapse of the S.D.F. electoral hopes
after the Barings crisis in the City late in 1890; and the explanation of the later improvement in income may be found almost
as much in the firmer state of the stock-and-share market as in
the growth of interest in Socialism. It should be added that
there was usually a small profit from a tea-trading depot which
was run by the central office.²

There is little doubt that, although Hyndman was in temporary eclipse after the fiasco of the 1892 election,³ he and his
supporters maintained full control over the machinery of the
S.D.F. throughout this period. The weekly journal *Justice* was
in their hands, through the ownership of the Twentieth Century
Press, a company constituted in 1891 with the purpose of off-
setting the loss on its publication by the profits of a general publishing business. The editor of *Justice* throughout this period
was Harry Quelch, a self-educated labourer, who was the
staunchest of Hyndman's clique; and he was also the managing
director of the press, which by 1900 had subsidized the paper
to the extent of about £500.⁴ But there was little sign of improvement in its quality, and it remained as unworthy as it had
always been, never tolerating real controversy in its columns
and always bitterly criticizing those former members of the
Federation who had seen fit to leave its ranks. At the end of
1889, Burns and the other leaders of the dock strike were accused
of malversation of the strike funds⁵; and this tradition of attack-
ing former associates was carried on in the 1890's with gusto,

¹ Thus the 1897 *Conference Report* tells us that out of a central office income of
£1,259 the dues from the branches under Rule 27 (1*d*. per month per member)
amounted to only £61.
² In 1898 it was reported that central office trading had made a profit of £108 for
the organization, and that a tobacco licence was being taken out (*Conference Report*,
1898, p. 17). In 1899 an analysis of the balance-sheet shows that the receipts by
dues were altogether, £134; donations amounted to £106 and trading profit to
£38, but there is no explanation of how the money was found for central office
expenses and organizing, which do not appear in the balance-sheet (*Labour Leader*,
12 Aug. 1899).
³ Hyndman was more or less forced to retire temporarily in 1892. See Engels to
Bernstein, 17 Sept. 1892 (*Labour Monthly*, 1934, pp. 631 f.).
⁴ *Justice*, 16 June 1900. Some of the conference delegates were worried by the
fact that the press was owned and controlled not by the S.D.F. but by individual
shareholders. See *Conference Report*, 1897, pp. 14 f.; 1899, p. 21.
⁵ *Justice*, 14 Dec. 1889.

Ramsay MacDonald and the Fabian leaders being especially singled out for criticism. In all this *Justice* simply represented the views of the Hyndman group, who greeted with scorn and vituperation the slightest sign of deviation from an attitude of uncompromising hostility to all other parties. In 1895 George Lansbury, who stood for Walworth as an S.D.F. Parliamentary candidate, ventured to speak in his manifesto of 'the transformation of society by peaceful means', and was severely taken to task by Hyndman for this abandonment of the true revolutionary attitude.[1]

Yet in spite of all its defects the S.D.F. continued to provide a serious challenge to the I.L.P., and at first sight it may seem surprising that this was so. In 1898 it claimed a total of 137 branches, which was twice as many as it had had in 1893, and roughly two-thirds the contemporary I.L.P. figure[2]; and since the General Election of 1895 it clearly gained ground at the expense of the I.L.P. It was because of this that its leaders were willing to support proposals of fusion with the I.L.P., for they now knew that they would no longer be submerged.

The reasons for the comparative success of the S.D.F. are to be found, first, in the fact that it was an older and more firmly established body. The I.L.P. had grown up very quickly but in many areas it had not set up a strong organization, and so it sometimes rapidly broke up when the reaction came. Then, secondly, the S.D.F. was, much more obviously than the I.L.P., a Socialist party; and those who were converted to Socialism whether by Hyndman or by Blatchford or anyone else, might well feel that there was an element of compromise about a party which failed to call itself 'Socialist' in its title. Members of the Federation were expected to make a real attempt to master the theory of Marxism, and even Lansbury's Bow and Bromley Socialists 'wearily struggled with *Das Kapital* and Engels's *Socialism, Utopian and Scientific*'[3]: this was much more than the I.L.P. branches were usually prepared to do. Thirdly, there were those who joined the S.D.F. because for one reason or another they were hostile to the I.L.P.: they might have been

[1] R. Postgate, *Life of George Lansbury* (1951), pp. 47 f.
[2] *S.D.F. Conference Report*, 1898 .   [3] G. Lansbury, *My Life* (1928), p. 79.

expelled on personal grounds, like Aveling; or they might have withdrawn of their own accord, feeling that the I.L.P. was not sufficiently democratic, as Blatchford kept saying. The S.D.F., with all its faults, was the only real alternative body for such persons to join if they wanted to remain in the political Socialist movement, for the Fabians had no national organization and their local societies had faded away. It was no doubt this fact that brought William Morris back to the S.D.F. for a short time before his death in 1896. Morris now accepted the need for political action, but his suspicions of Hardie, which dated from the days when Hardie was in Champion's pay, appear to have prevented him from associating with the I.L.P.[1] It was, therefore, to the S.D.F. that he made his palinode on the subject of the necessity of sending Socialists to Parliament; and it was to the S.D.F. election funds that he made a contribution in 1895.[2]

Thus it was that the S.D.F. continued to exist—a rather weedy growth in the political garden, with few attractive features at the best of times, but able to survive in the most parched conditions owing to its strong roots. It established a firm grip on the London Trades Council, which it virtually controlled after James Macdonald was elected its secretary in 1896. It also had one or two important members in the wider trade-union world, notably Will Thorne, secretary of the Gas-workers, who eventually elbowed Keir Hardie out of West Ham and replaced him as the prospective candidate.[3] George Lansbury was one of the most successful S.D.F. propagandists: he fought two Parliamentary elections at Walworth in the course of 1895, and for several months acted as a paid organizer.[4] Then there was an able leader in Lancashire, Dan Irving, originally a member of the Bristol Socialists, who moved to Burnley and made possible Hyndman's creditable election poll there in 1895. Irving had been a railwayman, but had lost a leg in an accident for which he received very little compensation, a fact which left him with strong feelings against the capitalist

[1] Glasier, *William Morris and the Early Days*, p. 15.
[2] *Labour Leader*, 25 Jan. 1896; *Justice*, 10 Aug. 1895.
[3] *Labour Leader*, 4 Mar. 1899. Thorne was defeated in 1900 but elected in 1906.
[4] *Social-Democrat*, Jan. 1900.

system.[1] For all that, he was not anything like as intransigent as Hyndman and Quelch and the other members of the governing group in London, who formed a unique 'old guard' of bitter, dogmatic sectaries.[2]

(2)

As for the I.L.P. there can be no doubt that it lost ground after the 1895 election. Hardie's personal prestige naturally suffered by his electoral defeat, and his paper the *Labour Leader* ran into financial difficulties. He himself was in poor health, and he decided to recoup himself by taking a trip abroad. He accepted an invitation from Henry Demarest Lloyd, the leading antagonist of the American trusts, to make a lecture tour of the United States, and he was away for nearly four months. On his return he was unable to exert the same influence on the Socialist movement as before. Because it had no member of parliament, the I.L.P. seemed to have narrowed down to the proportions of a sect comparable only with the S.D.F. At its 1896 conference, the title of Hardie's office was altered from 'President' to 'Chairman' and was very nearly abolished altogether. This was largely a result of the influence of Blatchford, who, on the grounds of so-called democratic theory, was suspicious of anyone who appeared to be a 'leader'.

On questions of policy, too, Blatchford was a real thorn in the flesh to Hardie. Their relations were rendered difficult by the contrast between their personalities and interests and the fact that their respective newspapers, the *Clarion* and the *Labour Leader*, were competing for the favour of the membership. The *Labour Leader* was dull and unadventurous; the *Clarion* was gay and reckless. Hardie deplored the fact that 'the fibre of the Socialist movement was almost totally destroyed by a spirit of irresponsible levity',[3] and he thought that the whisky-drinking habits of Blatchford and his friends were positively sinful.

[1] A brief biography of Irving appeared in *Social-Democrat*, Jan. 1899.
[2] See, for instance, for instance, Irving's friendlier attitude towards the I.L.P. (*Conference Report*, 1894, p. 26); and his views on co-operation with the Liberals in 1899 and 1900 (*Conference Report*, 1899, p. 24, and 1900, p. 10).
[3] *Labour Leader*, 24 Jan. 1903, quoted L. Thompson, *Robert Blatchford* (1951), p. 117.

Blatchford regarded the movement as 'somewhat deficient in humour', and privately put this down to the influence of the 'lily-livered Methodists' who controlled the I.L.P.[1] This was the background to their political differences, which were sharp enough in themselves. Blatchford had taken up the idea of a United Socialist Party to be formed by the fusion of the I.L.P., the S.D.F. and the Fabians—though neither the Fabians nor at first the S.D.F. were in favour of the proposal. It had originally been hoped by the founders of the I.L.P. that they would be able to absorb the S.D.F.; but this had not happened, and the S.D.F. had in fact grown in size. Hardie thought that nothing was to be gained, and a good deal lost, by uniting on equal terms with the leaders of the Federation, who had shown themselves, he thought, deplorably out of touch with the temper and social environment of labour as a whole.

The 1895 I.L.P. conference instructed Mann as secretary to open negotiations with the other parties, but the S.D.F. rejected the overture outright.[2] A year later, in spite of Hardie's opposition, the conference of the I.L.P. demanded the reopening of negotiations, and the question whether the party's name should be changed at once was very seriously discussed. Hardie felt his general policy of cautious appeal to labour and trade-union sympathies to be perpetually in the balance. The Aberdeen by-election in May 1896 was almost the last straw to him. There seemed a reasonable chance of success, but the local I.L.P., still loyal to the memory of Champion, refused to accept Hardie as their candidate and would only consider Tom Mann or Ramsay MacDonald. The rebuff was unpleasant, and Hardie seriously contemplated resigning and was only dissuaded by the insistence of Mann and his other colleagues.[3]

In the sequel, the approach to the other Socialist bodies took a form which Hardie could happily approve. They were invited to a joint conference to which the T.U.C. Parliamentary Committee was also invited, for the I.L.P. leaders had obtained a mandate from their annual conference to act 'in conjunction

---

[1] *Clarion*, 3 Dec. 1892; information from Mrs. K. B. Glasier.
[2] I.L.P. *Report*, 1896, p. 16.
[3] See Hardie's letter to Lowe, 22 May 1896 (Lowe, *From Pit to Parliament*, p. 104).

with other Socialists and Trade Union bodies' in calling a British Socialist Congress. This was consonant with Hardie's views. Although sceptical of success in forming a united body including both S.D.F. and I.L.P.—'Any attempt', he said, 'to join those whom nature meant to keep asunder can only produce discord'[1]—he was thoroughly in favour of a federation of Socialist and trade-union bodies. The Parliamentary Committee, however, finally returned a negative reply, as might have been expected. They had waited until after the September T.U.C. before answering, and so it was not until just before the I.L.P. Conference of 1897 that delegates of the S.D.F., Fabians and I.L.P. met to consider collaboration.

Hardie's position was now strengthened by the changes on the I.L.P. Council which took place in 1896 and 1897. Its compositions had been altered less since 1894 than the extreme 'democrats' would have liked; and what adjustments had taken place left the control more fully than before in the hands of Hardie, whose time was no longer taken up with Parliamentary work. Brocklehurst, who had been financial secretary in 1895–6, fell ill and was not active again for two years; and, more important still, Tom Mann at the end of 1896 had made up his mind that the construction of national and international trades federations was a task more worthy of his attention than the slow and painful consolidation of a small political party. Although Mann consented to continue as secretary until the 1898 conference, he acted on a part-time basis only, and the running of the office devolved more and more on his assistant, John Penny, while Hardie had to look around for other talent capable of supervising the work.

In 1896 Ramsay MacDonald, who was a political journalist and Fabian lecturer, became a member of the Council. Although of obscure birth and upbringing—he was the illegitimate child of a Morayshire servant girl—he had succeeded in educating himself to a very competent standard of attainment, and he was clearly a man of great administrative ability.[2] He had been attracted to Socialism in his late teens, while living in

[1] *Labour Leader*, 22 Feb. 1896.
[2] The best available life is G. Elton, *Life of James Ramsay MacDonald* (1939).

Bristol; but before he joined the I.L.P. in 1894 he had been employed as agent to a Liberal M.P. His marriage to Margaret Gladstone, a grand-niece of Lord Kelvin, relieved his financial stringency, and he was able to devote plenty of time to his work for the I.L.P. In 1897, with Brocklehurst ill and other members actively engaged in trade-union work, more and more of the party's business was executed by Council sub-committees, of which MacDonald was usually a member. Pete Curran, an organizer of the Gasworkers Union, objected to this, and threatened to resign if the committee work was not equalized as far as possible over all the members of the Council.[1] He was persuaded to stay, but it was clear that if he was to do effective work he would have to choose between political and industrial activity. He chose the latter, and left the Council in July 1898.[2] These changes had important consequences. The old direct link with New Unionism was severed: the party was now being run, under Hardie's direction, by a new type of Council member— the full-time journalist-politician, such as Ramsay MacDonald, Snowden or Glasier, who had no trade-union ties and was free to devote all or most of his time if necessary to the activities of the party. Hardie was sorry to see this change take place, and he was always demanding a greater proportion of trade union- ists on the Council. However, it certainly made for greater efficiency, and for some years Hardie was able to make good use of the talents of the new-comers without having to fear any challenge to his authority except from outside.

This internal discipline of the I.L.P. was important in view of the awkward political decisions that had to be made in 1897– 8. In July 1897 a joint informal conference of I.L.P. and S.D.F. rerpesentatives recommended fusion of the two bodies and set up a joint committee of arrangement pending decision on points of difference, such as the name of the new organiza- tion. Hardie was still sceptical of success, but could not prevent the matter being put to a joint referendum of the membership. The result showed a majority of 5 to 1 in favour, in a total poll of 6,000 members of both parties; but the I.L.P. Council

---

[1] Minutes, I.L.P. Council, 3 July 1897.
[2] In 1900 Curran became Chairman of the General Federation of Trade Unions.

I.L.P. Council, 1893

Left to right, sitting: P. Curran, J. Shaw Maxwell (Secretary), K. St. John Conway; *standing:* G. S. Christie, A. Field, J. W. Buttery, J. Burgess, W. Drew, E. Aveling, J. Settle, W. Johnson, J. Kennedy, J. Lister (Treasurer), W. Small, C. Robertson, G. Carson

From Emrys Hughes's Keir Hardie (*Lincolns-Prager*)

I.L.P. Council, 1899

Left to right, front row: J. Bruce Glasier, J. Keir Hardie (Chairman), H. Russell Smart, P. Snowden; *behind:* J. Ramsay MacDonald, J. Burgess, J. Parker, J. Penny (Secretary), F. Littlewood (Treasurer)

refused to act until the annual conference had discussed the question, arguing that only one-third of the I.L.P. paying membership had voted. When the conference took place, the Council recommended, not immediate fusion, but a federation of the two bodies as a first step, to be followed by fusion if this was successful. Hardie, in his Chairman's address, warned the conference of the perils of losing the growing good-will of the trade unions; and Bruce Glasier read a paper which put up a powerful barrage of arguments in favour of the official recommendation. The kernel of his case against fusion was as follows:

> There is no disguising that the ways of the S.D.F. are not our ways. If I may say so, the ways of the S.D.F. are more doctrinaire, more Calvinistic, more aggressively sectarian than the I.L.P. The S.D.F. has failed to touch the heart of the people. Its strange disregard of the religious, moral, and aesthetic sentiments of the people is an overwhelming defect. The I.L.P. position, moreover, is better understood by the public. There is, in truth, no party in the land whose aims are more clearly defined in the popular mind than ours. The trades unions have begun to rely upon us, and are depending upon our lead, and were we to abolish ourselves another I.L.P.—perhaps, owing to our desertion, a less resolute one —would inevitably take up our ground.

The conference was bewildered by the situation, and not without reason criticized the Council for its earlier indecision. A resolution was carried to refer the question of federation or fusion to a ballot of the membership, with the proviso that a three-fourths majority should be required if fusion was to take place. The proviso virtually killed all hope of fusion. When the ballot took place, the poll was not appreciably larger than before, but there was a fair-sized majority in favour of federation.[1] As the S.D.F. refused to consider this alternative, the negotiations came to an end, and although the I.L.P. Council made a further attempt in 1899 to bring all the Socialist organizations together on a federal basis, the project came to nothing. There were a few secessions of I.L.P. branches after the 1898

---

[1] The figures were: in favour of federation with S.F.D. and other independent Socialist bodies, 2,397; in favour of fusion with S.D.F., 1,697.

conference and again early in the following year,[1] after a *Clarion* referendum of its readers had resulted in a slight majority for fusion.[2] Following Hardie's lead, however, the I.L.P. Council regarded the whole question in the light of the much more important problem of how to secure the assistance of the trade unions and co-operative societies in a joint movement for independent labour representation. Fusion with the S.D.F., it was thought, would prejudice the solution of this problem; so, on the principle of first things first, it was decided to postpone indefinitely the question of fusion while the major issue was still pending.

(3)

After the 1895 election, as before it, the local branches lived their lives without much attention to the problems that worried the national leaders. Conferences and referenda were of course matters for serious consideration, but in parochial affairs it was quite common for I.L.P. and S.D.F. branches to work together without any reference to the constitutional niceties debated at the national level. The influence of the *Clarion* tended to encourage this local co-operation: the Clarion Scouts organization brought together Socialists of all sorts and made them put aside their party affiliations in joint activity for the common cause. From 1896 onwards the 'Clarion Van', a horse-drawn speaker's platform in imitation of the Georgite Yellow and Red Vans, toured northern England and South Wales advertising Socialism, and was almost invariably sure of a hearty welcome from every type of Socialist organization.[3]

---

[1] I.L.P. Reports from Head Office June–July 1898; Oct. 1898; Jan. 1899.

[2] For fusion, 4,429; for federation, 3,994. The voters were also required to choose a number of measures to form a 'practical' political programme (*Clarion*, 3 Dec. 1898).

[3] The first Clarion Van was presented by William Ranstead, a Liverpool business man who invested £1,000 in the *Clarion*. Its first appearance was in 1895, when it was set up in front of St. George's Hall, Liverpool, and used as a soup kitchen for the unemployed. It was supported by subscriptions from *Clarion* readers, but was replaced in 1897 by a new van specially built for the task of mobile propaganda, and named in memory of the I.L.P. lecturer Caroline Martyn (see illustration facing p. 134). By 1904 it had proved possible to run two vans, and in later years (up to 1914) there were several more, including a motor van. See *Liverpool Labour Chronicle*, Mar.-Apr. 1895; Countess of Warwick *et al.*, *All About the Clarion Vans* (1904), pp. 14 ff.; National Clarion Cycling Club, *Meet Programme and Year Book*, 1914.

By 1897, however, it was clear that the 'Socialist boom' was over. The rapid expansion of the I.L.P. had come to an end, and the total of affiliation fees, which forms the most reliable indication of its strength, dropped from a peak of £450 in 1897–8 to little more than £300 in 1900. Hardie, writing early in 1899, suggested that the departure of Tom Mann's 'strong personality' was largely responsible for this[1]; and it was true that John Penny, Mann's assistant, who took his place as Secretary, was not in the same class as Mann as regards ability and personal appeal. At the same time the main reason for the set-back was the change in the national political atmosphere. The imperialist fervour, which culminated in the South African War, was already growing, and the Socialists, with their emphasis on the principles of international brotherhood and on the problems of home reform, could not flourish in a climate of jingoism.

It had been Hardie's intention to give priority to winning over the English and Welsh miners, whose conversion to the I.L.P. gospel was in his view long overdue. The mining areas were thought to provide a good opening for Socialist propaganda; and when in 1896 it proved possible to appoint a paid national organizer, the applicant selected for the post, Tom Taylor, was chosen largely because he came from a mining area. He was required to devote his time principally to campaigning in the Yorkshire and Durham coalfields. It was uphill work, as was demonstrated by the failure of the I.L.P. candidate in the Barnsley by-election in 1897. Partly as a result of the great expense of this by-election, the party's general fund again ran heavily into debt, and the employment of a permanent national organizer had to be abandoned. A certain amount of organizing work was still carried on intermittently at the expense of the national office, and it was mostly concentrated on the mining areas of Yorkshire and South Wales.

The first wave of enthusiasm for the I.L.P. being at an end, in some districts the local branches went into decline and decay. In other districts the work was continued as actively as ever, and in a few places the pioneering spirit appeared for the first time. The Manchester I.L.P., already an important body,

---

[1] *Labour Leader*, 7 Jan. 1899.

reached a peak of local popularity in 1896 when their rights of meeting in Boggart Hole Clough, a public park, were disputed by the City Council. The I.L.P. speakers in the Clough were regularly summonsed, but their meetings continued and grew in popularity, until finally the Council was forced to give way. It was in the course of this affair that Mrs. Pankhurst, wife of the former I.L.P. Parliamentary candidate, gained the experience of public agitation that later served her so well in the suffragette movement. For many weeks she conducted the meetings herself, surmising correctly that although the magistrates had sent the male leaders of the local I.L.P. to prison they would not venture to sentence a woman for such an offence. All sorts of means were devised for evading the law: knowing that it was forbidden to take a collection, Mrs. Pankhurst would open her umbrella and stick it into the ground in a prominent position, and when she came to pick it up at the end of the meeting it would be full of pennies.[1]

In these years the movement in the West Riding of Yorkshire on the whole held together well. For one thing, its strongly radical traditions were not likely to be seriously affected by the growth of imperialist ideas. Moreover, a new prophet sprang up in the Keighley area: Philip Snowden, a crippled and anaemic young man, formerly a clerk in the Civil Service, appeared at I.L.P. meetings in 1895 and soon became the foremost propagandist in the neighbourhood. The thin lips, piercing blue eyes and pointing finger of Philip Snowden came to be feared by those who opposed him in debate, but the secret of his attraction for Labour supporters lay not so much in the biting criticisms that he could make of Liberals and Tories alike as in the strongly evangelical exhortations that he offered to the members of the party. Before the century was out, he had been elected to the Keighley Town Council, and in the General Election of 1900 he fought a remarkable campaign at Blackburn which the journalist A. G. Gardiner likened to 'a tide of spiritual revivalism'.[2]

If the efforts of the I.L.P. propagandists had no great effect

[1] Pankhurst, *The Suffragette Movement*, pp. 136 ff.
[2] Snowden, *Autobiography*, i. 98.

as yet among the miners of South Yorkshire and the Midlands—
fairly prosperous areas for the most part at this time—in South
Wales the signs of change were more evident. The Welsh miners'
strike of 1898 lasted six months, and led to a great development
in the political attitude of the men concerned. Here again was
an area by tradition strongly radical and Nonconformist, and
therefore potentially favourable to the I.L.P. brand of Socialism. The mixture of politics and religion which Hardie special-
ized in was very popular in Wales. Hardie wrote powerful and
moving articles for the *Labour Leader* on the distress which he
encountered among the strikers' families, and as a result a good
deal of money was raised by the paper's readers to provide
meals for the children. In the following year the 'Clarion Van'
spent most of its season in South Wales, and did considerable
propaganda work[1]; but it was a misfortune that the I.L.P. Head
Office was too poor to provide the South Wales Federation with
enough financial help to give it a good start. Not many of the
thirty branches that were founded as a result of the campaigns
of 1898 can have survived very long, although at least a few
remained, and there was support in Merthyr strong enough to
sponsor Hardie as a Parliamentary candidate in 1900.

(4)

After the disappearance of most of the local Fabian Societies
in the I.L.P. upsurge, the London Fabians were content to
exert influence in the provinces through the medium of ideas
rather than by any formal organization. The only important
local Fabian Society, apart from those that grew up among
university undergraduates, was that at Liverpool which published its own series of tracts in the 1890's. The London Fabians
were meanwhile developing new interests to add to their commitments in metropolitan government. In 1894 the death
occurred of Henry Hutchinson, who had provided the funds
for the Lancashire campaign of 1890, and by his will he left over
£9,000 to a trust consisting of his daughter and four of the
leading Fabians.[2] The money was to be spent within ten years:

[1] *I.L.P. News*, Sept. 1899.
[2] Pease, *History of the Fabian Society*, pp. 123 f.

and as the daughter died within fifteen months, leaving her more modest estate also to the trust, the Fabians were free to do what they wanted with a sum equivalent to perhaps seven times the average annual income in the nineties of the central offices of the I.L.P. and S.D.F. combined. It was decided to allot some of the money to lecturing and some to the purpose of the Fabian Society organization, but most of it was to be spent on a scheme which Sidney Webb was very enthusiastic about: the foundation of the London School of Economics and Political Science, and its library. Webb met with opposition, for Ramsay MacDonald, who was a member of the Fabian executive, had other plans for the disposal of the money, and was strongly opposed to its use for a primarily academic purpose. He held that the trustees should 'throw themselves more open to provincial influences', by which he meant that they should subsidize the I.L.P. 'The Hutchinson Trustees', he wrote, 'have a most unique opportunity of consolidating the Socialist movement.'[1]

The conflict between Webb and MacDonald on this question reflected the difference between the political tactics of the Fabian Society and the I.L.P., and echoed the disagreements over General Election policy. Mrs. Webb summed up the points at issue between her husband and MacDonald as follows: 'To bring about the maximum amount of public control in public administration do we want to organize the unthinking persons into Socialist societies, or to make the thinking persons socialistic? We believe in the latter process.'[2] MacDonald produced an elaborate scheme designed to 'discipline Socialist opinion' at a cost of £500 or £600 a year: it involved the extension of the programme of lecturing in London and the provinces and the appointment of a travelling secretary.[3] MacDonald's ideas were accepted by the Fabian executive, but somehow very little came of them: Webb, with his usual imperturbable technique, managed to get his way, and the money required for the establishment of the London School of Economics was duly found. This

---

[1] To Pease, ? 3 Apr. 1896 (Fabian Society Correspondence).
[2] Diary, 18 Apr. 1896 (B. Webb, *Our Partnership*, p. 132).
[3] Minutes, Fabian Executive, 5 Jan. 1896.

From W. Hill, Socialism and Sense *(1895)*

'Court Jester Shaw' by F. Carruthers Gould.

was because the Hutchinson Trustees, although members of the Fabian Society, were not responsible to its executive for their administration of the funds.

It was probably just as well for the Socialist movement that MacDonald was defeated in his attempt to use the money for directly political purposes. An extension of the activities of the Socialists as a result of heavy subsidy would not necessarily have borne fruit, and it was perhaps better that the main source of their income should be the dues of working-class members. Besides, the leading London Fabians would not have had the time for a new 'Lancashire campaign'. Shaw was now busy making a success as a dramatist; Mrs. Besant had taken up Theosophy at the beginning of the decade; and Sidney Webb was occupied with the committee work of the L.C.C. and, in collaboration with his wife, with the problems of research on the trade union movement, which led to the publication of *The History of Trade Unionism* in 1894 and *Industrial Democracy* in 1898. All the Fabian Society was fit for was to become a bureau of information for those engaged in following up the political programme that they had worked out in the eighties. And this is what it became: its secretary, the methodical and conscientious Edward Pease, was the ideal man for such a task.

The importance of this activity, limited though it was, must not be underestimated. It was in local politics, as we have seen, that Socialists of different groups found their best field of co-operation, and secured, in this unfavourable period, the most striking results. The London Fabians, albeit acting in alliance with the Liberals, had demonstrated how rapidly municipal Socialism could be extended, and there was always a plentiful supply of Fabian tracts to show how the town and county councils and the rural authorities could be goaded into activity. In many centres where they were comparatively strong, the Socialists branches got down in earnest to the task of securing a place on the councils, sometimes with the co-operation of local trades councils, but often without. At Glasgow, where this co-operation existed, there were by 1898 ten Labour men—'the Stalwarts' as they were known—in a city council of seventy; and they could claim to have already done much to improve the

wages of municipal employees and to extend the powers of the
council, especially as regards housing.[1] Elsewhere, of unique
value was the pioneer work done by Margaret McMillan on the
Bradford School Board in developing more enlightened methods
of child welfare and education.[2] There was one town council,
that of West Ham, where the Socialist and Labour representatives actually gained a majority in 1898. Great things were
expected of West Ham, but although considerable reforms were
effected, many mistakes were made, and the Labour majority
was soon defeated by a union of the parties opposed to Labour.[3]
It often happened that early Labour successes in municipal
contests were reversed when the Conservatives and Liberals
united their forces for the ensuing election—a development that
the Socialists had frequently predicted as the natural result of
their challenge.

The work that the branches were doing in local government
had little immediate reference to the objective of the Socialist
commonwealth. It was humdrum work, this task of sustaining
constant pressure on the authorities to exercise the limited
municipal powers afforded them by non-Socialist governments:
building public baths here, taking over a tramway there, and
generally endeavouring to improve the wages of the poorly
paid, while at the same time opposing increases in salaries for
the senior appointments. This attitude to local government
problems was often a dogmatic one: guided only by the latest
Fabian tracts, the Labour councillor sought, on principle and
sometimes without regard to local conditions, to extend municipal powers, and to reduce the disparity of wages and salaries.
Until the branches had obtained some experience of local
government their programmes were frequently not very practical. In general, however, the new approach to municipal
problems which they introduced was timely and valuable. For
the first time in many areas, local elections were vigorously con-
tested and the affairs of local government widely discussed.
People began to take an interest in what was going on in the

[1] See J. Connell, *Glasgow Municipal Enterprise* (Glasgow, 1898).
[2] See M. McMillan, *Life of Rachel McMillan* (1927).
[3] E. G. Howarth and M. Wilson, *West Ham* (1907), pp. 313 ff.; articles in *Economic Review*, 1899 and 1900.

council chamber, and well-established corrupt practices had to be abandoned for fear of the searching criticism of Labour representatives. Not that Labour men were immune from similar temptations: but with a continual conflict of party against party it became increasingly difficult for such practices to be maintained or developed anew without being at once exposed to public criticism. Furthermore, the Labour representatives were often a valuable element in the councils because they normally represented those sections of the community who were supposed to benefit most from municipal services. They knew, for instance, that houses built with privy middens were unpleasant and insanitary, and so they pressed with real vigour for the installation of water-closet systems in all new council houses.[1]

The extent of this municipal activity can be seen from the figures in the I.L.P. Annual Report for 1900, relating to the local elections of the previous year—by no means generally a favourable year for Socialist propaganda: 129 I.L.P. candidates were nominated; ten were returned unopposed and forty-six were elected; and the total vote, which was over 87,000, was twice as large as the poll of the I.L.P. candidates at the 1895 General Election. The Fabian Society realized the influence they could exercise through these representatives, and in 1899 they agreed to sponsor, with the I.L.P., annual conferences of Elected Persons, at which subjects of interest to those engaged in local government were discussed. They also agreed to set up jointly with the I.L.P. a Local Government Information Bureau as a permanent agency to supply literature and information to those interested in the subject.

The result, was in a sense, to Fabianize the local I.L.P. branches. Their idealism was modified by the training of municipal responsibility. As Brocklehurst said, comparing the 1900 I.L.P. conference with those of earlier years: 'The fiery element had departed, but it has given way to the deliberative and common sense.' He put this down to the effect of the party's work in local government. 'Men and women who are daily

---

[1] The best source for this is the press of the local I.L.P. branches: see e.g. *Pendlebury Pioneer*, Mar. 1899.

occupied in administering the Poor Law, educational, or civic affairs of the town cannot escape the sobering influences of responsibility.'[1] The party was, in fact, being tempered by political experience. Its leaders, who had for the most part been very young men in 1893—Hardie, at thirty-six, was older than most of the delegates at the inaugural conference—were now advancing into middle age. Realizing that they could not accomplish their aims as quickly as they had hoped, they began to have more respect for the cautious tactics of the Fabians. But the *rapprochement* was not to last: for it was just at this time that other issues not connected with home politics arose to dominate the national scene and to estrange the I.L.P. from the Fabians more completely than ever before.

(5)

The issues that came to the forefront in national politics in the last years of the century were connected with imperial expansion. Joseph Chamberlain had been appointed Colonial Secretary in the Unionist Government of 1895, and from that date onwards his post became one of the key offices in the government. The Jameson Raid at the end of the year, the Matabele Rising in 1896, the Colonial Conference of 1897, Omdurman and the Fashoda incident of 1898, and the outbreak of the South African War in 1899—it was a constant series of crisis and conflict leading up to the climax of a difficult large-scale colonial war, conducted by a truculent nation in defiance of the world. At home, the very isolation of Britain's position led to an upsurge of national sentiment, and foreign expressions of sympathy for the Boers stiffened the militant tone of public opinion.

The South African War caused a remarkable re-alignment of friendships and hostilities among the British Socialists. The Fabian Society, which had previously almost ignored external affairs, was suddenly faced with a crisis on this issue within its ranks. Shaw and the Webbs were anxious to avoid any

---

[1] *Clarion*, 21 Apr. 1900.

commitment on what Shaw called 'a non-Socialist point of policy'.[1] Bland, as a Tory, naturally took a similar view: the usefulness of the Society, he thought, would be entirely crippled 'if we throw ourselves dead athwart the Imperialist, or any other, strong stream of tendency'.[2] But Sydney Olivier, Graham Wallas and Ramsay MacDonald, among others, could not accept this limited conception of the Society's duty, and demanded a full-blooded denunciation of the war. The matter was submitted to a referendum of the Society's members, and by a small majority it was decided to make no official pronouncement on the issues raised by the war.[3] The result was that about fifteen members, including Ramsay MacDonald, resigned their membership; and Bernard Shaw drafted a manifesto entitled *Fabianism and the Empire*, the theme of which was that 'until the Federation of the World becomes an accomplished fact we must accept the most responsible Imperial federations available as a substitute for it'.[4]

With the exception of Hyndman, the leaders of the S.D.F. and the I.L.P. knew no more about foreign affairs than did the Fabians, but there was no question of their trimming their sails in the same way. They had always denounced imperial expansion and exploitation, and the link between Rand mining speculation and the outbreak of hostilities in South Africa convinced them that they were faced with a prime example of capitalist iniquity. They found themselves at one with a wing of the Liberal Party, which had failed to retain its unity on this question. The old 'Little-England' Radicals—who were not necessarily sympathizers with collectivism and were in some cases its bitter opponents—united with the anti-war Socialists to demand a cessation of hostilities. They hailed with enthusiasm the detailed criticisms of financial imperialism made by J. A. Hobson, whose work was later to provide much of the foundation for Lenin's *Imperialism*.[5]

It was, however, in some ways a misfortune for the Socialist

---

[1] To Pease, 30 Oct. 1899 (Fabian Society Correspondence).
[2] To Pease, 17 Oct. 1899 (ibid.).
[3] Pease, *History of the Fabian Society*, p. 131.
[4] Fabian Society, *Fabianism and the Empire* (1900), p. 24.
[5] See J. A. Hobson, *The War in South Africa* (1900); *Imperialism* (1902).

parties that the exigencies of politics had brought them into a major political controversy in which they could no longer rely on the support of Fabian research, and in which they found themselves in alliance with many of those Radicals and old-fashioned Liberals from whom they had recently been so anxious to establish their independence. There was danger in the fact that the Radical sympathies of many of the Socialists, especially those of the I.L.P., had been only submerged and not removed by their apprenticeship to Socialism.

Hardie's attitude to the South African War was so extreme as to be slightly absurd: 'As Socialists, our sympathies are bound to be with the Boers. Their Republican form of government bespeaks freedom, and is thus hateful to tyrants, whilst their methods of production for use are much nearer our ideal than any form of exploitation for profit.'[1] This seemed to reflect not Socialism, not even Cobdenism, but Jeffersonian Radicalism. It was not without reason that Sidney Webb called the I.L.P. leaders 'with regard to the British Empire, mere administrative Nihilists—that is to say, ultra-Nationalist, ultra-Gladstonian, Old-Liberal to the finger-tips'.[2]

That the Fabian Society should be accusing the I.L.P. of associating with Liberalism, instead of the other way about, indicates the remarkable change in political alignments caused by the issue of imperialism. It is true that Blatchford, the former sergeant of the 103rd Fusiliers, took a steady patriotic line— 'Until the war is over I am for the government'[3]—but even the other members of the *Clarion* team disagreed with him and opposed the war. So while the Fabians found themselves in agreement with the Liberal Imperialists, the great bulk of the Socialist movement united with the anti-war Liberals to sustain the South African Conciliation Committee, an *ad hoc* body established to demand an immediate peace. Naturally these attempts to oppose the government in war-time met with bitter public hostility. Conciliation Committee meetings, unless exceptionally well organized, were liable to be broken up by rowdies, and assaults on speakers became frequent. In London

[1] *Labour Leader*, 6 Jan. 1900. [2] *Nineteenth Century*, Sept. 1901.
[3] *Clarion*, 21 Oct. 1899.

there was a working agreement between the S.D.F. and the Radicals for the defence of anti-war meetings.[1] The I.L.P. also played its full part in fighting for free speech, and its Glasgow members especially distinguished themselves in defending Lloyd George at a Glasgow rally in March 1900. As it was, Lloyd George only just escaped from the violence of the jingo mob. Keir Hardie, who was in personal control of the stewards, announced that several flags had been captured from the rioters in the course of the fighting; but this was hardly compensation for the damage suffered by the *Labour Leader* office in Glasgow which was ransacked the same night.[2]

The rigours of such a hard-fought campaign against bitter opposition did much to revive the possibilities of electoral co-operation between the Socialists and at least some of the Liberals. Under the growing influence of Ramsay MacDonald, the I.L.P. had already been moving in that direction. Its 1899 conference had agreed that at the next election there should be only a restricted number of I.L.P. candidates. This change of policy was expounded in an article in the *Nineteenth Century* which was drafted by MacDonald, revised by Hardie, and fully authorized by the Council.[3] After adverting to the failure of Liberalism and emphasizing the evolutionary character of I.L.P. Socialism, the article goes on:

> We can now afford to identify ourselves with those questions of immediate reform upon which Radicals and Socialists are alike agreed, with less fear of allowing our aim to be obscured and the party to be swallowed up in the ranks of the shiftless opportunist. . . .
> We are in a better position than ever we have been to emphasize the fact that independence is not isolation, and in so far as co-operation with kindred sections is possible, while retaining our freedom, there is no barrier to it in our methods or tradition. We recognize that a mere pulling down of the old, although an indispensable preliminary, will never build up the new. . . .[4]

Observations of this type, if not unusual from the MacDonald pen, represented a new development of official I.L.P. policy.

[1] Hyndman, *Further Reminiscences*, p. 162.   [2] *Labour Leader*, 10 Mar.1900.
[3] Minutes, I.L.P. Council, 26 Oct. 1898.   [4] *Nineteenth Century*, Jan. 1899.

The Consolidation of Sectionalism

The change was endorsed by a large majority in a referendum of the branches,[1] and it received a warm welcome in Radical circles.

When the 1900 election came, even the S.D.F. abandoned their attitude of complete hostility to the Liberal Party, and agreed to support Radical candidates who shared their opposition to the 'Capitalist Imperialist policy in South Africa'.[2] The I.L.P., after considering a proposal to issue a 'White List' of anti-war candidates, decided to leave its branches free to use their discretion in the matter of supporting such persons. It must be observed, however, that these cautious modifications of policy did not amount to a complete reversal of the old policy of independence. There was no contact with the officialdom of Liberalism, which had not declared itself against the war; and what arrangements there were applied only to the immediate situation and were only made under the stress of the 'khaki election'. In any case, the Labour Representation Committee was by then in existence, and this represented a new electoral loyalty for most of the Socialists, which was in the long run to transcend any other consideration.

[1] Minutes, I.L.P. Council, 9 Sept. 1899. The vote was small—1,153 for, 94 against.
[2] *S.D.F. Conference Report*, 1900, p. 8.

CHAPTER X

The Conversion of the Unions

(1)

THE I.L.P. leaders had always been keen to persuade the unions to join in their political work, and in the early nineties, as we have seen, this object received the encouragement of the Fabians, who echoed their demand that the unions should take the initiative.

At the 1892 T.U.C. Hardie carried a resolution instructing the Parliamentary Committee to prepare a financial scheme for independent labour representation; and the scheme that the Parliamentary Committee produced was approved by the 1893 T.U.C. It was, however, a purely voluntary scheme, and since the Parliamentary Committee itself was so lukewarm about it, the unions did not elect to join and the scheme collapsed. But in 1894 the I.L.P. attempt to organize a compact Socialist *bloc* inside the Congress was more obvious than ever before. Tom Mann stood as a candidate for the Secretaryship, and secured about a third of the votes; and he was subsequently formally thanked by the I.L.P. Council for consenting to stand.[1]

Mann reckoned that out of the total of 370 delegates at the 1894 T.U.C., over eighty were I.L.P. members.[2] Quite a large number of these were trades council delegates, for the trades councils were more readily susceptible to Socialist influence than the large trade unions. It could be argued, however, that the trades councils had no right to be represented at Congress. To allow them at all was to duplicate the representation of their members, who were also members of trade unions; to exclude them would be to sacrifice little, for the trades councils had virtually no financial strength of their own.

In 1894, therefore, a group on the Parliamentary Committee,

[1] *Labour Leader*, 22 Sept. 1894.
[2] *Labour Annual*, 1895, p. 40.

alarmed by the growing strength of the Socialists, drew up new standing orders for the Congress which they proposed quite arbitrarily to bring into force before the next T.U.C. The new orders introduced the card vote, by which delegates voted according to the strength of their unions; in addition, the trades councils were to be excluded altogether, and no delegate was to be admitted who was not either a working trade unionist or an official of a union. Under these regulations neither Keir Hardie nor John Burns would be eligible to attend. Burns himself was Chairman of the Parliamentary Committee, but his ambitions in the sphere of trade-union politics were now satisfied. With Mawdsley, the Conservative leader of the Cotton Spinners, he formed an alliance against the I.L.P., and the two were largely responsible for proposing the new arrangements and putting them into force. The proposals were carried on the Committee by a majority of one only; but although Hardie attempted to organize an opposition to this *coup d'état*, even to the extent of writing to his old enemy Broadhurst in order to obtain his co-operation, he was quite unable to rally enough strength to prevent the changes taking place.[1] The 1895 Congress accepted the situation, and the I.L.P. seemed considerably farther off than before from their object of winning over the unions. The number of Socialist delegates dropped by a quarter, and Ben Tillett lost his place on the Parliamentary Committee.

It cannot be denied that the card system of voting, although it had its weaknesses, was the only way of giving the unions with large membership a share in the decisions to correspond to their strength. The conduct of the Trades Union Congresses compared very favourably with the international conferences of the Socialists. It had been customary for these 'Socialist and Labour' conferences, as thy were called, to be attended by a number of British trade-union representatives, but the inadequacy of the arrangements for the 1896 conference in London, the failure to achieve any proportion between the strength of delegations

[1] Hardie to Broadhurst, 28 Dec. 1894 (Broadhurst Correspondence, Brit. Lib. Pol. Sci.). See also *Labour Leader*, 29 Dec. 1894, where Hardie argues that Mawdsley's principal object was to exclude the Liberal Broadhurst. Elie Halévy has mistaken Broadhurst's attitude on this issue—see his *History of the English People in 1895–1905* (1926), p. 244.

and the size of the bodies they represented, and the absurd disorders of the debate on whether to admit the Anarchists, thoroughly justified the trade-union leaders who attended in calling
it a farce and refusing to participate again.[1] This sort of performance—in which Hyndman played a leading part—did not
improve the reputation of the Socialist cause in the trade-union
world.

The Trades Union Congress now seemed to be dominated by
the massive card vote of Coal and Cotton. Most of the unions
of these industries had accepted the demand for an eight-hour
day, but they were strongly hostile to independent labour representation. There were special reasons for hostility in each case.
The cotton industry included a high proportion of Conservative
voters, and the union officials feared that political action might
bring to the fore the party differences among their members,
which would jeopardize the safety of their organization.[2] The
miners, on the other hand, had already been more actively
engaged in Parlimentary representation than any other trade;
but they could elect their own members to Parliament without
outside assistance, for the mining vote was heavily concentrated
in a limited number of constituencies. They saw no reason for
mutual assistance, knowing that their position was much
stronger than that of the other unions. Ben Pickard, President
of the Miners Federation, expressed their attitude very lucidly
when he was confronted with the proposal to create a general
association for Labour representation. Addressing the members
of the Federation, he said:

> I should like to ask why we as a Federation should be called
> upon to join an Association to find money, time or intellect
> to focus the weaknesses of other Trade Unionists to do what
> you are doing for yourselves, and have done for the last four-
> teen years.[3]

The miners' political grievances against the landlords gave
them a preference for collaboration with the Liberal Party, and
the propaganda of the I.L.P. made little impression upon them

[1] *Conference Record*, 30 July 1896.
[2] See, e.g. T. Ashton in *T.U.C. Report*, 1899, p. 65.
[3] *Miners Federation Annual Report*, 1899, p. 25.

except in Scotland and, to a limited extent, in South Wales. This was shown convincingly at a by-election in October 1897 at Barnsley, the headquarters of the Yorkshire Miners Association. Pickard had pledged the union's support to the Liberal candidate, who was a mine-owner prepared to favour an eight-hours bill. In opposition to him the I.L.P. unwisely ran Pete Curran, an official of the Gasworkers Union. His campaign was an expensive failure, and at one village he was driven away by a hail of stones from the miners.[1]

Other sections of the trade-union world, however, were being powerfully influenced by the industrial and social changes of the time. There were, for instance, the developments in mechanization which threatened the established position of certain groups of skilled tradesmen. The most notable example of this was in the engineering industry. Indeed, the Amalgamated Society of Engineers soon found it necessary to alter its policy in the face of a reduction of the standard of skill required by employers in the trade. As early as 1891 Tom Mann had put up for election to the post of General Secretary on a programme which involved the extension of the boundaries of the Society's recruitment. He was narrowly defeated, but his campaign led to a rules revision in 1892, and eventually in 1896 to the election as General Secretary of George Barnes, also a member of the I.L.P. and Mann's principal lieutenant in the earlier contest. Barnes advocated, among other things, direct Parliamentary representation for the Society and a more militant trade policy.[2]

Another more general reason for the Engineers' change of attitude was the development of an employers' federation which seemed to be designed to limit the power of their Society. The growing tension between the Society and the federation led in 1897 to a six-months lock-out—a grim struggle which extended throughout the country and ended in the defeat of the Society. The course of this conflict was followed with alarm and dismay by the officials of the other unions. 'If the workmen are defeated', commented the monthly report of the Boot and Shoe Operatives just before the end of the lock-out, 'it will have

---

[1] R.P. Arnot, *The Miners* (1949), p. 302.
[2] Jefferys, *Story of the Engineers*, Part III *passim*.

far-reaching results to all other trades.'[1] A feeling had begun to grow that the employers in all trades were on the counter-offensive against the unions. Employers' federations were set up in many industries, and the unions sought to defend themselves in a similar way. Craft unions began to seek alliances with each other, so as to form a common front to their employers; and even international trades federations grew up—Tom Mann was active in this work after leaving the Secretaryship of the I.L.P.[2] Others took up the demand for a national federation of all trade unions, which would assist any threatened member union with the financial resources of the others.

But the conviction began to develop that purely industrial action was not enough. In America, the trusts and combines that had lately grown powerful had initiated an attack on the unions through the law courts and by the use of political power, and it seemed that the same thing might well be attempted in Britain. The British Socialists had for some time been pointing to the American trusts as the pattern towards which all capitalist industry was moving, and they did not fail to suggest that trade unions would be the first to suffer.[3] The trade-union leaders could get their own reports of what was happening in America through the regular correspondence of American branches of British unions,[4] and also through the system of fraternal exchanges with the American Federation of Labor which the T.U.C. initiated in 1894. The violent Homestead and Pullman strikes of 1892 and 1894 respectively did not pass unnoticed in this country, and it was observed that when the American employers could not get their way by industrial action alone they were able to make use of the legal injunction and also, on occasion, of Federal troops and state militia.

From the time of the 1897 Engineers' lock-out, the British interest in the American scene was intensified. The employers

---

[1] *N.U. Boot and Shoe Operatives Monthly Report*, Nov. 1897, p. 2.

[2] Mann, *Memoirs*, pp. 135 ff.

[3] E.g. Hyndman in *Social-Democrat*, Feb. 1898; *Justice*, 22 Aug. 1896, reports an American Socialist delegate as saying that 'the old trade unionism of America, inherited from Great Britain, is going to pieces'. See also William Clarke's contribution to *Fabian Essays*, mentioned above, p. 75.

[4] Some of the large British unions had American branches until as late as 1920: e.g. the Engineers and the Carpenters and Joiners (S. Gompers, *Seventy Years of Life and Labour* (1925), p. 55; Jefferys, op. cit. pp. 171 ff.).

hoped to emulate the success of their American rivals in reducing the power of the unions; the British trade-union leaders hoped to be able to defend themselves in time from the American methods. British industrialists were claiming that the weakness of American trade unionism accounted for the strong competitive position of American products in the world market. Colonel Dyer, leader of the Engineering Employers Federation during the 1897 lock-out, declared that 'The federated engineering employers are determined to obtain the freedom to manage their own affairs which has proved so beneficial to the American manufacturers as to enable them to compete . . . in what was formerly an English monopoly'.[1] Barnes, for the workers, retorted with a denunciation of the American 'boss system' and its 'attendant unrestrained brutality and lawlessness'.[2] It was significant that at almost the same time Henry Demarest Lloyd, the author of *Wealth Against Commonwealth*, which exposed the Standard Oil Trust,[3] announced in the course of a visit to England that 'English employers are getting the opinions of American lawyers as to the American methods of dealing with labour troubles'.[4]

Bearing in mind the feeling of insecurity which all this had created in the trade-union world, we can turn to consider particular unions which had special reasons for favouring political action. There were, first of all, the unions of heavy industry, including not only the Engineers but also the Blastfurnacemen, Shipwrights, Ironfounders and Steelsmelters. In these trades the severity of trade depression had been felt most acutely in earlier years: it was calculated, for instance, that in 1887

---

[1] *The Times*, 7 Sept. 1987. Col. Dyer's views on the disadvantages of British trade unionism were supported in a special article on 'The Engineering Industry in England and America', in *The Times*, 23 Sept. 1897.

[2] For this correspondence and many other documents relating to the lock-out, see the A.S.E.'s publication, *Notes on the Engineering Trades Lock-out*, 1897–8 (n.d., ? 1898).

[3] Published at New York, 1894. J. A. Hobson described it in a letter to Lloyd as 'by far the most powerful and convincing exposure of the natural working of developed Capitalism that has yet appeared' (22 Feb. 1895, H. D. Lloyd Correspondence).

[4] *New Age*, 28 Oct. 1897. A year later, in a letter to an English correspondent, A. G. Symonds, Lloyd said that he was 'profoundly impressed by the reactionary course which seems to be threatening in England, imitating America, with regard to trade unions' (28 Dec. 1898, H. D. Lloyd Correspondence).

unemployment among unionists in the engineering, shipbuilding and metal trades exceeded 10 per cent—a fact which goes far to explain the large number of Socialists among the younger workers.[1] Foreign competition, the introduction of new mechanical processes and the tendency towards amalgamation of firms all had an unsettling effect at the end of the century.

New machinery was also being introduced into the boot and shoe industry, which was now undergoing an 'industrial revolution' for the first time. There is no doubt that the dislocation caused by the destruction of the old home-working system sharpened the operatives' sense of political grievance: but they had been well known for generations for their interest in radical politics, and their centres at Leicester and Norwich had become strongholds of Socialism.[2] A strike on which they embarked in 1895 had ended unfavourably, and as a result of this the union membership had gone into a decline which lasted several years.[3] Somewhat parallel was the position of the two printers' unions, the London Society of Compositors and the Typographical Association, which had also recently suffered from the stresses caused by technical change.[4] The printers were the most literate and therefore, on the whole, the most politically interested workers in the trade-union movement: many of their members were prominent in either the S.D.F. or the I.L.P.

Another union which felt an urgent need for political action was the Amalgamated Society of Railway Servants. Its leaders realized the power of the 'railway interest' in Parliament and wanted to have representatives there to put their case against the companies. The A.S.R.S. was remarkable among the larger unions for its failure to obtain recognition from its employers. Consequently, conditions of work on the railways remained poor by comparison with other industries. An effort was made in 1897 to fight on a broad front, demanding improvements in all grades and from all companies, but this 'All-Grades Move-

---

[1] Clapham, *Economic History of Modern Britain*, iii. 7.
[2] 'Evolution of the Boot and Shoe Trade', *Social-Democrat*, Mar. 1898; Hawkins, *Norwich: a Social Study*, pp. 23 ff.
[3] Clapham, op. cit. iii, 332.
[4] Clapham, op. cit. iii. 191; P. de Rousiers, *La Question ouvrière en Angleterre* (Paris, 1895), pp. 85 ff., on the Scottish Typographical Association and the introduction of the linotype.

ment', as it was called, proved abortive.[1] From 1898 the Society's journal, the *Railway Review*, was edited by an active I.L.P. politician, G. J. Wardle; and in the same year it was decided to pay for an independent candidature for Parliament by the Secretary of the Society.[2]

Lastly, there were the 'new unions'—not so 'new' as they were in 1889–90 but still anxious to see the formation of a political party to represent them in Parliament. The Gasworkers, the London Dockers and the Liverpool Dockers all had Socialists as their General Secretaries.[3] There was also the new Workers Union, founded by Tom Mann in 1898 with 'the support of labour candidates on public elective bodies' prominent among its objects.[4]

This brief survey shows that there was a wide range of trades favourable to a policy of fuller political action. It was not merely the spread of Socialist ideas that was responsible for the swing in favour of this policy, for although the young Socialists of the eighties were now beginning to find their way into key posts even in the 'old' unions, they could not have done so without the backing of non-Socialist elements. It would be true to say that the attitude of the bulk of the unions now favouring independent labour representation was dictated more by fear for the security of their existing position than by the hope of any millennium. They wanted to hold on to what they had achieved by industrial action, and they were afraid that they might be deprived of their gains by indirect means—by Act of Parliament or by decision of the law courts. Already in 1893 a 'National Free Labour Association' had been established for the purpose of supplying 'blackleg' labour in case of strike action, and it was receiving the backing of the large employers.[5] There had

[1] S. and B. Webb, *History of Trade Unionism* (1920 ed.), p. 525.
[2] P. S. Bagwell, *The Railwaymen* (1963), p. 205.
[3] The Liverpool Dockers (National Union of Dock Labourers) had been formed in 1889 by two political friends of Davitt, R. McGhee and E. McHugh. A few years later James Sexton, himself a Liverpool Irish docker, became secretary. Sexton had been an Irish Nationalist, but abandoned the cause at the time of the Parnell crisis and became a foundation member of the I.L.P. See his autobiography, *Sir James Sexton, Agitator* (1936), pp. 107, 127.
[4] *Labour Leader*, 26 Feb. 1898; Mann, *Memoirs*, pp. 150 ff.
[5] W. Collison, *The Apostle of Free Labour* (1913), pp. 93 ff.; Anon., 'Free Labour Frauds', *Critic*, June-Aug. 1898; P. Mantoux and M. Alfassa, *La Crise du trade-unionisms* (Paris, 1903), pp. 194 ff.

been high-level discussion of the advisability of amending the Trade Union Act of 1871 in order to clarify the legal responsibilities of the unions: this had been advocated by a number of members of the Royal Commission on Labour, which reported in 1894.[1] In any case, the unions felt that their rights under existing legislation were being whittled away. One did not have to be a Socialist to take this view. The leader-writer of the Liberal *Daily Chronicle* wrote in January 1899 that he believed that at the time of the engineering dispute 'there was then a very strong militant party among the employers, not only in that but in other trades, which aimed at "union-smashing", and which was prepared to stake great amounts of capital in the venture'. Since then, however, it appeared to him that 'the field of action has been transferred to the law-courts, where there has been a well-arranged attempt to obtain decisions on various technical points of strike law, with the object of paralysing action by union officials in any future dispute'.[2] The case of *Lyons* v. *Wilkins* (1896 and 1899), which resulted in the conviction of a striker engaged in picketing, could be considered an example of this: it was an encroachment on what trade unionists had previously regarded as their rights under the Conspiracy and Protection of Property Act, 1875. The case was regarded as sufficiently important for the Parliamentary Committee of the T.U.C. to raise funds to take it to the House of Lords, but a solicitor's error allowed the appeal to lapse.[3] Another important case, *Allen* v. *Flood* (1897), concerned the right of trade unionists to strike in order to secure the dismissal of other workers. This was decided against the union in the Court of Appeal, but the Lords by a majority reversed the decision.[4] Thus even the right to strike was in jeopardy although not actually controverted; and the discretionary powers of the courts were seen to be very considerable.

Finally, the unions not only felt the need for increased poli-

[1] The group included the chairman, the Duke of Devonshire, and also George Livesey, the victor of the South London gas strike of 1889–90 (Royal Commission on Labour, Final Report: *Parliamentary Papers*, 1894, xxxv. 115 ff.).
[2] *Daily Chronicle*, 13 Jan. 1899.
[3] *G.F.T.U. Conference Report*, 1899, p. 17; *T.U.C. Report*, 1899, p 17, and 1900, pp. 33 ff.
[4] *The Times*, 15 Dec. 1897.

tical activity but also had the means at their disposal to ensure success. Their reserve funds had increased considerably in the prosperity of the last few years of the century—from less than £1,400,000 in 1893 to over £3,700,000 in 1900. The average reserves per member rose from £1 9s. 11¼d. to £3 4s. 2¼d.[1] This meant that the unions could afford an excursion into politics much more easily than before. In 1898 there was founded an Employers Parliamentary Council, which was designed to counteract the influence of the Parliamentary Committee of the T.U.C. as a pressure-group at Westminster and Whitehall, and which had as its object 'free contracts and free labour'.[2] The next move in the great struggle of Capital and Labour obviously depended on a new initiative from the T.U.C.

(2)

The policy of the I.L.P. as a result of the growing political consciousness among unionists became more and more definite as it became increasingly close to realization. Hardie had referred to the subject as early as 1896 in these terms:

I remember on the evening of the first I.L.P. Conference at Bradford, three years ago, talking this matter over with George Bernard Shaw. My opinion then was that periodically, say once a year, a Socialist conference should be called, and that all Socialist organizations, together with all Trade Unions and Co-operative organizations, should be invited to send delegates. I had in mind the Trade Union Congress as a model. That body is composed of representatives from all kinds of trade unions—skilled and unskilled alike. It formulates trade union opinions from year to year, though its findings are not binding on any of the unions represented. I still think this committee would be the recognized head of the Socialist movement in Britain, leaving the I.L.P., S.D.F.,

[1] Royal Commission on Trade Disputes, *Parliamentary Papers*, 1906, lvi, App. to Minutes of Evidence, p. 2.
[2] *The Times*, 18 Nov. and 21 Dec. 1898. Lord Wemyss was the President, George Livesey a Vice-President. These two, with Col. Dyer of the Engineering Employers Federation who had since died, had been associated in a project to form a 'Free Labour Protection Association' for the protection of the employers' interests against the 'mischievous and vexatious policy of the New Unionists' (Circular, quoted *Labour Leader*, 4 Sept. 1897).

Fabian Society, and other organizations to carry on their propaganda in their respective ways. The influence on trade-unionists would be very great.[1]

The difference between this scheme and the one expounded in Shaw's *Plan of Campaign for Labor*[2] was the emphasis that Hardie placed on the need for a national conference. Such a conference, to consist of Socialist societies and trade unions, was suggested by the I.L.P. Council later in 1896, at the time of the discussions of fusion with the S.D.F., and the Parliamentary Committee had been invited to raise the question at Congress: but nothing came of this. Then at the 1897 I.L.P. Conference John Edwards, an able Liverpool member, read a paper emphasizing the necessity for an electoral alliance with the trade unions.[3] He spoke of a 'labour representation conference', and no doubt drew upon personal local experience, for the Liverpool Trades Council had since 1894 been collaborating with the local I.L.P., S.D.F., and Fabians in a 'Labour Representation Committee'.[4] But the existing Parliamentary Committee of the T.U.C. was not interested in the idea, especially as it already had the problems of establishing a General Federation of Trade Unions to deal with.

The idea of a General Federation of Trade Unions for industrial purposes was one which had been strongly championed by the Socialists; and its successful foundation through the agency of a special committee appointed by the 1897 T.U.C., and a subsequent special Congress, was a valuable precedent for the similar establishment of a political federation. It was formally inaugurated in July 1899, and secured the immediate adhesion of forty-four unions, representing a quarter of the membership of the T.U.C.[5] But many unions remained doubtful of the value of this 'strike insurance fund', and preferred to remain outside it. As a result, it failed to acquire permanent importance.

After the 1898 T.U.C., therefore, the Parliamentary Committee had its hands free of the General Federation; and the

---

[1] *Labour Leader*, 22 Feb. 1896.   [2] See above, p. 160.
[3] Reprinted as J. Edwards, *Politics and the I.L.P.* (1897).
[4] See W. Hamling, *Short History of the Liverpool Trades Council* (Liverpool, 1948), pp. 27 f.; S. Maddock, 'The Liverpool Trades Council and Politics, 1878–1918' (M.A. thesis, Liverpool, 1959).
[5] W. A. Appleton, *Trade Unions* (1925), pp. 110 ff.

new Parliamentary Committee, it was clear, was much more independent of Liberalism than those that had preceded it—Hardie regarded four out of its thirteen members as Socialists.[1] The opportunity for securing T.U.C. support for the labour representation policy seemed to be at hand. At the 1898 Congress Hardie reckoned the majority of the ordinary delegates to be of the Socialist persuasion—and three-fifths of this majority members of the I.L.P.[2] Although this was probably an over-estimate, a resolution recommending trade unionists to support 'the working-class Socialist parties' was carried on a card vote by a large majority. Hardie's policy was now quite clear in his own mind: 'What we should aim at is the same kind of working agreement nationally as already exists for municipal purposes in Glasgow. Trade-Unionists, Socialists, and co-operators each select their own candidates, a joint programme having been first agreed upon, and then the expense of the campaign is also borne jointly.'[3] This was a more complete formulation of the type of alliance he was seeking than he had ever made before; and he now considered the time to be ripe for action. The I.L.P. Council met on the very day that this statement appeared in print, and decided at Hardie's request to make approaches to the Parliamentary Committees both of the T.U.C. and of the Scottish T.U.C. 'with a view to securing united political action'. This time, the approach was not made in vain.

Action followed very much more readily in Scotland than in England. The Scottish T.U.C. had been established as a protest against the new standing orders which Mawdsley and Burns had drawn up, and it met annually, with due representation from trades councils, from 1897 onwards. Political feeling among some sections of the organized working class in Scotland was considerably in advance of that in England—above all, the miners were strongly socialistic[4]—and before the third annual Congress its Parliamentary Committee responded to the I.L.P. suggestion by calling a special conference to which it

[1] *Labour Leader*, 10 Sept. 1898.   [2] Ibid.
[3] *Labour Leader*, 1 Oct. 1898.
[4] This was due to the exceptional weakness of their unions, partly as a result of Irish immigration; and to the need to find a third-party platform to reconcile supporters and opponents of Irish Home Rule.

invited the Scottish Co-operative Societies, the S.D.F., and the I.L.P. The Co-operators were undecided about participation, but a meeting was held with the political bodies, and the Scottish Parliamentary Committee, which contained an actual majority of I.L.P. members, was represented by three leaders, including Robert Smillie, the Scottish miners' leader, who was an old friend of Hardie and a former I.L.P. candidate, and George Carson, a mainstay of the Scottish Labour Party in earlier years.[1] With these men on the trade-union side, agreement was not difficult, and it was decided to place a resolution on the agenda of the next Scottish Congress empowering the Parliamentary Committee to call a special Congress 'to decide upon united working-class action at the next General Election'. Hardie attended the Scottish Congress which was accordingly held in April 1899, and after the resolution, moved by Carson, had been carried, Hardie was given an opportunity of addressing the Congress. When the Conference on Parliamentary representation was held—it took place in Edinburgh on 6 January 1900—it was attended not only by representatives of trade unions and trades councils and of the I.L.P. and S.D.F., but also by a number of delegates of co-operative societies. This conference was organized by Carson, and it duly adopted a resolution in favour of 'independent working-class representation', and enumerated a list of industrial reforms of pressing importance. It appointed a Scottish Workers Parliamentary Elections Committee to put its decisions into effect.

This was the path that the British T.U.C. was to be induced to follow, but the greater conservatism of the British trade-union leaders as a whole naturally made the task more difficult. The I.L.P. Council got in touch again with the Parliamentary Committee of the British T.U.C., but for definite action the initiative had to come from Congress itself. Hardie gave his backing to a resolution which the Railway Servants proposed to move at the 1899 T.U.C. as follows:

That this Congress, having regard to its decisions in former years, and with a view to securing a better representation of

---

[1] I.L.P. Report from Head Office, 17/24 Sept. 1898.

the interests of labour in the House of Commons, hereby instructs the Parliamentary Committee to invite the co-operation of all the co-operative, socialistic, trade union, and other working organizations to jointly co-operate on lines mutually agreed upon, in convening a special congress of representatives from such of the above-named organizations as may be willing to take part to devise ways and means for securing the return of an increased number of labour members to the next Parliament.

There is a strong tradition that this resolution was drafted by the I.L.P. leaders in London[1]; but there is no contemporary evidence to prove this. It appears rather to have been drafted by Thomas R. Steels, a member of the union's Doncaster branch and of the I.L.P.[2] The resolution was then put to the Railway Servants' committee by the branch. Its clumsy wording was designed to stress one essential point—that the scheme was to be taken out of the hands of the Parliamentary Committee, once it had obeyed its instructions to the extent of calling a conference of interested bodies. In plenty of time before the T.U.C. was held Hardie was urgently canvassing for support in the columns of the *Labour Leader*:

> Too much importance cannot be attached to this resolution, and should the Congress devote the entire week to discussing it in a manner worthy of its importance, it would be the best week's work ever performed in the interests of the classes represented. All who desire unity in the Labour movement will make it a point to be present at the Lodge meeting when the agenda is being discussed, and endeavour to see that the instructions to the delegate leave him no loophole of escape, even assuming that he would desire such.[3]

Two months before the Congress took place, a by-election at Oldham showed the contradiction of Liberal-Labour politics. Mawdsley, the leader of the Cotton Spinners and a member of the T.U.C. Parliamentary Committee, stood as Conservative candidate but was defeated, largely by the intervention of the

---

[1] E.g. Webb, *History of Trade Unionism* (1920 ed.), pp. 683 f.; Snowden, *Autobiography*, i. 88.
[2] F. Bealey and H. Pelling, *Labour and Politics, 1900–1906* (1958), p. 23; Bagwell, *The Railwaymen*, p. 206.
[3] *Labour Leader*, 1 July 1899.

'Lib-Labs'. The absurdity of this result caused many trade unionists to re-examine their political beliefs.

When the resolution came before the Congress on the initiative of James Holmes of the Railway Servants, it was earnestly debated for three hours. Sexton of the Liverpool Dockers, who seconded, pointed to the 'present disgraceful confusion' of elections at which 'prominent labour men had opposed each other on separate platforms'. Miss Bondfield supported the resolution because her union, the Shop Assistants, was a small body and could not get satisfactory legislative action alone. On the other hand, Thomas Ashton of the Cotton Spinners was reported as saying that 'if their Society were to interfere in politics, it would go down immediately'; and Harvey of the Derbyshire Miners argued for individual self-help by the unions instead of collective action: 'The matter was in their own hands, and each Society ought to get about teaching their members that it was their duty to pay for securing the end in view.'[1]

In the end, a card vote was taken, and the figures were read out in a deep hush: 546,000 in favour, 434,000 against. At once pandemonium broke out: the supporters of the motion, realizing the importance of their victory, expressed their feelings enthusiastically, climbing on the chairs to wave their hats and cheer.[2] The Engineers had retired from the T.U.C. after a trade demarcation dispute: but even without their help the great battalions of Coal and Cotton had been defeated, with about a sixth of the voting power absent or abstaining. It was a decision which revealed a real change in the attitude of the unions to political action.

(3)

In the months after the T.U.C. meeting there was a further slight but distinct shift of opinion in favour of forming a new party. It should be remembered that even at the end of the century the great majority of trade-union leaders were members of the Liberal Party, and Gladstonians at that. The outbreak of

---

[1] *T.U.C. Report*, 1899, pp. 64 ff.
[2] *Railway Review*, 20 Oct. 1899.

Parliamentary Committee of the T.U.C., 1899–1900, photographed at the 1900 T.U.C. with fraternal delegates of the American Federation of Labor

Left to right, front row: A. Wilkie (Shipwrights), E. Cowey (Miners' Federation), C. W. Bowerman (London Society of Compositors), S. Woods (Miners' Federation; Committee Secretary), F. Chandler (Carpenters and Joiners; Committee Chairman), W. J. Davis (Brassworkers), J. M. Hunter (A.F. of L.), S. J. Kent (A.F. of L.). *Behind:* W. C. Steadman (Bargebuilders), R. Bell (Railway Servants), W. Thorne (Gasworkers), W. B. Hornidge (Boot and Shoe Operatives), D. Holmes (Northern Counties Weavers), W. Mullin (Amalgamated Card and Blowing Room Operatives)

the South African War in October and the collapse of an effective Liberal opposition came as a great surprise to them. They could not agree with the Liberal Imperialists, and they found themselves drawn to the same conclusions as the Socialists, that the war had been brought about by unscrupulous financial interests. Even before the declaration of war, *Reynolds's Newspaper*, the great working-class newspaper which had formerly given a critical support to the Liberals, came out in favour of the formation of a new party: many of the members of the Liberal Party, it declared, were 'like Tories', and bogus company promoters were in control of politics.[1]

In due course the Secretary of the Parliamentary Committee called representatives of the Fabians, S.D.F., and I.L.P. into consultation with the four London members of his Committee, two of whom, Steadman and Thorne, were supporters of the idea. Hardie and MacDonald, for the I.L.P., went to the meetings with a simple scheme which MacDonald summed up in three points:

> 1. That the candidates be run by Trade Union, Socialist and other labour bodies and have no connection with either Liberal or Tory parties.
> 2. That each party run its own candidates and find its own money.
> 3. That a joint committee of the organizations running candidates should be the political committee of the combined forces.[2]

A series of seven resolutions was adopted to form an agenda for the conference. It embodied the three points which MacDonald had stated. To Hardie's annoyance, the full Parliamentary Committee revised this agenda before publishing it.[3] The main basis of the earlier arrangements remained, however, and the conference duly met on 27 February, 1900, in the Memorial Hall, Farringdon Street, London.

---

[1] *Reynolds's Newspaper*, 17 Sept. 1899.
[2] To Pease, 29 Nov. 1899 (Fabian Society Correspondence). The same principles are enunciated at greater length by J. Burgess in *I.L.P. News*, Feb. 1900. They differ from Hardie's statement of Oct. 1898 (see above, p. 203) only in that the parties to the agreement are to pay their candidates' expenses separately.
[3] *Labour Leader*, 13 Jan. 1900.

Unlike the foundation conference of the I.L.P., this first Labour Party conference was hardly noticed by the outside world. Home politics were not important news in the middle of a war; and in any case, bodies for labour representation had often been set up in the past, only to fade away after a short existence. There were but nine spectators in the gallery at the start,[1] and *The Times* on 1 March devoted less than a quarter of a column to its report. There was no notable enthusiasm for the conference in London, and there was nothing of any special significance in the meeting-place chosen, although the Memorial Hall, the 'Cathedral of Nonconformity' as the *Clarion* correspondent called it,[2] was in some ways peculiarly appropriate. The attendance of 129 delegates represented over half a million trade unionists: but while this was a number considerable enough to make the conference an important one, it was less than half the representation at the T.U.C. The only large unions to send delegates were the 'advanced' ones such as the Railway Servants, Gasworkers, Engineers and Boot and Shoe Operatives. As voting was according to membership, these four unions between them controlled over one-third of the votes.

The chairman of the conference was a fairly neutral figure— W. C. Steadman, of the Bargebuilders, a member of the T.U.C. Parliamentary Committee who was Radical M.P. for Stepney and also a member of the Fabian Society. The atmosphere of the conference was, on the whole, one of mutual reconciliation. The I.L.P. representatives steered a cautious and moderate course designed to give none of the trade unionists present an excuse for not supporting the new body. As G. N. Barnes of the Engineers put it, the idea was 'to keep in mind the need for the largest possible degree of unanimity'.[3] Where the resolutions accepted for discussion by the Parliamentary Committee did not suit their policy, they attempted before the conference met to get sympathetic trade unionists to propose amendments.[4] Thus Barnes was put up to amend the resolution designed to

---

[1] *Ethical World*, 3 Mar. 1900.
[2] *Clarion*, 3 Mar. 1900.
[3] *Ethical World*, 17 Feb. 1900.
[4] Minutes, I.L.P. Council, 8 Jan. 1900.

restrict Labour candidatures to members of the working class. This amendment was accepted without direct intervention by any I.L.P. delegate. Will Thorne of the Gasworkers, who was a member of the S.D.F., carried an amendment of another resolution in order to give the new body some control over the list of candidatures that it would be required to sponsor. On the other hand, the I.L.P. felt impelled to vote against the S.D.F. attempt to bind the conference to Socialism and 'a recognition of the class war'[1]: Hardie replaced this with an amendment to establish:

> . . . a distinct Labour group in Parliament, who shall have their own whips, and agree upon their policy, which must embrace a readiness to co-operate with any party which for the time being may be engaged in promoting legislation in the direct interests of labour, and be equally ready to associate themselves with any party in opposing measures having an opposite tendency. . . .

This was the most important resolution of the conference. It sketched the outline of an independent Parliamentary party, but left the details of programme and policy to be filled in later.

In addition, by what was a remarkable *tour de force*, an I.L.P. amendment was carried to reduce the size of the proposed Executive Committee from eighteen to twelve, leaving the I.L.P. and S.D.F. representation unchanged at two each but reducing the Fabians from two to one and the trade-union element from twelve to seven. This meant that if two out of the trade-union seven turned out to be Socialists—as was the case in the first year—there was a Socialist majority on the Committee. The main argument that the proposers of this amendment put forward in its favour was that a committee of twelve would be less expensive and more efficient than one of eighteen.

The other resolutions were either non-controversial or comparatively unimportant. Financial obstacles that might prevent unions joining the Committee were reduced to a minimum. The Committee was to be provided with working expenses, but

[1] The *Labour Leader* complained that the S.D.F. had not mentioned this resolution at the preliminary discussions, but had sprung it on the Conference 'in distinct bad taste' (*Labour Leader*, 10 Mar. 1900).

candidatures were still to be financed by the trade unions or political societies proposing them. The secretary of the Committee was to be an unpaid official; and the success of the I.L.P. in securing this post for their nominee, Ramsay MacDonald, was facilitated by the fact that only he could afford to accept an unpaid post—there were no other candidates.

In many ways the choice of MacDonald as secretary was an excellent one. It would have been very difficult to find an equally efficient administrator to take on the job; and Mac-Donald, if not a trade unionist, was at least of working-class origin. His past record of friendship with the Liberals suited most of the trade-union leaders, while it was a source of gratification to the I.L.P. to have one of their members in the key post of the new party. The S.D.F., which had always had a deep distrust of his opportunism, at once put it about that he had been elected by mistake for their own member, James Macdonald, the Secretary of the London Trades Council[1]; but this seems unlikely, as it is difficult to believe that the bulk of the unions would have favoured the election of a member of the S.D.F.

The I.L.P. rightly regarded the results of the conference as a great success for their policy. By careful examination of what was practicable they had carried all the proposals that they put before the delegates; and even John Burns, who was present as a representative of the Engineers, had been forced to support their amendments. Among the other Socialists, however, the significance of the conference was not rated so high. The S.D.F., with customary disregard for tactical considerations, denounced the I.L.P. attitude as 'treachery' to Socialism,[2] a remark which caused a complete break in all relations between the executives of the two bodies. The Fabian Society took very little notice of the conference or of the committee it set up, not expecting it to be a success. And R. B. Suthers, the correspondent of the *Clarion*, which had no connexion with the arrangements, summed up his attitude in a way which shows us how doubtful many of the Socialists were of the future: 'At last there is a United Labour Party, or perhaps it would be safer to say, a little cloud, no

[1] *Justice*, 10 Mar. 1900; Hyndman, *Further Reminiscences*, pp. 268 ff.
[2] *Justice*, 3 Mar. 1900.

bigger than a man's hand, which may grow into a United Labour Party. . . .'[1]

(4)

Ramsay MacDonald said of the 1900 conference that some of the delegates attended 'to bury the attempt in good-humoured tolerance' and a few even 'to make sure it was buried'[2]; and for many months afterwards it seemed that the funeral, although postponed, might take place at any moment. The new body was not yet called the 'Labour Party', or the 'United Labour Party' as Hardie suggested, but described itself more modestly as the 'Labour Representation Committee', which soon became abbreviated to 'L.R.C.'. Its meagre financial arrangements limited it to the very minimum of organization, for it had been feared that many trade unions would not have supported it if any considerable expense had been required of them. As it was, by no means all the unions represented at the inauguration decided to join at once. The Engineers' delegates had carefully avoided office because they were doubtful of being able to affiliate: and in fact the Society's executive at first did decide against joining. This blow to the early hopes of the L.R.C. may perhaps be explained by the fact that the Engineers were for the moment hostile to co-operation with other unions as a result of the dispute which had led to their temporary withdrawal from the T.U.C. Another union which decided not to affiliate was the Lancashire and Cheshire Miners Confederation, the only coal-miners' union to attend the inaugural conference. Their leader, Tom Greenall, had been elected vice-chairman of the L.R.C., but he was now obliged to resign. MacDonald, who had established the office of the L.R.C. in a room at his flat in Lincoln's Inn Fields, sent out circulars to all the unions inviting them to join. Naturally he made the most of the current arguments about the increased industrial and political strength of the employers as a result of combination and federation.[3] But the total

[1] *Clarion*, 10 Mar. 1900.
[2] J. R. MacDonald, *The Socialist Movement* (1911), p. 235.
[3] 'Today capital is federated for industrial as well as political purposes. . . . The control of capital over labour is enormously increased. This new power of capital is already represented in Parliament' (L.R.C. First Circular, 23 Mar. 1900).

union membership crept up very slowly at first, and after a full year had only just reached 350,000, whereas about 570,000 had been represented at the foundation. The principal unions that had joined were the Railway Servants, the two main dockers' unions, the Gasworkers, the two printers' unions, the Boot and Shoe Operatives, and a number of unions in heavy industry— Blastfurnacemen, Ironfounders, Steelsmelters and Shipwrights. Between them, these accounted for five-sevenths of the total numbers, and the rest were unions with memberships of less than 10,000 each.[1]

In September 1900 the South African War appeared to be coming to a victorious conclusion, and in October the Conservative government suddenly dissolved Parliament, rightly judging the moment opportune for a renewal of its mandate. It was not surprising that the L.R.C. was unable to organize the labour vote adequately at such an early stage of its career. There were as yet no central funds to finance contests, and the Committee could do no more than endorse the candidates, proposed by its constituent bodies. Out of a total L.R.C. expenditure in its first year of less than £200, only £33 was spent directly on the General Election.[2]

The candidatures endorsed by the L.R.C. were fifteen in number, eight of them being proposed by the I.L.P. and another one jointly by the I.L.P. and S.D.F. Four general secretaries of trade unions stood for election: Richard Bell, of the Railway Servants, at Derby; Thorne, of the Gasworkers, who had taken over Hardie's old constituency, West Ham South; John Hodge, of the Steelsmelters, at Gower, Glamorgan; and Alexander Wilkie, of the Shipwrights, who fought Sunderland. Hardie stood for two constituencies, Preston and Merthyr Tydfil, not deliberately but because in the rush of electoral preparations he had to consider more than one nomination and in the end found he could not withdraw from Merthyr, where he thought his chances were slight.[3] Nearly all his campaigning was done at Preston, but the strong pro-war feeling and the bitter antagonism between

---

[1] See below, Appendix B.
[2] *L.R.C. Report*, 1901, p. 11.
[3] *I.L.P. News*, Oct. 1900.

Catholics and Protestants worked to his disadvantage.[1] To the Nonconformist Welsh miners, on the other hand, imperialism had little appeal; and so it was at Merthyr that he was elected.

The other I.L.P. candidates were defeated, but they fared well under the circumstances of the election. Their average poll was double that of 1895, and Jowett was within 41 votes of winning West Bradford in a straight fight and with a total poll of almost 10,000. A considerable proportion of the improved voting figure, however, was due to Liberal support in some of the constituencies. The only other successful L.R.C. candidate besides Hardie was Richard Bell of the Railway Servants, who ran with one Liberal against two Conservatives in a double constituency. A party of two M.P.s—especially two who differed in political standpoint as did Hardie and Bell, for Bell was no Socialist—could hardly be expected to shape a new Parliamentary tradition.[2]

But it was just at this point that a new complexion was put on the problem of the L.R.C.'s future by the result of the Taff Vale case. This concerned a strike against the Taff Vale Railway Company by its employees, led by those who were members of the Amalgamated Society of Railway Servants. The company sought an injunction against the Society's officers, and won its case in the High Court. In the Court of Appeal the Society's plea for immunity under trade-union legislation was accepted, and the decision was reversed; but the company took the case to the Lords and there finally secured a judgement against the Railway Servants.

The judgement of the Lords was given in July 1901, but as early as September 1900, when the High Court made the initial decision against the Society, the case caused great agitation in the trade-union world: for if the funds of the unions were to be liable for damages caused by their members during strikes, they would not dare to undertake strike action for fear of financial ruin. The final effect of the Taff Vale case was reinforced by a further case decided by the Lords early in August 1901, that

---

[1] Glasier to Hardie, 8 Aug. 1900 (Glasier Correspondence).
[2] For Hardie's opinion of Bell—'a genial ass'—see his letter to Lowe, 26 Apr. 1901 (Lowe, *From Pit to Parliament*, p. 196).

of *Quinn* v. *Leathem*, in which judgement was given against a union for boycotting an employer.

The significance of these legal decisions was interpreted by the labour movement against the background of the employers' counter-offensive against the unions, to which reference has already been made, and which appeared at the time to be constantly gathering momentum. Already in 1900 *The Times* had reiterated the argument that the reason for the competitive advantage of American industry was its comparative freedom from trade unions[1]; and in 1901–2 this was followed by a series of articles, 'The Crisis of British Industry', in which the unions were blamed for 'ca' canny', opposition to mechanization and other restrictive activities.[2] The suggestion that Britain might fashion her economy on the American model alarmed the labour leaders. The Trades Union Congress echoed year after year to the complaints of the American fraternal delegates about the 'tyrannical conditions' which were being imposed by the trusts.[3] It was widely accepted by economists in this country that there was some truth in the forebodings: W. J. Ashley, for instance, said that 'the formation of a capitalistic combination undoubtedly puts the employers in a position of advantage in the bargaining for wages'[4]; and H. W. Macrosty wrote: 'American experience gives us reason for expecting that trusts . . . will be able to dispense with the services of a large number of workpeople, whose competition will tend to reduce wages.'[5] All these reasons combined to convince trade unionists that it was essential to prevent things in this country developing as in

[1] 'Militant trade unions have been the chief means of stopping the advance of British engineering industry, and in the interests of the men, as well as of the rest of the nation, their unreasonable and pernicious rule must be suppressed' ('American Engineering Competition: The Labour Problem', *The Times*, 11 June 1900 (continued 10 July 1900)).

[2] *The Times*, 21 Nov. 1901–16 Jan. 1902. The articles were actually written by E. A. Pratt, industrial correspondent of *The Times*, who published them as a book in 1904 under the title *Trade Unionism and British Industry*. But Collison of the National Free Labour Association was widely regarded as his source. The Management Committee of the General Federation of Trade Unions rapidly published a *Reply to* The Times *Attack on Trade Unionism* (1901). See also Mantoux and Alfassa, op. cit. pp. 85 ff., 316.

[3] *T.U.C. Report*, 1901, p. 55.

[4] Address to British Economic Association, Mar. 1899, reprinted in W. J. Ashley, *Surveys Historic and Economic* (1900), pp. 378 ff.

[5] H. W. Macrosty, *Trusts and the State* (1901), pp. 314 f.

America. The best way to defeat any attempt to tamper with the law was, of course, to build up a strong position in the legislature, and for this a separate Parliamentary party was necessary. Accordingly, we find the President of the Boot and Shoe Operatives telling his Society's general conference in June 1900:

> It may be necessary yet for the Trade Unionists of the country to support a separate Parliamentary body to look after the enactments as already there is a danger in America that the unions will not be allowed to use their funds for the protection of their members in times of strikes by paying their benefit. . . .[1]

This was before Taff Vale: the effects of that decision were to be seen in deeds rather than in words. The prospects of the Labour Representation Committee at once enormously improved. The affiliated membership rapidly increased from 375,000 in February 1901 to 469,000 a year later and to 861,000 in 1903. In 1902–3 the new accessions included several large unions: the Engineers made up their minds at last, and even the conservative Lancashire Textile Workers came in, alarmed at the threat to their massive funds. Moreover, this took place at a time when the commitments involved by membership were being heavily increased: for in 1902 the L.R.C. conference instructed its Committee to prepare a plan for raising a central fund to finance Parliamentary candidates and to maintain members of parliament. The acceptance in 1903 of arrangements made in accordance with these instructions was an indication that the L.R.C. was really being taken seriously by the trade-union movement; and the by-election successes of the L.R.C. at Clitheroe in 1902 and at Woolwich and Barnard Castle in 1903 showed what potential strength it had. It only required a fresh dissolution of Parliament and a General Election, and then the L.R.C. would be able to appear on the Parliamentary stage in its appropriate role of 'the Labour Party'.

[1] *N.U. Boot and Shoe Operatives Conference Report*, 1900.

CHAPTER XI
Conclusion

(1)

THE preceding narrative has examined the origins of the Labour Party almost entirely from the standpoint of the Socialists. This has been necessary because the Socialists were the one active political group interested in bringing the party into being. They alone could provide a programme which would make it distinct and separate from the existing parties. Without a programme, as Engels realized, there could be no such party on a permanent basis, and every attempt to found one would fail. Indeed, the political independence of the Labour Party always seemed to be in doubt until in 1918 it accepted a Socialist constitution. In addition, the Socialists possessed a faith in the righteousness and ultimate victory of their cause which acted as a powerful driving force. This faith was based, ultimately, upon the analysis of society first presented by Marx and Engels in the Communist Manifesto of 1848, and elaborated in their subsequent writings. However much the analysis was modified, as by Hyndman and the Fabians, and simplified for popular consumption, as by Morris and Blatchford, it still had a certain comprehensive reality for those who accepted it. To its working-class adherents it gave a sense of purpose and pride in class consciousness; to others it afforded the consolation that they were working in harmony with the tendencies of social change.

The history of the world has often shown the dynamic qualities of a faith devoutly held, like that of the early Christians, the Ottomans, or the Calvinists. It does not matter if the faith feeds on illusions, for it is capable of conquering reality. Socialism had this quality for the early members of the S.D.F., the Socialist League and the I.L.P. It led them at times into foolish misstatements, such as that of *Justice* in 1885: 'If Socialism were the

Conclusion

law in England every worker would get at least four times his
present wages for half his present work. Don't you call that
practical politics?'[1] or such as Blatchford's declaration in *Merrie
England* that 'this country is capable of feeding more than treble
her present population'.[2] But the faith did not stand or fall by
the accuracy of facts and figures: it depended much less for its
sources and strength upon reason than upon deeper and simpler
forces in human nature. 'Socialism', said Shaw in 1897, 'wins its
disciples by presenting civilization as a popular melodrama, or
as a Pilgrim's Progress through suffering, trial, and combat
against the powers of evil to the bar of poetic justice with para-
dise beyond.'[3] It was this crusading zeal which drew attention
to the Socialists in the eighties, and enabled them, like the
Narodniks in Russia with whom Kropotkin compared them,[4]
to have an influence in politics far beyond what their numbers
justified; it was this again which gave the early I.L.P. the
strength to play such an important part in the negotiations for
the making of the L.R.C. The Socialists made up in energy and
enthusiasm for their lack of numbers: in spite of their eccen-
tricities and discords, they formed, in a real sense, a political *élite*.
When it came to fighting elections—speaking at street-corners,
canvassing, delivering manifestos—the man with the red tie was
worth a score of his more easy-going fellow trade-unionists—a
fact that the union leaders were obliged to take into account in
drawing up the terms of the alliance in 1900.

Not all the Socialists, however, could claim to have made a
valuable contribution to the formation of the new party. The
S.D.F. originated in a labour revolt against the middle-class
National Liberal Federation: yet in the course of a few years it
came to embody an attitude of exclusiveness and hostility to all
save the initiates of its own narrow creed. Engels resented the
fact that it had 'managed to reduce the Marxist theory of
development to a rigid orthodoxy'.[5] Hyndman's was a doctrin-
aire radicalism, full of echoes of Tom Paine and the Jacobins,
but barren of revolutionary technique.

[1] *Justice*, 29 Aug. 1885.   [2] Blatchford, *Merrie England*, pp. 21, 28 ff.
[3] G. B. Shaw, 'The Illusions of Socialism', in E. Carpenter (ed.), *Forecasts of the Coming Century* (1897), p. 171.   [4] Kropotkin, *Memoirs of a Revolutionist*, ii. 314.
[5] To Sorge, 12 May 1894 (*Labour Monthly*, 1934, p. 755).

217

The fact was that the British working class as a whole had no use for the conception of violent revolution. Any leader who failed to recognize this could not expect to win widespread support. Economic grievances could temporarily arouse bitter discontent as they had done in the early years of the industrial revolution: the Norwich shoemakers who joined the Socialist League were, like the Chartist hand-loom weavers, making a protest against the harshness of the extending industrial system, which had no use for their craftsmanship. But dislocations of this type were for the most part transitory: a permanent political organization of the working class needed to disavow the use of violence. Only those who recognized this could effectively set on foot a movement to form a Labour Party.

The Fabian Society performed the essential service of adapting Marxist theory to a form compatible with British constitutional practice. For this purpose they drew heavily on indigenous Radical ideas, on Mill and the Benthamites, on the Positivists and on the historical economists. All this work of synthesis was a vital contribution to the British Labour movement. But the literary tradition of the past half-century which has favoured the Fabians so strongly should not lead us to conclude that they had much direct part in the establishment of the Labour Representation Committee. For their tactics were too subtle and too compromising for the working class to adopt as its own. In this period, the Fabians were never ready to believe that the time was ripe for the formation of a new party. It was not without reason that Hyndman and later Champion described them as 'the Micawber club'. The failure of permeation, in which they had placed such high hopes, turned their complacency to gloom, and by the end of the century the most prominent members of the Society were falling into that attitude of distrust of democratic processes that is so clearly reflected in Shaw's *Man and Superman* (1903). They thought that the L.R.C. would fail just as they believed the I.L.P. had failed, and in 1906 Shaw had so far despaired of it as to publicly 'apologise to the Universe for my connexion with such a party'.[1]

Apart from the early efforts of Engels and the Marx-Ave-

[1] *Clarion*, 2 Feb. 1906.

lings, therefore, it is Champion and his associates who deserve
the credit for devoting themselves to propaganda on behalf of a
Labour Party. The example of independence to which they
constantly pointed was that of the Irish Nationalists, who had
held Parliament to ransom in 1885-6. The Irish example held
good in the years leading up to the formation of the I.L.P. in
1893, and was repeatedly cited by Champion himself, by Keir
Hardie, and by others. But from 1893 onwards the I.L.P. began
to provide its own examples of the value of independence. It had
the initial support of Engels, and Aveling helped to draw up its
programme: yet it was steadfastly constitutional in its attitude,
although this was not explicitly stated at its foundation. Within
the limits of constitutionalism, however, it seemed to be determined to fight its battles without compromise. It paid for its
own politics, and was not afraid to publish its balance-sheet to
the world. It was this which made the political scientist Ostrogorski describe it as 'a novel phenomenon in the life of English
party organization'.[1] It governed itself by means of a supreme
annual conference—a democratic device inherited from the
trade unions, but not at that time accepted by any existing
political party, for we must remember that the conferences of
the National Liberal Federation had no control over the Liberal
Party machinery.[2] Further, the I.L.P. showed that, poor as it
was, it could fight elections against both Liberals and Conservatives and yet secure polls that were no discredit to the cause. It
was a party with a future; and, given the support of the trade
unions, it was obvious that the future would be rich in Parliamentary success.

The greatest achievement of Keir Hardie and his I.L.P. lay
in the capture of trade-union support as early as 1900. The
whole strategy of the party from its foundation in 1893 was
based on the conception of collaboration with trade unionists
with the ultimate object of tapping trade-union funds for the

[1] Ostrogorski, *Democracy and the Organisation of Political Parties*, i. 576.
[2] In any case, the N.L.F. Conference was mainly for propaganda purposes—as
Spence Watson, its President in 1891, put it, 'for making certain declarations. It
is not—and I want to be particularly clear on this point—for the decision of
subjects.' He said this in order to prevent Sidney Webb moving an amendment to
a resolution (*N.L.F. Conference Report*, 1891, p. 42).

attainment of Parliamentary power. It was primarily to defend this strategy that Hardie fought tooth and nail against fusion with the S.D.F. His attitude was justified by the behaviour of the S.D.F. leaders at the critical moment of the formation of the new party—their intransigence at the foundation conference and their decision eighteen months later to secede.

In 1900 Hardie retired from the chairmanship of the I.L.P., which he had held since the post was instituted. He had often previously made a show of wanting to give way to others, and he could no longer expect to be 'drafted' into office now that the immediate object of establishing an alliance with the unions had been achieved. Blatchford was continuing to demand that all officials of the party should be retired after a single year's service.[1] This was a conception of democracy that Hardie believed to be utterly impractical, for he had learned from his own experience in trade unionism and politics that '. . . for a long time to come democracy—even social democracy—will mean finding the fit person, and loyally and generously trusting him or her in the performance of the allotted task'.[2] He believed, with Carlyle, that history is made by great men, who can provide leadership for others. He was conscious that no one could guide the I.L.P. as well as himself, and in spite of all the principles of 'democracy' he was determined to continue giving it that guidance in the pages of the *Labour Leader*, which remained in his personal control. It was significant that whenever conference time came round he was careful to insert a note in the paper urging the branches not to follow the practice of binding their delegates to strict instructions, but to leave them free to be influenced by the debate, which would of course be dominated by himself and his colleagues.

Now that he had to leave the chairmanship, Hardie retired with good grace. The party was still devoted to his policy, and he was succeeded by a close personal friend, Bruce Glasier, a mild-tempered propagandist who had had a long career of activity since the early days of the Socialist League. Glasier had

---

[1] *Clarion*, 3 Nov. 1894, for his enunciation of this doctrine at the outset of Hardie's career as President of the I.L.P.
[2] *Labour Leader*, 10 Apr. 1897.

Conclusion

been a Clarion Van lecturer, and was in the almost unique position of being friendly with Blatchford as well as with Hardie. The I.L.P. was at this time deeply in debt, so deeply that the Council was only saved from bankruptcy by the generosity of wealthy supporters such as George Cadbury, who as a Quaker appreciated their stand against the war, and gave £500 to the election fund.[1] But with Hardie's re-election to Parliament, and, in the following years, the reaction against imperialism, the I.L.P.'s position steadily improved, and it began to build itself up again and to gain fresh recruits. By 1906 it was as strong as it ever had been, even though it had not yet felt the full force of the Socialist revival of that time.

By contrast, the resignation of Hyndman from the leadership of the S.D.F. was pathetically undignified. At the turn of the century the impatient pioneer was in very low spirits, seeing the decline in numbers that the Federation had suffered and the weakening of its members' intransigence towards the Radicals.[2] In September he admitted privately his 'utter disgust with the workers here in general, and with our own party in particular', and he added in a phrase all too typical of his own personal arrogance, 'Neither deserve to have men of ability from the educated class to serve them. . . . Liebknecht at any rate had the satisfaction of feeling the movement going well under him all his life.'[3] In August 1901 he withdrew from the S.D.F. executive, complaining sadly of the lack of 'class consciousness and class antagonism' even among the members, and declaring himself 'deeply discouraged at the results of our long-continued propaganda'.[4] Yet he too had left his closest associates in control of the organization; at the very time that Hyndman retired, they were withdrawing the Federation from participation in the L.R.C.; and it was not long before he was again in office,

[1] *I.L.P. News*, Nov. 1900; P. Snowden, 'The Rise of Labour', *New Leader*, 1 Feb. 1924. That this assistance endangered the I.L.P. policy of independence is clear from Cadbury's letter to Herbert Gladstone, the Liberal Chief Whip, on 8 Oct. 1900: 'I hope that any influence that I have acquired will be used to prevent the I.L.P opposing Liberals; if this is not the case they will get no more from me.' (Herbert Gladstone papers, B.M. Add. MSS. 46048.)
[2] For his opposition to the S.D.F. decision to support certain Radical candidates, see his letter to *Ethical World*, 18 Aug. 1900.
[3] To Neil Maclean, 3 Sept. 1900, quoted *Socialist*, Dec. 1904.
[4] To S.D.F. Executive, quoted *Labour Leader*, 17 Aug. 1901.

flaying the rest of the Socialist movement with his incessant, bitter denunciations.

(2)

But the Labour Representation Committee represented an alliance of forces in which the Socialists, organized as such, were only a tiny fraction. Some attempt has been made above, especially in the last chapter, to show what were the factors impelling the trade unions to join in the new political party: and many of these factors could be fully appreciated by men who did not respond to the Socialist appeal. The Labour Party was in fact not committed to Socialism as a political creed until 1918; and both before and after that date, but especially in the early years of its existence, it contained many who were hostile to it.

All along, there is little doubt that most of the non-Socialist trade-union leaders would have been happy to stay in the Liberal Party—which most of them had belonged to in the past —if the Liberals had made arrangements for a larger representation of the working class among their Parliamentary candidates. Again and again, it was the fault of the official Liberal Party constituency caucuses that this did not happen; and it was the behaviour of these caucuses that set many of the leaders of the workers thinking in terms of a separate party. Even Keir Hardie's revolt at Mid-Lanark in 1888 had been directed, not against the policy of Gladstone, but against the system by which the local association chose its candidate. The subsequent success of the I.L.P. was largely due to the failure of its rivals, the Labour Electoral Association, to make any satisfactory terms with the Liberal Party for the fuller representation of Labour. Threlfall himself, the trade-union leader who ran the L.E.A. and was responsible for the whole attempt to bargain with the Liberals on behalf of Labour, was forced to confess the complete failure of his policy. He wrote in 1894:

> Theoretically the caucus is a perfect machine, but in practice it is one-sided. . . . It is a curious commentary upon this 'ideal system' that of the thirteen Labour members representing

Conclusion

England and Wales in the present House, four ran in opposition to or without recognizing the existence of the caucus, five represent constituencies where the miners absolutely dominate the position . . . and only four either captured the caucus or out-generalled it. It is only a waste of time to advise the working classes to attend and make the caucus what they want it to be. The fact is they distrust it—they regard it as a middle-class machine; they have neither the time nor the inclination to compete with the wire-pullers who work it, and they have a decided objection to being made the puppets of anyone. It has served its purpose, and it has carried the people through one state of their development: but as it exists to-day it is too narrow and too much hampered with class prejudice to be a reflex of the expanding democratic and labour sentiment.[1]

It is true that the stubborn attitude of the local caucuses was realized and regretted by the principal leaders of the Liberal Party. Herbert Gladstone, for instance, later to be Liberal Chief Whip, admitted: 'The long and short of it is that the constituencies, for social, financial, and trade reasons are extremely slow to adopt Labour candidates'.[2] But the leaders could do little, the constitution of the party being what it was. Thomas Burt, himself a Liberal-Labour M.P., testified to their powerlessness in spite of their goodwill.[3] They could not force a Labour candidate on to a constituency: all that they could do, as Schnadhorst said, was to 'earnestly bespeak for him the generous support of the Liberal Association'.[4] Further, as the Fabians discovered, the usual type of local association did not respond satisfactorily to attempts to permeate it with 'advanced' men, for, as they had to admit, the moment permeation was carried beyond a certain point it was nullified by 'the bankruptcy of the swamped caucus'—that is to say, the people with the money refused to go on financing it.[5]

The principal reason why money was required was that there existed at this time no system for the payment of members of

[1] *Nineteenth Century*, Feb. 1894.   [2] *Albemarle*, Feb. 1892.
[3] *Daily Chronicle*, 13 Jan. 1893.
[4] Letter to Metropolitan Radical Federation, quoted *Yorkshire Factory Times*, 27 Mar. 1891. The M.R.F. had demanded the withdrawal of fifty Liberal candidates to make room for working men (*N.L.F. Conference Report*, 1891, p. 18).
[5] *Fabian Election Manifesto* (Tract No. 40, 1892), p. 8.

223

parliament: and here again the Liberal Party was found wanting. This was a reform that the Liberal leaders might well have taken up at a much earlier date than they did. If carried or at lest urgently pressed by the 1892–5 Liberal government, it might have removed a main factor in the support given by the smaller unions to the idea of a separate Labour Party.[1] E. Cowey of the Yorkshire Miners, a prominent Liberal-Labour leader, made this clear when he moved a resolution at the 1897 T.U.C. in favour of State payment of M.P.s:

> Mr. Cowey said that money was still the golden key that opened the door to a seat in the House of Commons. Only large and powerful societies could have their own members in the House, for only such societies could afford to keep their representatives in such a responsible and expensive position. For this reason he claimed that the payment of members was absolutely necessary to the success of the Labour movement.[2]

Yet although it had figured in the Newcastle programme of 1891, it was not until 1911, after the Osborne judgement, that the Liberal Party found it desirable to give priority to this reform and to pass it into law; and in the meantime the small unions had wedded themselves to the Labour Party idea.

For these reasons it is not difficult to see why the Liberal Party failed to retain the popularity that it had once had among the responsible leaders of trade unionism. There was justice in Ramsay MacDonald's observation to Herbert Samuel: 'We didn't leave the Liberals. They kicked us out and slammed the door in our faces.'[3] The failure of the Liberals to make any gesture of response to the growing electoral power of Labour was directly responsible for the early demise of the Labour Electoral Association. Founded originally in 1886, it reached the climax of its activities in 1891, when it was claimed that the delegates at its Congress represented an aggregate of 750,000 members of trade unions, of trades councils, and of ten local branches of the Association.[4] The first two points in its political

---

[1] Lord Rosebery, when Prime Minister, met a T.U.C. deputation on this issue, but refused to give it any high priority (*The Times*, 21 Nov. 1894).
[2] W. J. Davis, *British T.U.C.* (1916), ii. 137 f.
[3] To Samuel, 16 Aug. 1895 (quoted Samuel, *Memoirs*, p. 26).
[4] *L.E.A. Conference Report*, 1895.

programme were demands for the State payment of M.P.s and the payment of Returning Officers' fees out of the rates. Yet the Liberal Party took almost no notice of it, and the result was that after the ignominy of two General Elections in which it secured no concessions, it faded away in 1895–6. In inverse ratio to the decline of the L.E.A., the I.L.P. steadily established itself in those years as the hope of the working class for a say in Parliament.

(3)

The early components of the Labour Party formed a curious mixture of political idealists and hard-headed trade unionists: of convinced Socialists and loyal but disheartened Gladstonians. The great difficulty the L.R.C. had to face was the maintenance of an independent political line by all its members. Richard Bell, one of the only two M.P.s representing the party in the 1900 Parliament, saw no need to hold himself aloof from the Liberals, and in 1904–5, when he refused to sign the Labour Party constitution, he had to be expelled.[1] Similar trouble, though not leading to expulsion, was experienced with the three Labour M.P.s elected at by-elections before 1906: two of them—Shackleton and Arthur Henderson—had to be reprimanded in 1904 for appearing in support of a Liberal by-election candidate.[2] It was only in 1906, with the election of a substantial group of thirty M.P.s who drew a regular salary from the L.R.C. fund, that the Labour Party was put on a firm footing inside Parliament.

Part of the trouble had arisen from the extreme weakness of the Socialist societies both numerically and financially, as compared with the trade unions. The contributions to the party funds were computed on the basis of the membership of the

---

[1] It was lucky for Hardie and the Socialist wing that Bell was the only non-Socialist L.R.C. candidate to win in 1900. Wilkie, for instance, although the Vice-Chairman of the L.R.C., allowed himself to be completely identified with the Liberal Party in the course of the election campaign. He was adopted as an official Liberal candidate, and fought the Sunderland constituency, which was a double seat, on a joint platform with a Liberal-Imperialist shipbuilding employer, G. B. Hunter of Swan & Hunter (*Sunderland Herald*, 26 Sept. 1900).

[2] Minutes, L.R.C. Executive, 30 June 1904.

affiliated bodies, and even in 1901, before many trade unions had joined, the Socialist societies numbered less than one-sixteenth of the total affiliated membership. Matters were not improved in this respect by the secession of the S.D.F., for their two seats on the L.R.C. executive were assigned to extra union representatives, which considerably weakened the position of the Socialists. The Fabian Society had lost respect among the trade unionists for its willingness to compromise with jingoism; and the I.L.P. had so little support in the country that it was on the verge of utter bankruptcy. It is true that for reasons of prestige the I.L.P. regularly paid fees to the L.R.C. on a much higher figure of membership than it actually possessed: yet in 1906 this nominal figure was only 16,000, and the Socialist societies' proportion of the total contributing membership of the party had sunk to less than one-fiftieth.

Furthermore, many of the political difficulties of the Labour Party's early years arose from the fact that the I.L.P. itself, for all its insistence on the principles of independence, was frequently inclined to take the Liberal point of view. It was assumed as a matter of course that Free Trade was right and Protection wrong, since the latter was proposed by Joseph Chamberlain; and the strong Nonconformist ties of the party naturally led it to disapprove of the Education Act of 1902, which Sidney Webb had had a hand in designing. The *Manchester Guardian* was able to say of the 1901 I.L.P. conference that: 'What must strike a Liberal . . . is, one would say, how much of the proceedings is devoted to the advocacy of traditional Liberal principles.'[1] After Champion was finally discredited, the ex-Liberals had it all their own way in the leadership. Ramsay MacDonald, whom Hardie described as the party's 'greatest intellectual asset', sided with the Liberals against the Fabian 'old gang' on almost every immediate issue of the time; and Hardie, who had been much more friendly to the Radicals since the outbreak of the South African War,[2] in

[1] *Manchester Guardian*, 10 Apr. 1901.
[2] Hardie, in a letter to Henry Demarest Lloyd of 13 Dec. 1900, privately delared his eagerness to win Liberal support. 'The Radicals of the old Bright and Gladstone school are thoroughly disgusted with their party and this war, whilst the semi-Socialist Radicals here have strong leanings our way. I am hopeful therefore that

October 1901 publicly advocated a 'frank, open, and above-board agreement . . . for well-defined purposes' with the anti-war Liberals.[1] There was little enthusiasm for this among the Socialist rank-and-file; yet eighteen months later Hardie was apparently prepared to connive at MacDonald's secret electoral understanding with the Liberal whips.[2] With the leaders of the Socialist wing acting in this fashion, how could the non-Socialist elements be expected to keep clear of Liberalism?

(4)

Still, by 1903 the new party machine was in existence, and whatever the political views of its officers, it soon began to build up among them a vested interest in its maintenance. The officials of the great trade unions had made up their minds in favour of a distinct party of their own, and so long as their industrial strength continued to grow, the strength of the political organization would also increase. In the years that followed, there were doubts at times about the value of political action; there were personal feuds among the leaders as well as disagreements on policy; there were stresses and strains arising from war and revolution in Europe. Some of the unions, such as the Miners, suffered much in the vicissitudes of the British economy and became more radical; others, such as the new unions of 1889, moved in the opposite direction. But the unity of the party, once established, remained substantially intact, and in the first half-century of its life, every General Election but two that it fought resulted in an increase of the aggregate Labour poll. The association of Socialist faith and trade-union interest, of hope for an ideal future and fear for an endangered present, seemed on the point of disruption at times: yet it survived, for a variety of reasons which lie outside the compass of this book,

---

by careful cultivation of all these different elements we may between now and another General Election have the nucleus of the Party of the future' (H. D. Lloyd Correspondence).

[1] *Labour Leader*, 26 Oct. 1901.

[2] For an account of this, see Bealey and Pelling, *Labour and Politics, 1900–1906*, chap. vi.

but also because in the years before the party's birth there had been men and women who believed that the unity of the working-class movement, both in industry and politics, was an object to be striven for, just as now most of their successors regard it as an achievement to be maintained.

APPENDIX A

MEMBERSHIP OF NATIONAL SOCIALIST SOCIETIES TO 1901

A = Membership paying dues to central office (normally
1s. per year).
B = Total membership claimed by officers.
Unless otherwise stated, the figures, are drawn from the
annual reports of the national organizations concerned.

Date	Social Democratic Federation		Socialist League		Fabian Society	
					London	Provincial Societies
	A	B	A	B	A and B	B
1884	...	500[a]	...	...	...	...
1885	...	...	...	...	...	...
1886	...	...	?280[b]	550[b]	c.90[c]	...
1887	689[a]	...	...	c.700[b]	...	...
1888	c.790[a]	...	...	...	...	...
1889	?900[a]	1,926[a]	...	...	130[c]	...
1890	...	...	...	...	173	...
1891	...	...	...	...	361	350–400
1892	...	...	*Independent Labour Party*		541	c.1300
1893	...	...	A[d]	B	640	...
1894	...	4,500[e]	4,504	...	681	...
1895	...	10,536[f]	10,720	{50,000[g] / 35,000}	699	...
1896	...	...	6,300	20,000	739	...
1897	1,220[h]	...	8,632	...	816	...
1898	...	...	8,980	...	835	...
1899	2,680[h]	...	7,092	...	861	...
1900	...	...	6,084	...	811	...
1901	...	9,000[i]	5,145	13,000[i]	861[i]	...

[a] See above, p. 44, n. 1.　　　　[b] See above, p. 44, n. 2.
[c] See above, p. 45, n. 1.
[d] Figures in this column are calculated from the total of dues given in the annual balance-sheet. In the first two years (to 1895) the fee was only 3d. per year per member.　　　[e] See above p. 169.
[f] International Socialist Workers and Trade Union Congress, *Report of Proceedings* (1896), p. 66.
[g] See above, p. 164, n. 1.　　　　[h] See above, p 170, n. 1 and 2.
[i] Number on which affiliation fee to L.R.C. was based.

APPENDIX B

LIST OF PRINCIPAL TRADE UNIONS AFFILIATED TO L.R.C., MARCH 1901

(arranged in order of size)

		Affiliation Membership	Date of Foundation
1.	Railway Servants, Amalgamated	60,000	1871
2.	Gasworkers and General Labourers	48,038	1889
3.	Boot and Shoe Operatives, National Union	32,084	1874
4.	Ironfounders	18,357	1809
5.	Shipwrights, Associated	18,000	1882
6.	Typographical Association	16,000	1849
7.	Dock, Wharf, Riverside and General Workers	13,829	1887
8.	Dock Labourers, National Union	12,000	1889
9.	Compositors, London Society	11,415	1785
10.	Steel Smelters, British Amalgamated	10,509	1886
11.	Blastfurnacemen, National Federation	10,000	1881
12.	Brassworkers, National Amalgamated	10,000	1872
13.	Builders' Labourers, United	9,000	1889
14.	Shop Assistants, National Union	8,000	1891
15.	Miners, North Yorks and Cleveland	7,283	1872
16.	Decorators and Painters, Amalgamated Society of House	5,245	1873
17.	Coal Porters	5,000	1887
18.	Dyers, Amalgamated Society of	5,000	1878
19.	Navvies, Bricklayers' Labourers, &c.	5,000	1889
20.	Enginemen and Cranemen, National Amalgamated Society	4,016	1893
21.	Labourers Union, National Amalgamated	4,000	1889
22.	Railway Workers, General	4,000	1889
23.	Workers Union	4,000	1898
24.	Gasworkers, Brickmakers, &c., Amalgamated Society	4,000	1889
	Total affiliated membership of 24 largest unions	324,776	

Total affiliated membership of all 41 unions, 353,070.

(The total number of trade unions in Britain at the end of 1900 was 1,272, with an aggregate membership of 1,905,116.)

Appendix B

In addition, three Socialist Societies were affiliated with a total membership of 22,861 (see Appendix A) and also the following Trades Councils:

Leeds	15,000
Leicester	20,000
Woolwich	?
Bradford	10,000
Birmingham	25,000
Sunderland	7,000
Manchester	24,000

(There were 171 Trades Councils in existence at the end of 1900.)

Sources.—*L.R.C. Annual Report*, 1901; *Board of Trade Report on Trade Unions, 1900* (1901).

APPENDIX C

LIST OF UNPUBLISHED SOURCES CONSULTED

I. OFFICIAL DOCUMENTS

Labour Representation League, Minutes 1873–8; Labour Representation Committee, Executive Minutes, from 1900; Fabian Society Special Conference, June 1886, Minutes—Brit[ish] Lib[rary of] Pol[itical and Economic] Sci[ence].

Fabian Society Executive Minutes, from 1884; Secretary's Correspondence. By courtesy of the Fabian Society.

Socialist League, Secretary's Correspondence, 1885–8, and other official documents comprising the Nettlau Collection—Int[ernational] Inst[itute of] Soc[ial] Hist[ory, Amsterdam].

Socialist League, Statement of Membership, etc., 1886. By courtesy of Mr. John Mahon.

Hammersmith Branch, Socialist League, Minutes 1884–8—B[ritish] M[useum] Add[itional] M[anu]s[cript]s 45891–4.

I.L.P., National Administrative Council Minutes from 1893; London District Council, Minutes 1892–8; Reports from Head Office to N.A.C. Members, 1897–8; Preston Branch, Correspondence referring to 1900 Election. By courtesy of Mr. Francis Johnson.

Meltham Branch I.L.P., Minutes from 1899, and Contribution Book from 1893. By courtesy of Mr. J. Parker.

Keighley Branch I.L.P., Minutes from 1897. By courtesy of Keighley I.L.P.

Bradford Labour Church, Minutes 1892–4. By courtesy of Bradford I.L.P.

Birmingham Labour Church, Minutes 1894–8, 1903–10—Birmingham City Library.

London Trades Council, Minutes from 1891. By courtesy of London Trades Council.

II. PRIVATE DOCUMENTS

Correspondence of Marx, Engels, Eleanor Marx-Aveling, Scheu; manuscript autobiography and other documents of Joseph Lane—Int. Inst. Soc. Hist.

Correspondence of Henry Broadhurst; Mill-Taylor Correspondence; lecture notes of Philip Wicksteed, 1882–9; certain papers of J. Ramsay MacDonald and Margaret MacDonald; certain correspondence of George Lansbury—Brit. Lib. Pol. Sci.

Appendix C

Correspondence of Joseph Cowen—Newcastle-upon-Tyne City Library.

Correspondence of Thomas Davidson—Yale University Library, New Haven, Conn., U.S.A.

Correspondence of Henry George—New York Public Library, U.S.A. (Microfilm copy of letters exchanged with correspondents in Britain, kindly arranged by Professor Louis M. Hacker of Columbia University; now deposited at Brit. Lib. Pol. Sci.)

Papers of Edward Carpenter—Sheffield City Library.

Diaries and correspondence of John Burns (46281–46345); Socialist Diary of William Morris (45335); Correspondence of Herbert Gladstone (45985–46118)—B.M. Add. MSS.

Correspondence and other papers of Graham Wallas. By courtesy of Miss M. G. Wallas. Now at Brit. Lib. Pol. Sci.

Correspondence of Sidney and Beatrice Webb. By courtesy of Passfield trustees.

Manuscript History of Halifax I.L.P. by John Lister; documents relating to William Morris, Edward Carpenter, etc.—Mattison Collection, Brotherton Library, Leeds.

Diaries of Alf Mattison—Leeds City Library.

Correspondence of Alf Mattison. By courtesy of Mrs. Mattison.

Diary fragment of Keir Hardie; Correspondence and other documents relating to Mid-Lanark by-election, 1888; Correspondence of David Lowe. By courtesy of Mr. Francis Johnson.

Diary fragment and correspondence of Bruce Glasier. By courtesy of the late Mrs. K. Bruce Glasier.

Certain correspondence of Cunninghame Graham with H. H. Champion. By courtesy of Mrs. H. H. Champion.

Correspondence of G. B. Shaw and R. Blatchford with William Johnson. By courtesy of Mrs. William Johnson.

Correspondence of Henry Demarest Lloyd—Wisconsin State Historical Society, Madison, Wis. U.S.A. (I am grateful to Mr. R. V. Clements for extracts from letters exchanged with British correspondents.)

III. UNPUBLISHED RESEARCH THESES

D. W. Crowley, 'Origins of the Revolt of the British Labour Movement from Liberalism, 1875–1906'—Brit. Lib. Pol. Sci., 1952.

D. Good, 'Economic and Political Origins of the Labour Party, 1884–1906'—Brit. Lib. Pol. Sci., 1936.

E. J. Hobsbawm, 'Fabianism and the Fabians, 1884–1914'—Cambridge University Library, 1950.

R. D. Howland, 'Fabian Thought and Social Change in England, 1884 to 1914'—Brit. Lib. Pol. Sci., 1942.

W. K. Lamb, 'British Labour and Parliament, 1865 to 1893'—Brit. Lib. Pol. Sci., 1933.

S. Maddock, 'The Liverpool Trades Council and Politics, 1878–1918'—Liverpool University Library, 1959.

H. M. Pelling, 'Origins and Early History of the Independent Labour Party, 1880–1900'—Cambridge University Library, 1950.

C. T. Solberg, 'The Independent Labour Party, 1893 to 1918'—Oxford University, 1939. (I am grateful to Mr. Solberg for sending me a copy of his thesis.)

D. F. Summers, 'The Labour Church and Allied Movements of the late 19th and early 20th centuries'—Edinburgh University Library, 1958.

BIBLIOGRAPHICAL ESSAY

THIS essay is primarily a guide to further reading, in books and in current periodicals. It is not a comprehensive list of sources used in the preparation of this book. It omits the great bulk of primary sources, some of which are listed in Appendix C, and others of which are referred to in the footnotes. On the other hand, it includes many recently published works which were not available when the first edition of this book was in preparation. Although in the course of revision I have taken these works into account and have had occasion to refer to some of them in the footnotes, it will be obvious that I have not done so as much as I should have done had they been available when the first edition was being written.

Books mentioned below are published in London, unless otherwise stated.

1. GENERAL: BRITISH HISTORY IN THE LATE NINETEENTH CENTURY

The present generation of historians has so far produced no general study to replace those which were already in use twenty-five years ago. This is partly because the standard of the best earlier work was so high. Sir Robert Ensor's *England, 1870–1914* (Oxford, 1936), in the Oxford History of England series, is written with great insight and lucidity; in deaing with political and social history the author was able to draw upon knowledge derived from his own participation in the Socialist movement at the turn of the century. Elie Halévy's *History of the English People in 1895–1905* (1926) provides by far the best existing account of the main trends in social and political life for the years that it covers.

2. ECONOMIC HISTORY

Sir John Clapham's *Economic History of Modern Britain*, vols. 2 and 3 (Cambridge, 1932, 1938) is full of keen observation and cautious generalization which would be difficult to render obsolete. W. Ashworth, *Economic History of England, 1870–1939* (1960) contains, in shorter compass, the conclusions of more recent research. For a study of problems of trade and the trade cycle see W. W. Rostow, *British Economy of the Nineteenth Century* (Oxford, 1947) and A. E. Musson, 'The Great Depression in Britain: A Reappraisal', *Journal of Economic History*, vol. xix (1959). On agriculture, see the new edition of Lord Ernle's classic, *English Farming, Past and Present* (ed. G. E. Fussell and O. McGregor, 1961) and T. W. Fletcher, 'The Great Depression of English Agriculture, 1873–1896', *Economic History Review*, 2nd ser., vol. xiii (1960). On wages and living standards, A. L. Bowley, *Wages and Income in the United Kingdom since 1860* (Cambridge, 1937) has been supplemented by P. Deane and W. A. Cole, *British Economic Growth, 1688–1959* (Cambridge, 1962) and B. R. Mitchell, *Abstract of British Historical Statistics* (Cambridge, 1962).

3. SOCIAL AND INTELLECTUAL HISTORY

Much remains to be done in both these fields. The social investigators of the late nineteenth century provided much material. One thinks particularly of Charles Booth's *Life and Labour of the People* (17 vols. in the edition of 1902–3), which is an investigation of London only, but his interest at the time was largely confined to problems of poverty. On Booth, see T. S. Simey and M. B. Simey, *Charles Booth* (Oxford, 1960). B. S. Rowntree, *Poverty* (1902) is a study of York; on Rowntree, see A. Briggs, *Social Thought and Social Action* (1961). Study of other aspects of the period is only beginning, with such works as J. A. Banks, *Prosperity and Parenthood* (1954) and P. T. Cominos, 'Late Victorian Sexual Respectability and the Social System', *International Review of Social History*, vol. viii (1963). On urbanization, a pioneering work is A. Briggs, *Victorian Cities* (1963), and the same historian has been responsible for the most useful particular study, in his *History of Birmingham*, vol. 2, *1865–1938* (1952). The only comparable work is T. C. Barker and J. R. Harris, *A Merseyside Town in the Industrial Revolution: St. Helens, 1750–1900* (Liverpool, 1954); but H. J. Dyos, *Victorian Suburb: A Study of the Growth of Camberwell* (Leicester, 1960) is also of much value.

Mrs. H. M. Lynd's *England in the Eighteen-Eighties* (New York, 1945) is an attempt to trace the emergence of new attitudes of mind about social policy. Apart from Halévy's work, there is nothing comparable for the 1890's. Holbrook Jackson's *The Eighteen-Nineties* (1913), albeit a work of classic quality, is largely confined to literary and aesthetic matters.

4. WORKING OF THE ELECTORAL SYSTEM

H. J. Hanham, *Elections and Party Management* (1959) throws much fresh light on the politics of parliamentary elections in the 1870's and 1880's. There is no comparable work for the succeeding period; and the student who wishes to obtain a picture of the parliamentary system at the end of the century must turn to A. L. Lowell,

Bibliographical Essay

The Government of England (2 vols., New York, 1912). On franchise reform and the redistribution of seats, see C. Seymour, *Electoral Reform in England and Wales* (New Haven, Conn., 1915), which covers 1832 to 1885, and H. L. Morris, *Parliamentary Franchise Reform in England and Wales, 1885–1918* (New York, 1921). The financial aspects of politics are dealt with by W. B. Gwyn, *Democracy and the Cost of Politics* (1962) and, more narrowly, by C. O'Leary, *Elimination of Corrupt Practices in British Elections* (Oxford, 1962).

5. THE POLITICAL PARTIES

For extra-parliamentary political organization, M. Ostrogorski's *Democracy and the Organisation of Political Parties*, vol. 1 (1902) has not been superseded for this period. On the Conservative Party, there is a stimulating essay by R. B. McDowell, *British Conservatism, 1832–1914* (1959). Otherwise, information about policy and organization has to be gleaned from biographies, of which the most useful standard works will be found listed in Ensor, *England, 1870–1914*. Two recent studies throw light on these questions: E. A., Lord Chilston, *Chief Whip* (1961), which is about A. Akers-Douglas, and R. R. James, *Lord Randolph Churchill* (1959). For the history of the Liberal Party, we are similarly dependent on biographies, and it is regrettable that the recent works by Sir Philip Magnus, *Gladstone* (1954) and Roy Jenkins, *Sir Charles Dilke* (1958) have so little fresh to say on political questions. R. R. James, *Rosebery* (1963) is much more useful. For Liberal organization, see F. H. Herrick, 'Origins of the National Liberal Federation', *Journal of Modern History*, vol. xvii (1945) and B. McGill, 'Francis Schnadhorst and Liberal Party Organisation', ibid. vol. xxxiv (1962). On the party's relations with Nonconformity see Herrick's article and also J. F. Glaser, 'English Nonconformity and the Decline of Liberalism', *American Historical Review*, vol. lxiii (1958). For Wales and the Liberal Party, see the excellent study by K. O. Morgan, *Wales in British Politics, 1868–1922* (Cardiff, 1963). More light has been thrown on the career of Joseph Chamberlain by C. H. D. Howard, 'Joseph Chamberlain and the Unauthorised Programme', *English Historical Review*, vol. lxv (1950), by Chamberlain's own *Political Memoir, 1880–1892* (ed. C. H. D. Howard, 1953), and by M. C. Hurst, *Joseph Chamberlain and West Midland Politics, 1886–1895* (Dugdale Society, Stratford-on-Avon, 1962).

6. THE IRISH QUESTION

Important works on this subject have been published in recent years. C. C. O'Brien's *Parnell and His Party, 1880–1890* (Oxford,

237

1957) must rank high as a work of political analysis. It has been provided with an epilogue of matching quality in F. S. L. Lyons, *Fall of Parnell, 1890–91* (1960). Less dramatic, but valuable for details of political organization and parliamentary tactics, is F. S. L. Lyons, *The Irish Parliamentary Party, 1890–1910* (1951). The effect of the Irish question on British politics has been discussed in a provocative article by Sir Robert Ensor, 'Some Political and Economic Interactions in Later Victorian England', *Transactions of the Royal Historical Society*, 4th ser., vol. xxxi (1949). E. R. Strauss, *Irish Nationalism and British Democracy* (1951) exaggerates the importance of the economic factor but makes some interesting suggestions. For a valuable recent study of Unionist policy in Ireland, see L. P. Curtis, *Coercion and Conciliation in Ireland, 1880–1892* (Princeton, N.J., 1963). On the political role of the Irish in Britain, some information may be obtained from J. A. Jackson, *The Irish in Britain* (1963) and from J. E. Handley, *The Irish in Modern Scotland* (Cork, 1947). On the Unionist alliance in British politics see G. L. Goodman, 'Liberal Unionism: The Revolt of the Whigs', *Victorian Studies*, vol. iii (1959) and P. Fraser, 'The Liberal Unionist Alliance: Chamberlain, Hartington and the Conservatives, 1886–1904', *English Historical Review*, vol. lxxvii (1962).

7. LOCAL GOVERNMENT

The study of this subject can usefully start with K. B. Smellie, *History of Local Government* (1946). A fuller study is J. Redlich and F. W. Hirst, *Local Government in England* (2 vols., 1903). B. Keith-Lucas, *English Local Government Franchise* (Oxford, 1952) is of considerable historical value. For London, see G. Gibbon and R. W. Bell, *History of the London County Council, 1889–1939* (1939), and the less official H. Haward, *The London County Council from Within* (1932). On the Progressives, see A. G. Gardiner, *Sir John Benn and the Progressive Movement* (1925). E. G. Howarth and M. Wilson, *West Ham* (1907) has a section on local government.

8. THE SOCIALIST REVIVAL: IDEAS

The history of British Socialism in the nineteenth century may best be traced in M. Beer, *History of British Socialism* (1919) and in G. D. H. Cole, *History of Socialist Thought* (vols. 1–3, 1953–6). H. Pelling (ed.), *The Challenge of Socialism* (1954) is a selection of documents. A. B. Ulam, *Philosophical Foundations of English Socialism* (Cambridge, Mass., 1951) is a study of Socialist thought against the background of contemporary Idealism. The evolution of Social-

Bibliographical Essay

ist ideas is also very well described on a personal basis in Beatrice Webb's *My Apprenticeship* (1926).

9. RELATIONS WITH RADICALISM

On relations between Radicalism and Socialism see S. Maccoby, *English Radicalism, 1853–1886* (1938) and the sequel, *English Radicalism, 1886–1914* (1953). H. Pelling, *America and the British Left* (1956), chap. iv, deals with attitudes to America in the 1880's as a touchstone of sympathy for Socialism. For a valuable discussion of London politics, see P. Thompson, 'Liberals, Radicals and Labour in London, 1880–1900,' *Past and Present* no. 27 (1964). On Henry George's influence, which had an important catalysing effect, C. A. Barker, *Henry George* (New York, 1955) and E. P. Lawrence, *Henry George in the British Isles* (East Lansing, Mich., 1957), are complementary. For the secularist movement, see J. Eros, 'Rise of Organised Freethought', *Sociological Review*, new ser., vol. ii (1954); J. E. McGee, *History of the British Secular Movement* (Girard, Kansas, 1948); and H. B. Bonner and J. M. Robertson, *Charles Bradlaugh* (1898).

10. SOCIALIST ORGANIZATION AND PERSONALITIES: GENERAL

Cole's *History of Socialist Thought* has a good deal to say about organization. But perhaps the best book for conveying the atmosphere of British Socialism in the 1880's and 1890's is J. Clayton, *Rise and Decline of Socialism, 1884–1924* (1926). Also of value is G. Elton, *England Arise!* (1931). S. Bryher, *An Account of the Labour and Socialist Movement in Bristol* (Bristol, 1929) is a useful local study. Biographies which are important include Edward Carpenter, *My Days and Dreams* (1916); A. S. Tschiffely, *Don Roberto* (1927), for Cunninghame Graham; H. S. Salt, *Company I Have Kept* (1930); and Harry, Lord Snell, *Men, Movements and Myself* (1936).

11. ANARCHISM

On this subject see W. C. Hart, *Confessions of an Anarchist* (1906); M. Nettlau, *Anarchisten und Sozial-Revolutionaire* (Berlin, 1931); and R. Rocker, *The London Years* (1956). A recent summary of the history of the Anarchist movement in Britain and other countries will be found in G. Woodcock, *Anarchism* (1963). P. Kropotkin, *Memoirs of a Revolutionist* (New York, 1899) gives an impression of early Socialism and Anarchism in London in the 1880's.

The Origins of the Labour Party, 1880–1900

12. MARX AND ENGELS IN BRITISH POLITICS

A starting-point for the study of Marx and Marxism is I. Berlin, *Karl Marx* (1939). On Engels see G. Mayer, *Friedrich Engels* (1936). A useful compendium of reminiscences of Marx and Engels is that recently published in Moscow under the title *Reminiscences of Marx and Engels* (n.d.). The role of Engels in the British labour movement is carefully traced by S. Bünger, *Friedrich Engels und die britische sozialist-ische Bewegung, 1881–1895* (Berlin, 1962). The most useful collections of Marx and Engels correspondence in English are as follows: *Marx-Engels Selected Correspondence* (Moscow, 1956); *Marx Engels on Britain* (Moscow, 1953); K. Marx and F. Engels, *Selected Correspon-dence* (ed. D. Torr, London, 1934); and *Engels-Lafargue Correspondence* (3 vols., Moscow, 1959–).

13. THE SOCIALIST INTERNATIONAL

For the First International, see G. M. Stekloff, *History of the First International* (1928), and H. Collins, 'English Branches of the First International' in A. Briggs and J. Saville, *Essays in Labour History* (1960). The Second International is briefly analysed in J. Joll, *The Second International, 1889–1914* (1955); both the international con-gresses and the national parties are considered in G. D. H. Cole, *History of Socialist Thought*, vols. 2 and 3 (1954, 1956). Sir Robert Ensor's *Modern Socialism* (1904) is a valuable documentary source. Also of help are M. Beer, *Fifty Years of International Socialism* (1935) and E. Bernstein, *My Years of Exile* (1921). P. Gay, *The Dilemma of Democratic Socialism* (New York, 1952) is a study of Bernstein's revi-sionism.

14 THE SOCIAL-DEMOCRATIC FEDERATION

The only book on the S.D.F. as such is H. W. Lee and E. Archbold *Social-Democracy in Britain* (1935), a work of reminiscence rather than research. H. M. Hyndman's memoirs, *The Record of an Adventurous Life* (1911) and *Further Reminiscences* (1912) both contain readable and evocative material. A recent study, C. Tsuzuki, *H. M. Hyndman and British Socialism* (Oxford, 1961) is based on the files of *Justice* and Hyndman's extant correspondence, as well as other sources. For other personalities, see H. Quelch, *Literary Remains* (1914); E. B. Bax, *Reminiscences and Reflections* (1912). John Burns has been somewhat unfortunate in his biographers; there is more to be said on his behalf than will be found in J. Burgess, *John Burns* (Glasgow, 1911) and W. Kent, *Labour's Lost Leader* (1950). Tom Mann's *Memoirs* (1923) has been supplemented by D. Torr, *Tom Mann and*

Bibliographical Essay

His Times (1956). On Champion, see H. Pelling, 'H. H. Champion', *Cambridge Journal*, vol. vi (1952). On Lansbury, see R. Postgate, *George Lansbury* (1951). Also of value is W. S. Sanders, *Early Socialist Days* (1927).

15. WILLIAM MORRIS AND THE SOCIALIST LEAGUE

J. W. Mackail's *Life* of William Morris (2 vols., 1899) is of little help on the political side. L. E. Grey, *William Morris* (1949) is an attempt to remedy the deficiency; but the outstanding work, based on all available evidence, is E. P. Thompson, *William Morris, Romantic to Revolutionary* (1955). This book contains some letters which are not in the useful collection by P. Henderson, *Letters of William Morris* (1950). See also May Morris, *William Morris, Artist, Writer, Socialist* (Oxford, 1936) and J. B. Glasier, *William Morris and the Early Days of the Socialist Movement* (1921). Morris's own writings appeared in 24 volumes, *Collected Works of William Morris* (1910–15), with useful preface by May Morris.

16. FABIANISM AND THE FABIANS

E. R. Pease, *History of the Fabian Society* (1916) is a careful study by its secretary; this has hardly been improved upon, for the early years, by Mrs. M. Cole in her *Story of Fabian Socialism* (1961). By far the best analysis of Fabian influence in the period is A. M. McBriar, *Fabian Socialism and English Politics* (Cambridge, 1962). For Thomas Davidson, see W. Knight (ed.), *Memorials of Thomas Davidson* (1907). For Bernard Shaw, the literature is very extensive, the most comprehensive biography being A. Henderson, *George Bernard Shaw, Man of the Century* (New York, 1956), which contains correspondence with the Webbs. Shaw's *Collected Letters, 1874–1897* (ed. D. H. Laurence, forthcoming) should be of great value. A. West, *A Good Man Fallen Among Fabians* (1950) contains an interesting analysis of his political views; see also C. E. M. Joad (ed.), *Shaw and Society* (1953). For Annie Besant, see her *Autobiography* (1908) and A. H. Nethercot, *The First Four Lives of Annie Besant* (1961). For the Webbs, see M. Cole (ed.), *The Webbs and Their Work* (1949), and the second volume of Mrs. Webb's diaries, *Our Partnership* (1948). Some account of other leading Fabians is to be found in H. Burrows and J. A. Hobson (ed.), *William Clarke* (1908); in D. L. Moore, *E. Nesbit* (1933), which is interesting also on Hubert Bland; and in M. Olivier, *Sydney Olivier* (1948).

17. THE INDEPENDENT LABOUR PARTY

There is no general study of the I.L.P., and for its national policies we must turn at once to biographies. For Keir Hardie,

241

The Origins of the Labour Party, 1880–1900

there is an old biography by W. Stewart, *J. Keir Hardie* (1921), which may be supplemented by E. Hughes, *Keir Hardie* (1956) and D. Lowe, *From Pit to Parliament* (1913); but none of this takes us beyond the stage of hagiography. For Joseph Burgess, see his own books, *Will Lloyd George Supplant Ramsay MacDonald?* (Ilford, 1926) and *A Potential Poet?* (Ilford, 1928). For Ramsay MacDonald, the best work is G. Elton, *Life of James Ramsay MacDonald* (1939); but a new study, based on his papers, is being prepared by Mr. David Marquand. Philip Snowden's *Autobiography*, vol. 1 (1934) gives a good account of the early days of the I.L.P. in the North. For Blatchford and the *Clarion*, see L. Thompson, *Portrait of an Englishman* (1951) and two earlier books of memoirs, R. Blatchford, *My Eighty Years* (1931) and A. M. Thompson, *Here I Lie* (1937). For the movement in Bradford, see the life of Jowett by A. Fenner Brockway, *Socialism over Sixty Years* (1946), and D. Cresswell, *Margaret McMillan* (1948). On the West Riding more generally, see E. P. Thompson, 'Homage to Tom Maguire', in A. Briggs and J. Saville (ed.), *Essays in Labour History* (1960); and also Ben Turner, *About Myself* (1930). The I.L.P. at Manchester receives some attention in E. S. Pankhurst, *The Suffragette Movement* (1931). The movement in Scotland may be traced in D. W. Crowley, 'The Crofters' Party, 1885–1892', *Scottish Historical Review*, vol. xxxv (1956), in D. Lowe, *Souvenirs of Scottish Labour* (Glasgow, 1919), in R. Smillie, *My Life for Labour* (1924) and in W. M. Haddow, *My Seventy Years* (Glasgow, n.d.). S. G. Hobson, *Pilgrim to the Left* (1938) throws some light on the growth of the I.L.P. nationally.

18. LABOUR AND THE CHURCHES

Little has so far been written on the churches' hold over the working class in this period, and on regional variations of religious practice. There are some interesting suggestions in E. J. Hobsbawm, *Primitive Rebels* (Manchester, 1959), and there is one valuable local study, E. R. Wickham, *Church and People in an Industrial City* (1957), which deals with Sheffield. The need for further work is emphasized by K. S. Inglis in his *Churches and the Working Class in Victorian England* (1963); and in view of this it is perhaps surprising that his book is so definite about religious apathy among the Victorian workers. Yet Professor Inglis does provide here a series of valuable chapters on the reaction of the churches in the 1880's and 1890's to the need for social reform.

On the development of religious thought in general, see L. E. Elliott-Binns, *English Thought, 1860–1900: The Theological Aspect* (1956). On the Church of England and social reform, see D. O.

242

Bibliographical Essay

Wagner, *Church of England and Social Reform since 1854* (New York, 1930) and G. C. Binyon, *The Christian Socialist Movement* (1931). For the Guild of St. Matthew, see F. G. Bettany, *Stewart Headlam* (1926). For the settlement movement, see H. O. Barnett, *Canon Barnett* (2 vols., 1918). For Methodism, see D. P. Hughes, *Life of Hugh Price Hughes* (1904); and there is a study of the links between Methodism and labour in R. F. Wearmouth, *Methodism and the Struggle of the Working Classes, 1850–1900* (Leicester, 1954). For Congregationalism, see J. W. Grant, *Free Churchmanship in England, 1870–1940* (1955). For the Catholic Church, see S. Leslie, *Henry Edward Manning* (1921) and G. P. McEntee, *The Social Catholic Movement in Great Britain* (New York, 1927). On the Salvation Army, see *History of the Salvation Army*, vol. 3 by R. Sandall (1955) and vol. 4 by A. R. Wiggins (1964). Many of these works are uncritical in character.

For the Labour Churches, John Trevor's autobiography, *My Quest for God* (Manchester, 1897) is particularly useful. Also of assistance are C. H. Herford, *Philip Henry Wicksteed* (1931) and P. Redfern, *Journey to Understanding* (1946). The subject has attracted increasing attention from historians in recent years: see Inglis, op. cit.; Hobsbawm, op. cit.; and S. Pierson, 'John Trevor and the Labour Church Movement in England, 1891–1900' *Church History*, vol. xxx (1960).

19. TRADE UNIONISM: GENERAL

A bibliography of trade unionism in this period will be found in H. Pelling, *History of British Trade Unionism* (1963). But this does not mention an important recent work, H. A. Clegg, A Fox and A. F. Thompson, *History of British Trade Unionism since 1889*, vol. 1 (Oxford, 1964), which goes far towards replacing G. D. H. Cole, *Short History of the British Working-Class Movement* (new edn., 1948), at least for this period. S. and B. Webb, *History of Trade Unionism* (1894) and *Industrial Democracy* (1898), although in many respects out-of-date, retain their interest as documents of Socialist interpretation. E. J. Hobsbawm's *Labour's Turning Point, 1880–1900* (1948) is a selection from sources, with a Marxist slant. B. C. Roberts, *The Trades Union Congress, 1868–1921* (1958) is an authoritative study. On the 1889 dock strike, Ann Stafford, *A Match to Fire the Thames* (1961) is impressionistic but useful. But new unionism did not begin in 1889, as is pointed out in A. E. P. Duffy, 'New Unionism in Britain, 1889–90: A Reappraisal', *Economic History Review*, 2nd ser., vol. xiv (1961). See also H. Pelling, 'The Knights of Labour in Britain, 1880–1901', ibid. vol., ix (1956). E. J. Hobsbawm, 'General Labour

Unions in Britain, 1889–1914', ibid., vol. i (1949) is of considerable interest on the later history of the new unions.

20. TRADES UNIONS: INDIVIDUAL STUDIES

On individual unions, see in particular R. P. Arnot, *The Miners*, vol. 1 (1949), and B. McCormick and J. E. Williams, 'The Miners and the Eight-Hour Day, 1863–1900', *Economic History Review*, 2nd ser., vol. xii (1959); P. S. Bagwell, *The Railwaymen* (1963); J. B. Jefferys, *Story of the Engineers* (1945); A. E. Musson, *Typographical Association* (Oxford, 1954); A. Fox, *History of the N.U. of Boot and Shoe Operatives* (Oxford, 1958); and H. G. Swift, *History of Postal Agitation* (1929). For other unions, the best account will probably be found in the general work by Clegg, Fox and Thompson.

The most useful books of memoirs or biography, apart from those of Burns, Mann, Smillie, and Turner already mentioned, are: G. N. Barnes, *From Workshop to War Cabinet* (1924); *Sir James Sexton, Agitator: An Autobiography* (1936); W. Thorne, *My Life's Battles* (1925); B. Tillett, *Memories and Reflections* (1931); and J. Havelock Wilson, *My Stormy Voyage Through Life* (1925). There is an excellent autobiography by the 'free labour' organizer W. Collison, entitled *Apostle of Free Labour* (1913). This question is also ably dealt with by J. Saville, 'Trade Unions and Free Labour', in A. Briggs and J. Saville (ed.), *Essays in Labour History*.

21. TRADE UNIONISM: LOCAL STUDIES

There is scope for considerable development in the sphere of local studies. The London Trades Council deserves better than the official study, *London Trades Council, 1860–1950* (1950). In fact, there is only one thorough study of the history of a trades council: K. D. Buckley, *Trade Unionism in Aberdeen, 1878–1900* (Edinburgh, 1955). S. Pollard, *History of Labour in Sheffield* (Liverpool, 1959) is of more general value. On Birmingham', see A. Fox, 'Industrial Relations in 19th Century Birmingham', *Oxford Economic Papers*, vol. vii (1959). L. J. Williams, 'New Unionism in South Wales, 1889–92', *Welsh Historical Review*, vol. i (1963) is of some interest. W. H. Marwick, *Scottish Labour* (Glasgow, 1949) is a brief summary. An impression of Jewish unionism may be gained from L. P. Gartner, *The Jewish Immigrant in England, 1870–1914* (1960).

22. LABOUR REPRESENTATION

The best account for this period is to be found in Clegg, Fox and Thompson, *History of British Trade Unionism since 1889*, vol. 1. Also

Bibliographical Essay

of use are G. D. H. Cole, *British Working Class Politics, 1832–1914*
(1941) and A. W. Himphrey, *History of Labour Representation* (1912).
Two important autobiographies of 'Lib-Labs' are *Henry Broadhurst,
M.P.* (1901) and *Thomas Burt: an Autobiography* (1924). F. Bealey
and H. Pelling, *Labour and Politics, 1900–1906* (1958) traces the
history of the Labour Representation Committee. P. P. Poirier,
Advent of the Labour Party (1958) covers much the same ground, with
a summary of the politics of the 1890's. For an essay on 'The Amer-
ican Economy and the Foundation of the Labour Party' see H.
Pelling, *America and the British Left*. Some of the documents of the
electoral agreement between the Liberals and the L.R.C. are
printed in F. Bealey, 'Negotiations between the Liberals and the
L.R.C.', *Bulletin of the Institute of Historical Research*, vol. xxix (1956).
On relations with the Irish Nationalists, see T. W. Moody, 'Michael
Davitt and the British Labour Movement', *Transactions of the Royal
Historical Society*, 5th ser., vol. iii (1953).

23. IMPERIALISM AND SOCIAL REFORM

For the role of imperial issues in domestic politics, see R. E.
Robinson, 'Imperial Problems in British Politics, 1880–1895' and
A. F. Madden, 'Changing Attitudes and Widening Responsibilities,
1895–1914', both being chapters in the *Cambridge History of the British
Empire*, vol. 3 (Cambridge, 1959). B. Semmel, *Imperialism and Social
Reform* (1960) shows the connexion between the two topics, but per-
haps also exaggerates it, as for instance in the case of the Fabians.
F. Bealey, 'Les Travaillistes et La Guerre des Boers', *Le Mouvement
Social*, no. 45 (1963) examines labour and Socialist attitudes to the
South African War.

24. FURTHER BIBLIOGRAPHY

For a recent general bibliography see J. Clive, 'British History,
1870–1914, Reconsidered', *American Historical Review*, vol. lxviii
(1963). Detailed bibliographies of labour history, and information
about work in progress, may be found in the Bulletins (mimeo-
graphed) of the Society for the Study of Labour History (twice
yearly, from the University of Sheffield, 1960–). Also of value is J.
Brophy, 'Bibliography of British Labour and Radical Journals,
1880–1914', *Labor History* (New York), vol. v (1962).

INDEX

R

Index

Davidson, Thomas, 33, 36
Davitt, Michael, 48 n., 67, 70, 102, 199 n.
Delahaye, Victor, 82
De Mattos, W. S., 83
Democrat, 41
Democratic Club, 110, 147 n.
Democratic Fedn. *See* Social-Democratic Fedn.
Demos (Gissing), 43 n.
Deptford, 59
Derby, 212
Derbyshire Miners Assn., 206
Deville, G., 36
Devonshire, Duke of, 200 n.
Disraeli, Benjamin, Earl of Beaconsfield, 6, 19, 21
Dock Labourers, National Union of (Liverpool Dockers), 199, 206, 212, 230
Dock, Wharf, Riverside and General Workers Union (London Dockers), 83, 95, 110, 199, 212, 230
Donald, A. K., 53 f., 67, 83, 115, 118 n., 122
Doncaster, 205
Drew, W. H., 95, 110 f., 112, 115, 117, 119
Dulwich, 59
Dundee, 102, 112, 135 n., 149
Durham, 78, 93, 179
Dyer, Col. H., 197, 201 n.

Eastern Question, 5, 16, 24 n.
Eastern Question Assn., 23
Economic Circle, 133
Economic Review, 128
Edinburgh, 24, 25, 36 n., 204
Education Act (1902), 226
Edwards, John, 202
Eight Hours League. *See* Legal Eight Hours League
Eight hours movement, 23, 24, 59 f., 70, 72, 79, 85, 93, 104, 119, 195
Egypt, 24
Employers Parliamentary Council, 201
Engels, Friedrich, 7, 18 n., 20, 28, 29, 30, 44 n., 53, 63, 71, 85 f., 87, 93, 123, 171, 216, 217, 218, 219
Engineering Employers Fedn., 197, 201 n.
Engineers, Amal. Society of (A.S.E.), 82, 90, 195, 196 f., 206, 208, 210, 211, 215
England for All (Hyndman), 19
English Land Restoration League (*formerly* Land Reform Union), 23, 27, 128 n.

Ethical Union, 136
Evangelical Union, 63, 140

Fabian Essays in Socialism, 74–77, 94, 98, 196 n.
Fabianism and the Empire, 188
Fabian Society, 9, 39, 44 f., 46, 57, 74 f., 80, 86, 101, 107, 123, 126, 137, 139 f., 161, 171, 175, 181–6, 192, 202, 216; foundation, 33–36; favours constitutionalism, 37, 49–51, 56, 217; policy of permeation, 52 f., 73 f., 86 n., 99, 100, 117, 128, 147, 218, 223; doubts about I.L.P., 114, 120, 148, 157, 160; opposes Socialist unity, 112, 174; limited part in formation of L.R.C., 207–9, 210, 218; use of Hutchinson Trust, 94, 181–4; assistance to local Labour representatives, 157 f., 184 f., 186; attitude to South African War, 187–9, 226; provincial societies of, 81 n., 94, 97, 99, 116, 117, 123, 137, 148 n., 157, 172, 181, 229; Fabian Church, 137
Facts for Londoners, 74
Facts for Socialists, 74
Fair Trade campaign, 8
Fair Trade League, 42
Fashoda, 187
Faulkner, Charles, 30
Fay, F., 110
Fellowship of the New Life, 33 f., 137
Fenwick, Charles, 62, 88
Ferguson, John, 70, 71, 102
Fielding, John, 40
Figures for Londoners, 74
Fitzgerald, C. L., 41, 50
Fors Clavigera (Ruskin), 10 f., 15
Fortnightly Review, 147 n., 168
Fourth Clause, 97, 121, 153
France, 24, 125. *See also* French Revolution
Franchise Reform Acts (1832), 2; (1867), 1, 2; (1884), 1, 38, 39, 47, 57, 123
Freedom, 51 n.
Freedom Group, 51 n., 55 n.
Freethought Publishing Company, 46
Freiheit, 14
French Revolution, 46, 143. *See also* Paris
Frost, R. P. B., 23, 29 n.

Gardiner, A. G., 180
Garvin, J. L., 168
Gas Stokers Union, 4, 78
Gasworkers and General Labourers Union, 80, 81, 83, 86, 93, 112, 172, 176, 195, 199, 208, 209, 212, 230

249

R*

Index

Hyndman, H. M.—*contd.*
Engels, 20 f., 86; with Morris, 27–31; with Champion, 56 f., 60, 84; with Burns, 84; with Lansbury, 171; in 'Tory Gold' scandal, 40 f.; on trial, 43; loses money in Barings crisis, 103, 170; role in International, 86, 194

Illingworth, Alfred, 92
Imperialism (Lenin), 188
Independent Labour Party (I.L.P.), 81 n., 212, 216, 222; emergence, 109–15; foundation 115–24; early development, 145–65; fights 1895 election, 165–8; setback after 1895, 173 f., 179–81; relations with S.D.F., 145, 174–8; municipal work, 157 f., 186 f.; and South African War, 188–91; and unions, 98, 201–11, 219 f.; and religion, 135, 137 f., 140 f., 181; membership statistics, 163 f., 226, 229; contribution assessed, 217, 219 f.
Industrial Democracy (Webb), 184
Industrial Remuneration Conference, 36
International, First, 5, 13 n., 40; Second, 86; Congress (1889), 45 n., 86; (1896), 193 f.
International Labour Union, 13 n.
Ireland, 10, 15, 17, 18, 21, 23, 47, 116, 161, 163
Irish Home Rule, 21, 41, 47, 48 f., 51, 59, 71, 100; Land League, 22; Nationalist Party, 47 f., 48 n., 51, 55 n., 58, 66, 68, 102, 199 n., 219
Ironfounders, Friendly Society of, 197, 212, 230
Irving, Dan, 172 f.

Jameson Raid, 187
Jevons, W. S., 132; Jevonian Theory of Marginal Unity, 37, 75
Johnson, William, 112
Jowett, Fred, 92 n., 95, 115, 134, 213
Joynes, J. L., 23, 25, 45
Justice, 24, 27, 29, 30, 39 f., 40 n., 41, 45, 56, 170 f., 216 f.
Kapital, Das (Marx). See *Capital*
Keddell, F., 36
Keighley, 180
Kelvin, Lord, 176
Kennington, 40
Kingsley, Charles, 126
Kitson, James, 92
Kitz, F., 14 n., 22 n.
Knights of Labor, 80 f.
Kropotkin, P., 14, 51 n., 55 n., 161, 217

Labor Leader, 101, 109
Labouchere, H., 38

Labour, Royal Commission on, 119 n., 200
Labour Army, 101
Labour Churches, 97, 114, 116, 131–143, 155; *Labour Church Record*, 138; Labour Church Union, 135 f., 152
Labour Elector, 59 f., 80, 83, 91, 102, 109, 124, 146, 150
Labour Electoral Committee, *later* Assn. (L.E.A.), 57 f., 60, 65 f., 69, 72, 97, 104, 164, 222, 224 f.; Metropolitan Section, 58, 69, 112
Labour Emancipation League (L.E.L.), 22, 25, 26, 28, 29, 30, 55
Labour Leader, formerly *Miner*, 64, 71, 102, 152, 159, 166, 173, 181, 190, 205, 209 n., 220
Labour Literature Society (Glasgow), 103, 167
Labour Party, 11, 53, 77, 208, 211, 215, 216, 218, 219, 222, 224, 225, 226; *and see* Labour Representation Committee
Labour Prophet, 135, 136, 138
Labour Representation Committee (L.R.C.), 191, 211–15, 217, 218, 221, 222, 225–7, 230 f.
Labour Representation League, 2 f., 5, 47, 58
Labour Standard, 53
Labour Union (Hoxton), 55, 58, 60, 83, 110
Lambeth, 39 n.; Democratic Assn., 16
Lanarkshire, 62, 65, 121 n.; *see also* Mid-Lanark
Lancashire, 6, 78, 92, 93, 94, 116, 131, 134, 135, 143, 152, 153, 163, 169, 172, 181, 184, 215
Lancashire and Cheshire Miners Confedn., 211
Land and Labour League, 5
Land Nationalisation (Spence), 21
Land Reform Union. See English Land Restoration League
Lane, Joseph, 22, 26, 29, 54 n.
Langley, Ald. B., 164
Lansbury, George, 171, 172
Law and Liberty League, 46
Lee, H. W., 124 n.
Leeds, 30, 81 n., 93, 231
Leek (Staffs.), 141
Legal Eight Hours League, 103, 116, 148
Leicester, 32 n., 139, 164, 198, 231
Lenin, V. I., 188
Leslie, Cliffe, 8
Liberal Imperialists, 189, 207, 225 n.
Liberal-Labour M.P.s ('Lib.-Labs'), 3 f., 15, 23, 47, 49, 62, 66, 148, 164, 205 f., 223

The Origins of the Labour Party, 1880-1900

Liberal Party, 1, 3, 4, 5, 6, 7, 11, 15, 22, 38, 47, 48 f., 52, 58, 59, 65, 67, 71, 72, 73, 97, 100, 102, 106, 107 f., 117, 125, 128, 143, 145, 156, 165, 191, 194, 206 f., 219, 222, 224, 225; *see also* National Liberal Fedn.
Liberal Unionists, 40, 48, 97, 100
Liebknecht, W., 81, 221
Link, 45 f., 80
Linnell, Alfred, 43 f.
Lister, John, 121, 146 f., 164
Liverpool, 18 n., 24, 110, 178 n., 181, 199 n., 202
Liverpool Dockers. *See* Dock Labourers, N. U. of
Livesey, George, 200 n., 201 n.
Lloyd, H. D., 75 n., 173, 197, 226 n.
Local Government Information Bureau, 186
London, politics of, 15–18, 39–41, 52, 73 f., 77, 91 f., 100 f., 104 f., 110 f., 117, 158–60, 184
London County Council (L.C.C.), 74, 77, 82, 91, 103, 104 f., 108, 116, 158 f., 184
London Dockers, *See* Dock, Wharf, Riverside and General Workers Union
London dock strike (1889), 81–83, 104, 126
London I.L.P., 110 f., 113, 121, 122 n., 146 f., 148, 159 f.
London Liberal and Radical Union, 74
London Reform Union, 151
London School Board, 39, 74, 159
London School of Economics, 182
London Tailors, 112
London Trades Council, 85, 92, 100 f., 106, 172, 210; Representation League, 101
London Working Men's Assn., 2
Longfellow, H. W., 136
Looking Backward (Bellamy), 101, 134
Lord, J., 17
Lynn (Mass., U.S.A.), 141
Lyons v. *Wilkins*, 200

McCarthy, Tom, 110
McDonald, Alexander, 4, 15
Macdonald, James, 24 f., 112, 121, 172, 210
MacDonald, J. Ramsay, 112 n., 136 f., 142, 167, 171, 174, 190, 207, 211, 224; joins Socialist Union, 41; joins I.L.P., 156 n., 165; on I.L.P. Council, 175 f., 190; differences with Fabians, 182 f., 188, 226; secretary of L.R.C., 210, 211 f., 227

MacDonald, Mrs. J. Ramsay (*née* Gladstone), 176
McGhee, R., 199 n.
McHugh, E., 199 n.
McKinley, William, 94
McMillan, Margaret, 185
Macrosty, H. W., 214
Mahon, J. L., 29, 53 f., 55, 67, 70, 83, 115, 118 n., 122
Mainwaring, S., 29
Man and Superman (Shaw), 218
Manchester, 92, 95, 97, 102, 133, 150, 151–3; I.L.P., 97, 110, 112, 121, 137, 153, 167, 179 f., 231; Labour Church, 97, 116, 133 f.; Labour Union, 41, 50; Socialist Union, 50
Manchester Guardian, 226
Manhood Suffrage League, 13, 22 n.
Mann, Tom, 90, 91, 100 f., 110, 117, 133, 145, 165 f., 192, 195; aids Champion, 58, 60, 67; helps new unions, 81, 82 f., 84, 85, 126; secretary of I.L.P., 151 f., 154, 155 f., 158, 160, 163 f., 168, 174; returns to union work, 175, 179, 191
Manning, Cardinal, 83, 84, 126
Manningham Mills (Bradford), 94 f., 115
Mansfield, 110
Martyn, Caroline, 155, 178 n.
Marx, Karl, 5, 9, 11, 13 n., 14, 16, 19 f., 24 n., 26, 28, 31, 36 f., 86, 216
Marx-Aveling, Eleanor, 28, 29, 53, 55, 63, 81, 86, 89, 159, 218
Marxism *and* Marxists, 12, 21, 31, 39, 40, 53, 55, 64, 75, 77, 78, 86, 120, 146, 161, 171, 218
Marylebone, 16, 21, 39 n.; Democratic Assn., 22, 24 f.
Massingham, H. W., 74
Masterman, C. F. G., 130 n.
Matabele rising, 187
Mattison, Alf, 81 n.
Maurice, F. D., 126
Mawdsley, J., 193, 205 f.
Maxwell, Shaw, 70, 71, 101, 103, 110 f., 120 f., 122, 146, 149, 151
Mazzini, Joseph, 140
Merrie England (Blatchford), 156, 161, 217
Merthyr, 140, 181, 212 f.
Merton Abbey, 30
Methodists, 125, 129 f., 131, 155, 174. *See also* Wesleyans
Methodist Times, 129 f.
Metropolitan Radical Fedn. (M.R.F.), 73, 86 n., 223 n.
Middlesbrough, 106

252

Index

Mid-Lanark by-election, 65–68, 150, 164, 222
Midland Social Democratic Assn., 14
Mile End, 22, 55 n.
Mill, J. S., 8, 15, 37, 218
Miner. See *Labour Leader*
Miners Fedn. of Great Britain, 194, 227
Modern Thought, 14
Moir, John, 103
Morayshire, 175
Morley, Arnold, 59
Morpeth, 4
Morris, William, 50, 51, 52, 57, 86, 98, 140, 141, 155, 216; joins Fedn., 23 f., 25, 26, 27; founds Socialist League, 28–32; opposes Parliamentary group, 54 f.; retires from League, 55; change of attitude, 124, 172; Socialist songs of, 44, 136
Morris, Rev. W. A., 81
Most, Johann, 14
Municipal Corporations Act (1882), 47
Murdoch, John, 67, 70
Murray, Charles, 13, 15, 23 n.
Murray, J. F., 13

Narodniks, 217
National Fedn. of Labour, 80
National Free Labour Assn., 199, 214 n.
Nationalisation News, 101
Nationalization of Labour Society, 101
National Liberal Fedn., 15, 17, 49, 65, 73, 100, 217, 219. *See also* Caucus *and* Schnadhorst, F.
National Reform League, 13
National Secular Society, 26 f., 28 n., 131
Navvies, Bricklayers' Labourers, &c., Union of, 152, 230
Neo-Malthusianism, 37
Nesbit, E. (Mrs. Hubert Bland), 35, 46
Newcastle, 16, 17, 24, 53 n., 100, 106, 110, 164
Newcastle Programme, 100, 147, 224
News from Nowhere (Morris), 98
New Trades Unionism (Mann and Tillett), 85
New Unionism, 60, 64, 79–94, 101, 126, 176, 199, 201 n., 227
New Zealand, 141 n.
Nine Hours League, 80 n.
Nineteenth Century, 19, 106, 190
Nonconformity, 1, 6, 38, 125, 128–33, 134, 141, 143, 159, 181, 208, 213, 226
Northcote, Sir Stafford, 39
North London Press. See *People's Press*
North of England Socialist Fedn., 54
Northumberland, 78, 79, 93

Northwich, 60
Norwich, 139 n., 198, 218
Nottingham, 24, 25, 41, 94 n.

Oastler, Richard, 6, 13 n.
O'Connor, T. P., 15, 74
Old Cumnock (Ayrshire), 63
Oldham, 205 f.
Olivier, Sydney, 37, 76, 188
Omdurman, 187
Osborne judgement, 224
Ostrogorski, M., 219
Our Corner, 45, 49
Owen, Robert, 33, 34
Owenism, 5, 6 f., 14, 33
Oxford, 23, 30
Oxford House, 127

Paine, Tom, 217
Pall Mall Gazette, 41
Pankhurst, Dr., 51, 167
Pankhurst, Mrs., 180
Paris, 14; Commune of (1871), 5, 82, 123 n.; Socialist Congresses of (1889), 45 n., 86
Parke, Ernest, 91
Parnell, C. S., 21 f., 47, 48, 66 f., 150, 199 n.
Pease, Edward, 33, 34, 35, 36, 53 n., 80, 184
Pease, Sir Joseph, 92
Penny, John, 175, 179
People's Press, 101, 103
Philipps, J. W., 65, 67, 68
Phoenix Park murders, 22
Pickard, Ben, 194, 195
Plan of Campaign for Labor, 160, 204
Plymouth, 110, 116
Podmore, F., 34 f., 36
Positivists, 17, 143, 218
Postmen's Union, 83
Potter, George, 5
Practical Socialist, 45, 50
Pratt, E. A., 214 n.
Preston, 212 f.
Principles of Social Democracy, (Sketchley), 13
Progress and Poverty (George), 10, 18, 36
Progressive Party (on L.C.C.), 74, 91 f., 104 f., 108, 124 n., 145, 151, 159
Providence (R. I., U.S.A.), 141
Pullman (Ill., U.S.A.), 196

Quakers, 129, 221
Quelch, Harry, 39 n., 110, 170, 173
Quinn v. Leatheam, 213

Radical, 15, 22 n.
Railway Review, 199

Index

Spencer, Herbert, 11
Stacy, Enid, 155
Stafford, 4, 110
Staffordshire, 24, 141
Standard Oil Trust, 197
Star, 74
Steadman, W. C., 207, 208
Steels, T. R., 205
Steelsmelters, British Amal., 197, 212, 230
Stepney, 208
Stockton, 115
Stratford Radical Club, 23
Sunday Chronicle, 92, 96
Sunderland, 212, 225, 231
Suthers, R. B., 210 f.
Swansea, 62
Swinton and Pendlebury, 110
Syndicalism, 31

Taff Vale case, 213 f., 215
Tattersall, Ald. J., 152
Taylor, Helen, 15, 23 n., 25, 39, 40 n.
Taylor, H. R., 106
Taylor, Tom, 179
Tea Operatives Union, 81
Temple, William, 139
Tennyson, Alfred, 136, 140
Textile Factory Workers Assn., United 215
Textile Workers, General Union of, 94
Theophilanthropy, 143
Thompson, William, 11
Thorne, Will, 80, 81, 84, 88, 93, 172, 207, 209, 212
Threlfall, T. R., 57 f., 65, 66, 222 f.
Tichborne case, 14
Tillett, Ben, 81, 83, 91, 95 f., 107, 110, 116, 117, 118, 133, 134, 152, 154, 193
Times, The, 14, 59, 105, 208, 214
To-day, 24, 37, 45, 52
Tory Democracy, 38 f.
'Tory Gold' scandal, 40 f., 50, 56, 67, 150
Tory Radicalism, 6, 15 f., 56
Tower Hamlets, 39 n., 74
Toynbee, Arnold, 8, 9, 127
Toynbee Hall, 127
Trades Union Congress (T.U.C.), 4, 6, 25, 58, 62, 64, 72, 78, 87 f., 90, 100, 102, 112, 113, 122, 149, 151, 175, 192, 193, 194, 196, 202 f., 204 f., 211, 214, 224 n.; Parliamentary Committee, 4, 113, 151, 152, 174 f., 192 f., 200, 201, 203, 204, 207; secretary, 15, 62, 88, 202 f., 204 f., 207 f.
Trade Unionism and British Industry (Pratt), 214 n.
Trade Unionist, 101

Trade-union Acts (1871), 4, 200; (1875), 4
Trafalgar Square, 42 f., 50, 56, 60, 67, 82
Travis, Henry, 14
Trevor, John, 97, 116, 132–4, 135, 136, 137, 138, 141, 143 f.
Trusts, 75, 77, 196 f., 214
Tunis, 24
Turner, Ben, 94
Twentieth Century Press, 170
Tyneside, 80
Typographical Assn., 198, 212, 230
Tyrone, 22

'Unauthorised Programme', 38, 48
Unemployed demonstrations, 42–44, 56, 147
Unitarianism, 97, 129, 131, 132 f.
United States, 1, 14 n., 18, 19, 33, 53, 75, 77, 80 f., 94, 98 n., 101 n., 141, 173, 196, 197, 214 f.
University Hall, 133
Unto This Last (Ruskin), 10 f.
Urquhart, David, 56

Veblen, T., 131
Victoria, Queen, 1, 43
Vorwärts, 118

Wales, 100, 116, 130 n., 140, 143, 163, 178, 179, 181, 195, 213, 223
Wallace, Prof. A. R., 18
Wallace, Rev. J. B., 128 n., 134
Wallas, Graham, 75 n., 76, 160, 188
Walworth, 171, 172
Ward, Mrs. Humphry, 133
Wardle, G. J., 199
Watson, R. Spence, 219 n.
Watts, J. Hunter, 41
Wealth against Commonwealth (Lloyd), 197
Webb, Sidney, 37, 51, 52, 74, 75, 76 f., 89, 91, 99, 182, 184, 187 f., 189, 219 n., 226
Webb, Mrs Sidney (*née* Beatrice Potter), 89, 131, 144, 160, 167 f., 182, 184, 187 f.
Weekly Dispatch, 35, 52
Wemyss, Earl of, 201 n.
Wesleyans, 115, 125, 129. *See also* Methodists
West Bromwich, 25
West Ham, 172, 185
West Ham, South, 103 f., 106, 166, 212
Whigs, 1, 3, 15, 48, 100
Whitechapel, 14, 127
Whitman, Walt, 140
Why are the Many Poor?, 36

255